# THE POPULATION OF
# THE CALIFORNIA INDIANS
## 1769 - 1970

# THE POPULATION OF
# THE CALIFORNIA INDIANS
# 1769-1970

### SHERBURNE F. COOK

*With a foreword by*
*WOODROW BORAH* and *ROBERT F. HEIZER*

UNIVERSITY OF CALIFORNIA PRESS

BERKELEY • LOS ANGELES • LONDON

University of California Press
Berkeley and Los Angeles, California
University of California Press, Ltd.
London, England
Copyright © 1976, by
The Regents of the University of California
ISBN 0-520-02923-2
Library of Congress Catalog Card Number: 74-27287
Printed in the United States of America

*Published with the assistance of the*
Center for the History of the
American Indian
*of the Newberry Library*

# CONTENTS

# FIGURES

# TABLES

# FOREWORD

This volume is posthumous. Its author, Sherburne F. Cook, died 7 November 1974 on the Monterey peninsula, ending a remarkably creative and productive life that still was reaching out in new directions. Although he would have been 78 on 31 December and had been formally retired for ten years, he was working actively at the time of his death upon more sophisticated analysis of California mission records and upon further studies of population characteristics, morbidity, and aboriginal diet and nutrition in California and Mexico. He also had been gathering notes on the history of Mexican-Americans in Santa Clara County, using hitherto untapped sources.

Cook was born in Springfield, Massachusetts, in 1896. His father was for many years editor of *The Springfield Republican*. The son was reared in New England, with a year of study in imperial Germany, that left a lasting impression upon him. College education at Harvard was interrupted by the certainty of entrance of the United States into the First World War. Young Sherburne volunteered and served with the A.E.F. in France until 1919, when he returned to Harvard for his A.B. He had begun study as a history major, but finding the department stuffy, he changed to a major in biology. He went on to an A.M. in 1923 and a Ph.D. in 1925, with a thesis on ''The Toxicity of the Heavy Metals in Relation to Respiration.'' His doctorate was supplemented by two years as a National Research Fellow in Biological Sciences, with study at the Kaiser Wilhelm Institut in Berlin-Dahlem and at Cambridge University. In 1928 he came to the University of California, Berkeley, as Assistant Professor of Physiology, and was promoted more slowly than normal course until he became full professor in 1942. He retired in 1964 but was recalled for two more years of active service.

Until the middle 1930s Cook's career was the normal one of an able man in physiology, with a series of studies of the toxic effects of heavy metals, the spleen, and the effects of various kinds of feed upon poultry. He later went on to further studies in oxygen absorption by human beings, the effects of high altitudes, and the fossilization of bone. The first sign of an interest out of the ordinary was an article on ''Diseases of the Indians of Lower California in the Eighteenth Century,'' published in 1935 (*California and Western Medicine*, vol. 43, no. 6). This was followed by historical studies of outbreaks of disease and methods of treatment in California and Mexico. A Guggenheim fellowship and sabbatical leave in Mexico in 1939 led to an extension of interest to the Indians of the Mixteca Alta. In 1940 Cook published his first monograph in the Ibero-Americana series of the University of California, to which he became a distinguished and frequent contributor (*Population Trends among the California Mission Indians*, no. 17). A great deal of his future research was prefigured in that monograph and in an article published in 1945 in the *Annals of the American Academy of Political and Social Science* ("Demographic Consequences of European Contact with Primitive Peoples"). With the publication of the four volumes of *The Conflict between the California Indian and White Civilization* (Ibero-Americana: 21-24) in 1943, Cook entered fully into the fields of California anthropology and history. For years thereafter any large scholarly meeting was apt to wind up in heated debate upon these volumes, with their acute and at times astringent perceptions on contact, treatment, and the meaning of missionization. The volume of essays here published represents a continuation of Cook's interest in the California Indians, with a reworking of some themes and an extension to new ones. At the time of his death he was applying new techniques of analysis to California mission records, the preliminary results of which would indicate a more favorable verdict on California missions in terms of demographic impact than his previous studies.

Cook was always, in whatever he did, at heart a social biologist. The human effect, action, or result in some aspect or other was central to his research. He brought to his studies, further, a most unusual breadth and competence in many different areas of science, anthropology, and history. Few other scholars could face up so resolutely to the challenge of unresolved problems, show equal ability to get to the heart of these, and come up with new insights and conclusions. Here his base in science helped to equip him with a knack of cutting through to the essential and a remarkable elegance and economy in dealing with it. His ingenuity in finding ways around barriers of apparent lack of direct evidence continually impressed colleagues. Many of his conclusions, which might first have appeared at best educated guesses, since have been verified by other scholars using techniques developed later. In the end Cook accepted the data, when verified, and went where they led. He might have had less controversy in his life had he held to the ideas of established scholars.

The contributions of Cook extended to developing new techniques in archaeology and anthropology. He soon found that direct population counts or census figures would not take the scholar far in determining the size of pre-Contact populations of California. He turned therefore to unexploited kinds of archaeological evidence, such as quantitative measure of the kinds and numbers of potsherds in ceramic cultural sites, the point being that there was surely some pattern of frequency, breakage, and disposal of cooking and storage pots. Another instance is his analysis of numbers and size of houses and the surface area of archaeological sites in order to determine the number of persons per house and per village. Cook spent approximately ten years in screening, separating, and identifying the palpable residues of discarded organic trash in occupation sites in California in order to learn about the prehistoric dietary and production practices of the people who left the wastes. He was the first present-day practitioner of this approach, which has now become a standard procedure in archaeology. He advocated the analysis of coprolites years before American archaeologists accepted the idea. As to Cook's contributions and eminence in historical demography and Mexican history and anthropology, there is no need to detail them here. They were recognized posthumously on 9 March 1975 when the Mexican National Institute of Anthropology and History awarded the gold medal of the Bernardino de Sahagun prize for 1971 for the two volumes of *Essays in Population History: Mexico and the Caribbean* (University of California Press, 1971-1974).

We believe that this volume will stand for a long time to come as the most authoritative analysis of native Californian demography in the period since discovery to the present decade. It represents the final and considered conclusions of a person who immersed himself in the data for a period of a third of a century.

*Woodrow Borah*
*Robert F. Heizer*

# INTRODUCTION

These essays complete one phase of a task begun more than thirty years ago, the establishment of the population trends exhibited by the Indians of California from aboriginal times down to the present day. The first publications, which appeared during the 1940s, emphasized the conflict attending the entrance of the white man into California, and the resulting disintegration of native society. Population was but a single aspect of this struggle, but it was an important one for it served as an index to the failure of the Indian to survive successfully in a cultural environment completely foreign to his experience.

The first serious attempt to determine the aboriginal population was that of Merriam in 1905. Using principally mission records he reached a total of 260,000 souls. With a vastly greater body of information, and with a keen although conservative approach, Kroeber reduced Merriam's value to 125,000 (Handbook, 1925). A reevaluation by the present author (1943), who used substantially the same sources as had Kroeber, raised the total moderately to 133,550.

The "Conflict" series in Ibero-Americana then devoted a great deal of space to the post-contact movements of population, in all cases reductions. These changes occurred during the Spanish-Mexican period 1770 to 1848, and during the initial occupation by the Americans, from 1848 to the early 1860s. For the latter era reliance was placed primarily upon statements offered by civil and military authorities, explorers, and reporters, many of whom were directly concerned with organizing the new state of California. These turbulent days were described up to the time when a more or less stable equilibrium was attained. By 1865 the Indian population had fallen to a figure upon which there is general agreement, somewhere near 25,000 or 30,000. At this date the period of intense physical conflict had ended, a very slow reconstruction had begun, and the consideration of the population decline by the early monograph series was brought to its conclusion.

The crucial figure is that of the aboriginal population, for the number of Indians has been reasonably well established in all decades since 1865. The great decline took place earlier, and its magnitude can be appreciated only if there is an adequate starting point. When we thought about the problem in 1940 the drop from 133,000 to 25,000 seemed enormous, and an even more precipitous fall was almost unbelievable. Nevertheless, in 1974 we now know much more about the destruction of the native races. For example, the recent paper by Dobyns (1966) shows that throughout the Western Hemisphere a decline to no more than 5 or 10 percent of the aboriginal number is by no means incredible. Indeed, it is the rule rather than the exception.

In order to obtain a clearer picture of the actual pre-contact population in California, a series of studies was undertaken during the decade following the Second World War. In the light of the earlier experience it was felt that a better job could be done by considering each region separately rather than by attempting to evaluate the number of inhabitants of the entire state at once. Accordingly three regions were selected—the north coast, the East Bay counties, and the San Joaquin Valley—and a monograph was written about each (1955, 1956, 1957). Within each area all possible sources of information were brought together and analyzed in detail—historical, ethnographic, and archaeological. It is probable that at least an approach to the truth was achieved.

However, the project was only partially completed, a fact which was impressed upon me when I undertook to write a short review of aboriginal California population for the International Congress of Americanists in 1962. Two large and important regions still remained unexplored, and without consideration of them no intelligent estimate could be made of the aggregate number of people in the state. These regions were the Sacramento Valley as far north as Oregon, and the missionized coastal strip from San Diego to San Francisco. Finally, two other areas were unaccounted for—the interior southern desert and the territory in California east of the Sierra Nevada, a region for which Kroeber's estimate is accepted as essentially valid. As a consequence of these factors, the first and longest essay of the present series attempts to survey the two main unresearched areas, the Sacramento Valley and the mission strip. With these new regions, therefore, and with some readjustment of the old areas, the total population of the state as a whole can be assembled. The total is set at a little over 300,000 souls, or almost three times the number originally postulated by Kroeber.

In the second essay, the course of change in number of California Indians is traced from the end of violent conflict at about 1865 to the census of 1970. For this period one must use very different sources from those employed for aboriginal and early contact conditions. The Bureau of Indian Affairs in Washington has issued reports annually for most of the century involved and has supplemented these by careful enumerations at intervals during the past fifty years. The reports are available at all major libraries, and the Great Rolls, as they are called, may be seen at the Office of Tribal Relations, Sacramento. The various

United States censuses are also of value, as is the special report by Kelsey in 1906. These are all official in character, and partake of both the strengths and the weaknesses of such documents. They are pure government-ese. There is no trace of the religious fervor which graces the mission reports, or of the personal reminiscence injected by miner, general, or politician, unless one wishes to consider as personal the oratory of various reservation agents during the nineteenth century.

In essays three and four, the decennial census reports, the files of the probate court for the Sacramento Agency, the Great Rolls of 1928, 1950, and 1970, and the birth and death files at the office of the state Bureau of Public Health are all employed for an analysis of the demographic features of the Indian population since 1865 and particularly since 1900. Here changes in age distribution and in mortality and natality are considered. These analyses deal exclusively with modern times, for there are no data which would elucidate such parameters in the prehistoric and early historic periods. The only possible exception is the file of internal mission baptism and death records, but these documents are only now being examined and their mine of information exploited.

The fifth essay considers a problem specifically Indian, the degree of interbreeding with other races. That there has been a great deal of hybridization was well recognized in the early nineteenth century. Very little new in principle is therefore contributed, but the survey is brought up to date. The reports of the Bureau of Vital Statistics are combined with the Roll of 1928, which remains the best store of information concerning the marital behavior of the Indians in recent decades. The probability for future interracial fusion is also discussed.

The sixth and final essay is short and seeks to show simply that the contemporary Indian, like his fellow citizens of other ethnic origin, is moving away from the traditional rural way of life. Some of the numerical data which provide this knowledge are very impressive, and indicate that urbanization is actually accelerating at the present time.

Although these essays are fragmentary, in the sense that they deal with disparate topics, the whole sweep of the facts contained in them and in the preceding monographs carries a set of clear messages. The aboriginal Indian was crushed and almost destroyed by white civilization, but in recent years he has recovered and is now on a rapid march toward gaining his proper position in the population spectrum. This idea is reiterated in the brief concluding summary to this series of essays.

# I. THE ABORIGINAL POPULATION OF CALIFORNIA

Estimates of the population of California have been made by several investigators during the present century. Merriam (1905) used mission data to get 260,000. Kroeber (1925) based his calculation mainly upon ethnographic findings and scaled down the estimate to 133,000 within the political boundaries of the state. Cook (1943) revised Kroeber's figures upward by about 7 percent and reached 133,500, but excluded the Modoc, Paiute, Washo, Mojave, and Yuma. More recently Baumhoff (1963:226), upon grounds of subsistence and ecology, suggested a total of 350,000. In view of the disparity of these opinions further study is clearly indicated.

The size of California and the enormous geographical and climatic diversity, as well as the range of cultures represented by its aboriginal inhabitants, requires that population estimates be based, not upon a general consideration of the entire area, but upon a detailed study of separate regions. Such an approach is also in conformity with the varied historical experience of the major portions of the state and the different types of information which may be derived from each.

The present writer has studied three areas in depth: the North Coast (1956), the San Joaquin Valley (1955a), and Alameda and Contra Costa Counties (1957). A renewed interest has prompted me to present briefly a consideration of two other primary areas—the Sacramento Valley north to the Oregon line, and the long coastal belt in which were placed the Spanish missions. If a reasonable value can be assigned to these two regions, we shall then come close to a definitive estimate of the aboriginal population of California. This essay is divided into two sections, each dealing with one of the primary areas mentioned.

## The Sacramento Valley and Northward

Beginning with the Sacramento River at its junction with the San Joaquin, we pursue a line running northward along the summits of the inner coast ranges to the Trinity Mountains. Thence it follows the boundary between the Karok and the Shasta tribes as far as Oregon. The limit on the south is the Sacramento River and the divide between the American and the Cosumnes Rivers. It extends east to the crest of the Sierra Nevada, and thence northward so as to separate the California tribes from those more properly regarded as inhabiting the Great Basin, the Washo and the Paiute tribes.

This great territory may be divided ethnographically and geographically into two sub-areas. The first consists of the group of linguistic stocks which cross the state parallel to its northern border—the Shastan complex, the Achomawi and Atsugewi, and the California Modoc. The second includes the peoples of the Sacramento Valley floor and the lower foothills to west and to east. Here are found the large aggregates—Maidu, Yana, Yahi, and Wintun—which contributed most of the population to prehistoric northern California.

The extreme north of the state was not touched by the white man prior to 1849, in which year, or shortly thereafter, the entire region was flooded with gold miners and associated teamsters, soldiers, traders, and camp followers. Within a decade Indian society was completely disrupted and the population was seriously reduced. Not until after 1900 was any systematic attempt made to secure knowledge of their cultures, which were at that time almost forgotten. As a result we possess no records whatever which could provide the basis for a population estimate of the Shastan groups prior to the work of Dixon (1907), Kroeber (1925), and Kniffen (1928). Since these studies, nothing new has appeared until recently, when Heizer and Hester (1970c) published C. Hart Merriam's list of Shasta villages. This list is valuable and will be discussed further. In the meantime we are obliged to fall back on the area-density method, one which may be applied to these populations with a fair degree of confidence.

A Shastan division for which there exist good data is that of the Achomawi and Atsugewi, who inhabited the Pit River from its source to the mouth of Montgomery Creek at the 122nd meridian. Eleven smaller groups constitute the stock as a whole, each of which is described by Kniffen (1928), who shows the territorial boundaries on his Map no. 2. Kniffen's delineation of the complete Achomawi holdings yields a greater area than does that of Kroeber (1925) on his tribal map of California. According to the linear scales shown on the respective maps, planimeter measurement gives 6,735 square miles for Kniffen and 5,770 for Kroeber. The difference lies principally in the greater extent of domain allowed by Kniffen at the zone of contact with the Paiute in the northeast. The eleven sub-groups fall naturally into an eastern and a western division, five in the west, six in the east. The former lay in the oak belt, enjoyed a higher rainfall, and had available better subsistence. By measurement, using Kniffen's map, the western sector included 2,120 square miles, the eastern 4,615 square miles.

Kniffen made an estimate of the aboriginal population of each subgroup. He based his figures upon numbers of former houses, and upon statements of informants. In support of this procedure he points out first that the Pit River Indians were not seriously disturbed in the 1850s—and previously not at all—and, second, that the present population is relatively great when compared with other California tribes. There is undoubtedly a good deal of subjective evaluation here, but Kniffen's estimates, which were accepted by his informants, and which carry back in memory almost if not quite to the aboriginal condition, probably come close to the truth. If they err at all it is on the side of underestimate. We may use them with substantial assurance. His totals give 1,450 for the eastern division and 1,550 for the western, hence 3,000 for the entire population.

If these figures are used, the population density for the eastern division is approximately 0.30 persons per square mile, for the western division 0.73. Since the habitats of the two divisions were quite distinct, it is preferable to keep the density figures separate.

It is well recognized that the Achomawi, in common with all northern California Indians, were territorially very unevenly distributed, because they maintained their permanent settlements only along the water courses, leaving great tracts of land uninhabited. How, then, can a density be valid when it is applied to all types of land indiscriminately? The answer must be that the tribal area embraced all land within the recognized boundaries. Regardless of fixed villages and long term habitation, as Kroeber has repeatedly demonstrated, each tribe, band, or clan had the use of a relatively large area within which it operated for the purpose of securing subsistence. The population, therefore, however it might be restricted in the orbit of its homestead, was actually dependent politically and economically upon its entire domain. Thus it is quite proper to relate number of people to total territory in order to calculate density.

The California Modoc lived in the barren, arid northeastern corner of the state in a territory which contained about 2,350 square miles. Kroeber (1925:320) thought that their number did not exceed 300-350 persons. However, it is possible to apply the density found for the eastern division of the Achomawi, close to 0.30 persons per square mile, since the topography and the available subsistence were almost identical in the two areas. Furthermore the fact that the Modoc frequently raided the adjacent Achomawi and captured prisoners indicates at least numerical parity. There would have been, consequently, 705, or call it 700, Modoc in the state.

To the Shasta and their related neighbors the density values for the Achomawi can not be directly applied, for the habitats of the two groups are by no means identical. On the other hand, it is possible to make adjustments for this difference. If we move in imagination from west to east across California between the 40th and 41st parallels of latitude, we encounter first the linguistic groups Tolowa and Yurok on the coast and the lower Klamath River. Then come the Hupa and the Karok on the lower Trinity and middle Klamath Rivers. They are followed by the Shasta, together with the New River Shasta and the Okwanuchu. Finally, to the eastward are the Achomawi and the Modoc. The environment progresssively changes from the wet coastal habitat, with dense forests and enormous resources of fish, to the drier hill and river country abounding in oaks and still carrying a heavy load of fish in the rivers. Ultimately the oaks disappear, as do the great runs of fish, to be replaced by juniper and sagebrush in the arid highlands of the southern Cascades. Population density changes with the climate.

For the western tribes, the areas and populations have been calculated in a previous study (Cook, 1956). The Yurok and Tolowa show respectively 4.66 and 3.56 persons per square mile. The Hupa on the lower Trinity River have 5.20 and the Karok, well upstream on the Klamath, have 2.42. The Shasta are as yet undetermined. The density of the western Achomawi is 0.73, and that of the eastern Achomawi and Modoc is 0.30 persons per square mile. Thus a steadily diminishing population density follows the impoverishment and increasing aridity of the habitat from the coast to the Great Basin, and the human capacity for utilization becomes the major factor in establishing the equilibrium population.

If this interdependence of variables is valid, then the Shasta must occupy a middle position, between the Achomawi on the east and to the Karok and Hupa on the west. We do not know the exact values for density but a fairly close approximation may be achieved. The three western Achomawi sub-groups, the Ilamawi, Itsatawi, and Madesi (Kniffen, 1928), have an aggregate area of 800 square miles with a population of 900 souls. The density is close to 1.13 persons per square mile. Then we may say that the Okwanuchu, just to the northwest, had the same density, and, with an area of 595 square miles, a population of 675. The Shasta proper and the New River Shasta lived under the same conditions and probably had essentially the same density. The value of the latter should be intermediate between the westernmost Achomawi, 1.1, and that of the Karok, 2.4. We take the median, 1.75, and reduce it slightly to 1.7. The total area by map measurement of these groups, including the Konomihu, is 3,105 square miles. If the density was 1.7 the population would have been 5,280. When the Okawanuchu are added, the total for all branches of the Shasta becomes 5,955.

A check on the Shasta is possible by means of the village lists published by Heizer and Hester (1970). These represent a consolidation and reconciliation of the lists previously published by Dixon (1907) and Kroeber (1925) with the list of Merriam (Ms. on file, Dept. of Anthropology, University of California, Berkeley). There are 156 names, of which five are stated to have been Karok, not Shasta, and three are designated camp sites. The remaining 148 may be regarded as villages in existence at or near the year 1850 on the Klamath and in the valleys of the Shasta and the Scott Rivers.

The use of villages for the purpose of computing populations depends upon their average size. In this instance the list published by Heizer and Hester gives no clue. However, we do have data from neighboring tribes. Kniffen (1928) counted villages among the Atsugewi and Achomawi. His total was 131, which, with a total population of 3,000, gives a mean of 22.9 persons per village. To the west, for the Karok, Cook (1956), using Kroeber's village list showing 118 villages and his own population estimate, also found 22.9 persons per village. If Kroeber (1925:109) is correct, the Chimariko on the Trinity had 6 villages and 250 people, or 41.7 persons per village. The comparable figure for the Yurok is 43.7 and for the Hupa 77.0 (Cook, 1956). By analogy with the Achomawi and the Karok, the average village size of the Shasta might be 25 persons. If so, for the 148 villages the total population would be 3,700. However, in the Heizer and Hester list ten villages are noted as "large" or "big". Hence they must have exceeded 25 persons each, and by a considerable margin. Perhaps a few reached 100 or more. Nevertheless, we should estimate for these ten places an average of no more than 75 persons. The total then becomes 4,200 for the Shasta proper. Since there are no village lists for the Okwanuchu and the New River Shasta, the values obtained by density will have to be retained. For the entire group the population then becomes 5,870.

The two results, 5,955 and 5,870 are very close, probably spuriously so. The methods used obviously involve considerable error, at least plus or minus five to ten percent. However, they agree in principle, and we may conclude that the Shasta had a population of 5,900, give or take 500 persons. If we add 3,000 for the Pit Rivers and 700 for the Modoc, the pre-contact population of northeastern California would have been approximately 9,600.

The Sacramento Valley province includes two sharply defined types of habitat. In the center we find the flat valley floor with two large rivers, the Sacramento and the Feather, along which Indian villages were strung like beads on a chain. There were few tributaries except Putah Creek and Cache Creek on the west and the American and Yuba Rivers on the east. Between these streams the arid plain extended uninhabited. The periphery is hilly or mountainous. The Coast Ranges, the rough country in Trinity and Siskiyou Counties, and the Sierra Nevada foothills ring the valley on three sides. There are numerous small streams, most of which saw planted on their banks villages of the type found among the Shasta and Achomawi, but frequently larger. In considering population it will be convenient to treat these habitats separately. This is particularly desirable because somewhat different methods have to be employed in the two cases.

The southernmost extension of the Sacramento Valley was occupied by a group which Kroeber (1932) called the Southern Patwin. It extends from Putah Creek to the Delta, Suisin, and San Pablo Bays and includes the lower few miles of the Napa River. There has been no detailed survey of living centers south and southwest of Putah Creek. A few villages may be assigned to this territory, but as Kroeber points out they are likely to have been the capitals of tribelets, from which they take their name.

One element which has almost nullified the efforts of ethnographers is the fact that the Southern Patwin were swept into the missions as early as 1810, long before the memory of modern informants. As a result, our principal source of information lies in the mission records.

These records are discussed in detail in connection with the Costanoans and other linguistic groups further south. Those which are pertinent here are three in number. First is the baptism book of the Mission San Francisco Solano, preserved in the Bancroft Library at Berkeley. The second and third are the copies of the mission books of San Francisco de Asis and San José made by Alphonse L. Pinart for H. H. Bancroft and also to be found in the Bancroft Library. In all three documents the village of origin is given for each gentile baptized, and the Pinart copies, although they have been criticized for inaccuracy, are sufficiently reliable for the present purpose. It is possible to allocate many of the village names to the appropriate linguistic stock, and thereby arrive at an approximation to the number of Southern Patwin natives who were baptized in the three missions. In addition there are roughly 700 baptisms of Indians from villages some of whose names are clearly, some only possibly, of Patwin origin.

There are four large villages, or tribelets as Kroeber would have called them, the names of which very frequently recur: the Suisunes, the Libaytos, the Canicaymos, and the Ululatos, the respective baptisms from which were 231, 217, 233, and 572. To these may be added the Napa, who may not have been entirely Patwin, but for whom are recorded 193 baptisms. The mean is 289. If we allow one half of the doubtful Patwin villages, or 350 souls, we get a total of close to 1,800.

Unlike the territory of the Costanoans and Salinans, missionization in this area was marginal. Mission Dolores did not reach northeast of the bay until 1810; San Francisco Solano not until after 1820. In the meantime proselyting effort declined and the missions were secularized in 1833-1834. As a result many natives escaped conversion. It is probable that not more than one third of the aboriginal number were recorded as baptized. Consequently we may double or triple the number of converts and count the pre-mission population as in the vicinity of 5,000.

This value receives indirect confirmation from two sources. The first is the diary of the expedition by Capt. Luis Arguello in 1821. A copy of this diary, kept by Fr. Blas Ordaz, is in the Bancroft Library (Santa Barbara Archive, Vol. IV, 161-190) and was published as a translation into English by Heizer and Hester (1970b). On Oct. 23, 1821, the party reached the rancheria of the Ululatos (near Vacaville). The Father was ''astonished at the small number of gentiles'' found there—only 30. The remainder had fled because of a local war. His astonishment implies the expectation of finding at least a few hundred souls. On the same day the rancheria of the Libaytos, on Putah Creek, was reached. There were only 50 Indians, the rest being away to gather seeds. However, ''according to the houses'' which the Spaniards could easily count, there might have been 400 persons. The recorded baptisms of the Ululatos and Libaytos were about 450. If the population of the two rancherias was near 1,000, as is indicated by the remarks of Father Ordaz, it was more than twice the number of conversions.

The second source of confirmation is the population density. Although it is true that the environment as well as the settlement pattern found for the Patwin is quite different from that which characterizes the Miwok, Pomo, and Yuki of the coast ranges, the probable densities might be more or less comparable. When the areas are measured on Kroeber's tribal map (1925), and when the populations are taken from Cook (1956), the results are: for the Yuki plus the northeastern Pomo, 5.3 persons per square mile; for the remainder of the Pomo, 6.4; for the Wappo plus Coast and Lake Miwok, 4.3. The Patwin, south of Putah Creek, had 1,130 square miles and 5,000 souls. The density, 4.4, is close to the range of the groups which border on the west. We may also compare the area to the east and south. According to the data given by Cook (1955a), the Delta, together with the lower courses of the Cosumnes, Mokelumne, Calaveras, Stanislaus, and Tuolumne Rivers, had an aggregate area of 3,200 square miles and supported a population of 27,070. The density would have been 8.4 persons per square mile, probably the highest in California. The density to the north and west of the lower Sacramento would be expected to fall far short of this value, although perhaps it might not be less than one half. On the whole, therefore, if we can rely upon density calculations, a population estimate of 5,000 for the southern Patwin is reasonable.

The main axis of the Sacramento Valley embraces a territory which runs from Putah Creek northward to Cottonwood Creek and then southward along the foot of the Sierra Nevada to the American River. The native linguistic stocks who lived here were, according to Kroeber's division (1932), the southern Patwin (those above Putah Creek), the Valley Nisenan, the River Patwin, the Valley Maidu, and the River Wintun. The Sacramento River between the city and Red Bluff, with the Feather River from Knight's Landing to Oroville, lie in the flat valley floor and constitute a sharply defined ecological province, which, with respect to human habitation, is dominated by the two wide rivers flowing through it. Their banks were studded with a series of villages that held almost the entire population of the region.

Some idea of the size of these rancherias can be obtained from the writings of men who saw them before their destruction by disease and the invasion of the whites. Father Blas Ordaz, in describing the expedition of Arguello, gives the number of inhabitants of several villages. One has already been mentioned—the rancheria of the Libaytos, with an estimated 400 souls. Then comes Ehita, not cited by either Kroeber or Merriam, on Cache Creek somewhere near Madison, with 900 souls according to the houses. Next is Goroy, apparently on the Sacramento near Grimes, with 1,000. Higher up the river was Guiribay with 1,600. About a mile or two south of Princeton was Cha, said to be the second largest Patwin village after Coru. These are called Chah-de-ha and Koroo by Merriam in Heizer and Hester, (1970:83). According to Ordaz, there were 400-500 children up to 14 years of age at Cha, with 1,000 older people, for a total of 1,400. Father Ordaz does not give a population for Coru, but if it was larger than Cha it must have held at least 1,500 persons. Thus, if we omit the Libaytos, who may already have been decimated by the Spaniards, there are five River Patwin villages with an average of 1,280 inhabitants.

Certain points should be kept in mind with respect to the Arguello account. Only the largest villages are mentioned by name, and probably they were the only ones to receive serious attention. It is impossible to say with precision how much smaller the many unmentioned villages were. However, few would have had less than 200 inhabitants, and many would have had several hundred. If we include the largest, the average size was probably of the order of 500 persons.

Further testimony comes from numerous later writers, but the only one who saw the Sacramento Valley himself, prior to 1834, was John Work, who described his trip south from Oregon in his journal (published by Alice Bay Maloney in 1945). In early January 1833, Work was on the lower Feather River, where, in a "short" day's journey, he passed or contacted seven Indian villages. "The inhabitants of each must amount to some hundreds" (1945:25). A few days later he counted 28 houses in one village and 40-50 houses in each of four others. This would mean an average of 300-400 persons in each. Apart from Work's journal, we find much hearsay, or second-hand evidence from explorers and travelers who visited the area between 1835 and 1845, to the effect that most native villages did contain or had contained from several hundred to over one thousand inhabitants. The unanimity of opinion is startling, for there seems to be not a single dissenting voice. Moreover, wholesale exaggeration or prevarication is extremely unlikely in the complete absence of any motive for such behavior. There can be little doubt, therefore, that an average of 500 is reasonable and even conservative.

Subsequent to 1833, and particularly in the years just preceding and following the discovery of gold, numerous counts and estimates of the Indian population in the Sacramento Valley were made by settlers and by government officials. Several of these are reproduced by Heizer and Hester (1970 a and b). Many more are cited by Cook (1943b: table 1 and notes). Here all of them must be ignored, for none of them gives a true picture of aboriginal populations. The change had been enormous since 1833.

During the years 1810 to 1845 there were repeated incursions into the lower Sacramento Valley by Spaniards and Mexicans, and these began the process of demoralization and disturbance of native society. In this activity they were assisted by the earliest settlers and holders of

---

**Map 1.** California north of the latitude of San Francisco Bay, and in particular the Sacramento Valley. The lighter lines delineate the counties. The heavy lines indicate the tribal divisions of the Indians, as discussed in the text, or as modified from Kroeber (1925, 1932). The boundaries cannot be and are not intended to be strictly accurate, but the error involved does not exceed a few percent. The broken lines represent the approximate boundaries of subdivisions within the main tribal entities, such as the Wintun or Maidu. The names of the counties are displayed on the map, but the tribal divisions are designated by numbers for a key to which reference is made to the list below. A few of the principal towns are shown for the purpose of orientation.

| | | | |
|---|---|---|---|
| 1. | Tolowa | 14. | Pomo |
| 2. | Yurok | 15. | Wappo and Coast Miwok |
| 3. | Karok | 16. | Northern Wintun, or Wintu |
| 4. | Wiyot | 17. | Yana and Yahi |
| 5. | Hupa | 18. | Hill Wintun |
| 6. | Chimariko | 19. | Valley, or River Wintun |
| 7. | New River Shasta | 20. | Valley, or River Maidu |
| 8. | Shasta | 21. | Hill Patwin |
| 9. | Modoc | 22. | Valley, or River Patwin |
| 10. | Okwanuchu | 23. | Valley Nisenan |
| 11. | Achomawi and Atsugewi (Pit Rivers) | 24. | Southern Patwin |
| 12. | Athabascans | 25. | Northeastern Maidu |
| 13. | Yuki | 26. | Hill Maidu |
| | | 27. | Hill Nisenan |

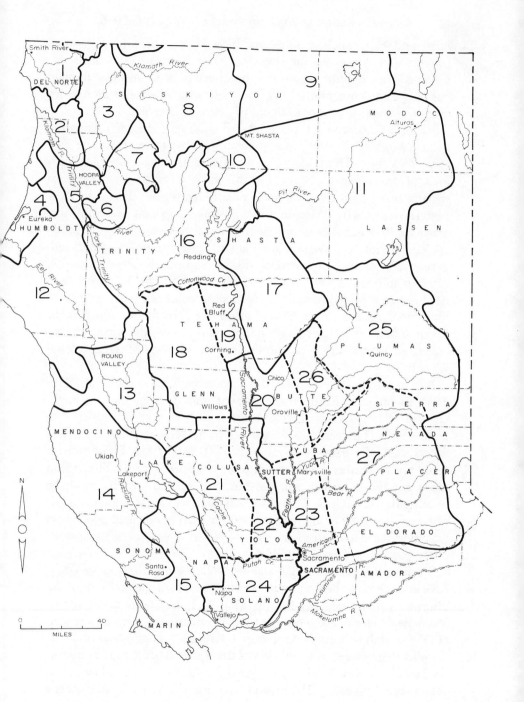

large land grants such as Sutter and Bidwell, together with occasional English and American fur trappers. None of these individuals entertained the slightest regard for the integrity of indigenous life and custom. The demographic effect was seriously adverse, although we can not assess the damage in rigorously numerical terms.

An even greater effect was produced by disease. In 1833 came the great "pandemic" which was extremely lethal throughout the Sacramento Valley. The principal facts concerning it have been set forth in a previous paper (Cook, 1955b) and the cause is ascribed to malaria brought in from the Columbia River region. The year 1837 saw the so-called "Miramontes epidemic", which was probably smallpox. It was particularly severe toward the coast, but apparently spilled over into the Wintun and Patwin. Later epidemics, and the all-pervasive syphilis, early introduced by the Spaniards, are discussed in detail in an essay of 1943 (Cook, 1943a: 11-12). The details on these need not be repeated here. It is adequate to point out that, because of introduced maladies, the natives along the Sacramento and Feather Rivers suffered extreme reduction in numbers, a decline which was accentuated by the disruption attending the physical entrance of the white man.

It is necessary to emphasize this demographic catastrophe of 1830-1845 in order to justify the statement that none of the twentieth-century ethnographers is to be trusted with respect to estimates of population. The reason is simple. Barrett, Kroeber, Merriam, and others used informants of no more than 70 years of age. These persons could not remember events much prior to 1850 or 1860. They could name and locate former villages, but they had no knowledge of the number of inhabitants. Therefore, although we can accept names and places indicated by modern informants, we can not depend upon them for reports of size. Instead, we are obliged to rely upon contemporary observers such as Ordaz and Work.

We now turn to other Sacramento Valley groups and in so doing have attempted to show the approximate location of the divisions of the Wintun, Patwin, and Maidu on Map 1. It has been necessary to reconcile differences between the tribal boundaries as given on the map of 1925 and those found on the map to Kroeber's monograph of 1932. Kroeber compiled a list of villages of the Valley Maidu and Wintun in the Handbook (1925). He later revised this list for his special essays on the Valley Nisenan (1929) and the Patwin (1932). Meanwhile

Merriam, using other informants, had accumulated a different list which was only recently published by Heizer and Hester (1970a; 79-93). The two lists overlap but do not coincide exactly, largely because informants remembered or had heard about different settlements. Merriam's list, as presented by Heizer and Hester, gives 77 places on the Sacramento and the Feather Rivers. Kroeber (1932) mentions approximately 50. By examining both lists, and by following Heizer and Hester's reconciliation, we get 17 villages listed by Kroeber but not by Merriam, 47 listed by Merriam but not by Kroeber, and 30 listed by both. The total is 94 places, the existence of which is reasonably assured. If the aboriginal inhabitants averaged 500 persons per village, the total population would have been 47,000. When we add 5,000 for the partially missionized Southern Patwin, we get 52,000. If the average of 500 persons per village seems too high, it should be borne in mind that the Kroeber-Merriam lists do not contain all the rancherias in existence prior to 1830.

When we consider the hill divisions of the Patwin, Wintun, Yana, and Maidu, we revert again to area-density determinations, but we support this method by means of village lists provided principally by Kroeber. The boundaries between these divisions and those of the river groups are not clearly defined on Kroeber's maps. Hence the areas can be only approximate. The Hill Patwin extended along the inner coast ranges from Putah Creek north to the sources of Stony Creek near Stonyford. The western boundary met the Pomo and the Lake Miwok east of Clear Lake. The eastern boundary was vague, but according to Kroeber's (1932) map it may be taken as a line connecting Winters with Dunnigan and thence continuing northward along the Southern Pacific Railway. This territory embraces somewhere near 1,600 square miles.

The density may be judged by comparison with the adjacent Pomo, Wappo, and Miwok. Area measurement, as has previously been stated, gives for the Yuki and Northeast Pomo 5.3 persons per square mile, for the Pomo proper 6.4, and for the Miwok and Wappo 4.3. The Hill Patwin cannot have exceeded the last value. Indeed, it is doubtful whether they even reached it. The reason lies in the fact that this group lived along narrow stream valleys in the relatively arid coast ranges. They possessed no lake front and no wide, fertile bottom lands such as characterized the Russian River system or the upper Napa Valley. The open land on the west side of the Sacramento Valley yielded little subsistence and was virtually uninhabited. Hence we can assign a maximum of no more than three persons per square mile. With 1,000 square miles this would mean a population of 4,800.

Kroeber (1932) lists 19 names of settlements for the Hill Patwin. However, he makes it very clear that these denote tribelets, or small, independent units of the linguistic stock as a whole. Each name also extends to the principal village of the tribelet, and thus, demographically applies to the people who live there plus any others who might be scattered in the vicinity. It is in this sense that we must use his list for the Hill Patwin and the Hill Wintun. With regard to the average number of persons per settlement (or tribelet), Kroeber thinks 100 is adequate. On the other hand, a thorough study of the more coastal tribes (Cook, 1956) shows that for them 200 is far more likely, with a distinct possibility of a higher value. Since the Hill Patwin resemble the Pomo and Wappo in many other respects, we may consider 200 to be a fair average value. The total then becomes 3,800.

The two estimates differ by 1,000 persons. However, the figure based upon villages is probably the more accurate. We shall therefore set the value at 4,000 and the density consequently at 2.5 persons per square mile.

The Hill Wintun extended northward of the Hill Patwin as far as the middle fork of Cottonwood Creek. To the west they fronted on the Yuki. To the east they reached the Southern Pacific Railway as far north as Kirkwood, just south of Corning. At this point they merged with the small group, the Valley Wintun, which according to Kroeber's account, held the Sacramento River from below Corning to several miles above Red Bluff. We are actually dealing, therefore, with two divisions of the Wintun. The strictly hill division occupied a large expanse of hill country which reached west as far as the headwaters of the Trinity and Eel Rivers. Their habitat and their settlement pattern resembled that of the Hill Patwin, whereas the River Wintun represented a northward extension of the River Maidu.

The density of the Hill Wintun was probably less than that of the Hill Patwin to the south and of the Yuki to the west. If we say 2.0 persons per square mile the estimate will be liberal. This would mean for approximately 1,950 square miles 3,900 persons. Kroeber found ten tribelets or settlements which appeared authentic. At 200 per tribelet the total population would be 2,000. However, there were several doubtful cases mentioned by informants which Kroeber rejected but which may have indicated some type of occupation. Furthermore, the territory was exposed to epidemics in the 1830s and was overrun by miners in the 1850s. It is likely, therefore, that the original number of tribelets was greater than ten. As a compromise, we may set the population at 3,000.

The River Wintun area covers not much more than 500 square miles. Kroeber's principal informants located five settlements, which may have been tribelets, all below Red Bluff. For the Valley Maidu and the River Patwin we used an average of 500 persons per village. The River Wintun were probably not quite so numerous. At 400 each the population would have been 2,000, and at 300 each it would have been 1,500. It is of interest that another informant who had lived most of his life in the valley near Chico mentioned four areas along the river which were Wintun tribelets. Again we get somewhere near 1,500. The entire region, Hill Wintun and River Wintun, would thus have contained 4,500 souls.

The group called by Kroeber in 1925 the Northern Wintun are also known on linguistic grounds as Wintu, or as the Trinity Wintu. They held the territory north of Cottonwood Creek, on the upper Trinity River and east to the Sacramento. As outlined on Kroeber's tribal map (1925) they covered about 3,550 square miles. There are no village lists available, and very little modern knowledge of any kind. The social organization was effectively destroyed by the miners in the 1850s. Consequently we are forced to almost an outright guess with respect to aboriginal population.

The habitat, along the headwaters of the Trinity and Sacramento Rivers, consisted of narrow stream canyons among high hills or mountains. The villages must have been of moderate size and number, perhaps resembling those of the Karok and western Shasta. We used a density of 2.4 for the Karok and 1.7 for the Shasta. Farther south the density of the Hill Patwin was estimated at 2.5 and of the Hill Wintun about 1.6 persons per square mile. The area of the Wintu must have been more sparsely inhabited than that of the groups which approached the open Sacramento Valley, and also of that held by the Shasta. Hence a value of 1.5 persons per square mile will not be excessive. The population may be put at 5,325, or, after rounding off, 5,300.

Similar considerations apply to the Yana and Yahi, who inhabited the broken lava country along the eastern affluents of the Sacramento from Chico north to the Pit River. The terrain was very inhospitable and even today is thinly settled. Environmentally the closest Indian stocks were the western Achomawi and the Okwanuchu. Since there are no village records and since the Yana and Yahi are extinct, the only basis for a population estimate is that of density. The Okwanuchu were assigned a density of 1.2 persons per square mile, and the western Achomawi one of 0.7. We may take the approximate median, 0.9. There were 2,035 square miles, hence the population estimate would be 1,830 persons, or, let us say 1,850.

With the Northeastern, or Mountain Maidu we again encounter data derived from villages. This division of the Maidu inhabited the headwaters of the North and Middle Forks of the Feather River, and extended north to Mt. Lassen and Susanville. To the east they reached the crest of the Sierra Nevada as far south as Sierraville. The settlements, however, were concentrated at and to the north of Quincy, leaving great tracts of land uninhabited.

Kroeber (1925) lists seven settlements, at the same time carefully explaining that these are actually territorial divisions, each one of which comprised several local hamlets or villages. He lists six places for the settlement at Quincy, called Silo-ng-koyo (1925:397), and three for Tasi-koyo in Indian Valley (p. 398). He also shows the number of houses. In Silo there were 18-23, or an average of 3.5 per hamlet; in Tasi there were 20-22, or an average of 7 per hamlet. If there were seven settlements, or tribelets, with an average of 20 houses each, the total houses would have been 140. Kroeber thinks the number of persons per house would have been between 5 and 10, and mentions the Yurok number of 7.5. Since these were single family dwellings, the Yurok number is applicable. The population then would have reached 1,050, with an average tribelet size of 150. The area was measured on Kroeber's maps and found to be 3,530 square miles. The density therefore was 0.34 persons per square mile. This is substantially the same value as was derived for the Modoc and eastern Achomawi, who lived in much the same type of country. If the value seems very low for the Northeastern Maidu, who were localized in the broad valleys of central Plumas County, it must be remembered that their entire living space included much high mountain and desert terrain. At any rate there is no evidence now available which would justify increasing the estimated population.

Two of Kroeber's original groups of Maidu were called the North-western and the Southern. From these he later established four branches, which he designated the Hill and the Valley Maidu, and the Hill and the Valley Nisenan. The valley divisions we have already included among the river inhabitants. We have left, therefore, the two divisions who lived in the foothill region and controlled the land to the crest of the high Sierra Nevada.

We first consult the village lists of Kroeber, and in so doing we consolidate the Hill Maidu and the Hill Nisenan into a single entity. Upstream from a line drawn five or ten miles east of Oroville, Marysville, and Sacramento, Kroeber gives the number of villages on the various river systems in the accompanying table.

| | |
|---|---|
| Feather River | 11 |
| Honcut Creek | 2 |
| Yuba River | 6 |
| Bear River | 1 |
| American River | 12 |
| Cosumnes River, North Fork | 5 |
| Total | 37 |

With regard to the size and importance of these places, Kroeber (1925:393) says: "In some regions minor villages have been included, in other tracts even the major towns have not been recorded." The 37 names therefore probably represent an intermediate magnitude. For the Northeastern Maidu, an average of 150 persons per settlement was assumed. In view of Kroeber's uncertainty, and because the larger villages were more apt to be remembered by informants, we may raise this value to 200. The population of the foothill strip would then reach 7,400.

An area-density calculation may be attempted. Simply for the purpose of making a check of consistency we may delineate an area bounded on the west by the border between the Hill and the Valley tribes, and on the east by the limit of Kroeber's village sites. The northern and southern boundaries are respectively Chico Creek and the North Fork of the Cosumnes. The high mountains are thus excluded. Very approximately, the area contains 2,800 square miles. With a population of 7,400, the density is 2.65 persons per square mile, a value not unreasonable in view of the densities found in similar hilly regions elsewhere.

Another possible check is by means of the distribution of population along streams, particularly since most of the Maidu lived on the banks of rivers. A basis for comparison is the set of calculations made by Baumhoff (1963), who has computed "fish-miles" for many of the North Coast and San Joaquin Valley tribes. By fish-mile he means a mile of river from which fish can be taken in significant amounts. The main streams in the Hill Maidu area were all plentifully stocked with fish, although the minor affluents can be ignored as a source of supply. Hence direct measurements of the primary streams yield stream lengths which are comparable with the aggregate fish-miles of Baumhoff. For population he uses the values given by Cook (1955a, 1956). Some of his results can be listed in the accompanying table.

| Stream or tribe | miles | persons per river mile |
|---|---|---|
| Lower Merced | 32 | 55 |
| Middle Kings | 75 | 67 |
| Lower Kings | 20 | 75 |
| Plains Miwok | 252 | 57 |
| Central Miwok | 88 | 24 |
| Southern Miwok | 60 | 45 |
| Average: | | 54 |

In the Hill Maidu territory there are three substantial river systems, those of the American, the Yuba, and the Feather. For these the approximate mileages, together with the population estimated from village counts, are given in the accompanying table.

| Stream | Miles | Population | Persons per river mile |
|---|---|---|---|
| American River | 60 | 2,400 | 40 |
| Yuba River | 60 | 1,200 | 20 |
| Feather River | 70 | 2,200 | 31 |
| Average: | | | 30 |

Although the values for the Maidu fall below those of the Yokuts on the Merced and the Kings River, they are not materially different from those of the Central and Southern Miwok. The consistency is reasonable, particularly when we consider the wide limits of error imposed by such a crude method. It appears, therefore, that the number 7,400 is not far wrong for the population of the Hill Maidu and the Hill Nisenan.

We can now put together the pieces and assemble the most probable aboriginal population of the Sacramento Valley and adjacent foothills. We compose the list according to the secondary linguistic divisions.

| | |
|---|---:|
| Southern Patwin, missionized | 5,000 |
| Southern Patwin, non-missionized | |
| Valley Nisenan | |
| River Patwin | |
| Valley Maidu | 47,000 |
| Hill Patwin | 4,000 |
| Hill Wintun | 3,000 |
| River Wintun | 1,500 |
| Northern Wintun or Wintu | 5,300 |
| Yana and Yahi | 1,850 |
| Northeastern Maidu | 1,050 |
| Hill Maidu | |
| Hill Nisenan | 7,400 |
| Total for the province | 76,100 |

In concluding this portion of the present essay, it is of interest to compare the population of the two great valleys of California, the San Joaquin and the Sacramento. In the San Joaquin, a study by the writer (Cook, 1955a) found 83,800 natives living on 33,400 square miles, or 2.51 persons per square mile. In the Sacramento, the present calculation indicates 76,100 on 22,700 square miles, or 3.35 persons per square mile. If we add the thinly populated northern tier of tribes, 9,600 people living on close to 12,800 square miles, we get for the entire northern interior 85,700 persons and 35,500 square miles. The density is 2.41 persons per square mile. The two regions are therefore remarkably similar in demographic character.

## The Mission Strip

Thirty years ago (1940, 1943a) I investigated the population of the coast which was controlled by the Spanish missions. Since that time, with the exception of the Chumash, no aboriginal group living within the area has been studied in detail, either ethnographically or demographically. In the meantime, however, the extensive mission village lists of Merriam have been published (1968, 1970), I have contributed a little on Alameda and Contra Costa Counties (1957), and a host of works have appeared which describe the missions themselves. The time is appropriate for a brief resume of existing knowledge concerning the aboriginal population which was brought under the control of the Franciscan Friars.

The area embraced by the mission system at the peak of its development began with San Francisco Bay and its extensions northeast as far as Mount Diablo. Thence it stretched down the coast to San Diego without interruption. The interior boundary was in places indefinite, but for the present purpose may be taken as the crest of the innermost coast ranges and the high mountain chain of Southern California. From Mount Diablo the line of full mission occupation followed quite closely the present eastern boundaries of Santa Clara, San Benito, Monterey, and San Luis Obispo Counties. Then it crossed the Tehachapi to the San Gabriel Mountains and the San Bernardino and San Jacinto Ranges. From San Jacinto Peak it followed a generally southerly course to the Lower California border. Thus the entire area includes a band of territory seven hundred miles long and from fifty to one hundred and fifty miles wide.

The population of this great region cannot be studied as a single unit, for its ethnographic as well as geographic diversity is too great. A division is necessary into subordinate parts. Of these there are three which naturally come to mind. The first is the region inhabited by the Costanoans and Salinans between San Francisco Bay and the headwaters of the Salinas River. To this may be added for convenience the local area under the jurisdiction of San Luis Obispo even though there is an infringement upon the domain of the Chumash. The second province includes the Chumash of the Santa Barbara Channel from Mission Purisima to and including San Buenaventura. The third division embraces all of Southern California from San Fernando to San Diego. We initially examine the northern division, but first there must be a few words concerning method and sources.

The mission area differs from other parts of California in an utter lack of ethnographic information with respect to native habitation. The original occupants were completely transferred to the mission centers prior to 1810. Hence few survivors were available as informants to modern students, and those few could contribute nothing with respect to the size and number of the pre-mission villages. A few contemporary accounts have survived, but they benefit our knowledge in only a few, restricted areas. Thus the Portola expedition of 1769-1770, through Crespi's diary, has helped to establish the status of the villages along the Santa Barbara Channel. Other expeditions around San Francisco Bay were utilized for estimating the aboriginal population of Alameda and Contra Costa Counties (Cook, 1957). On the whole, however, these sources are not sufficiently extensive to be of value for calculation of the number of inhabitants throughout the region in its entirety.

The method of comparing densities by restricted areas is feasible to a limited extent, and is used as far as is possible. Further details are discussed as they apply to specific areas.

The only major approach that remains is through the mission statistics concerning conversions of the native population. The primary source of these data is the baptism books of the several missions, from which may be derived the number of heathen who were drawn into the mission from the coastal region. These records are still extant for more than half the missions, although several have disappeared in the course of time. Nevertheless, copies have been made so that the pattern as a whole may be reconstructed reasonably well.

The first person to transcribe baptism records in detail was Alphonse L. Pinart, who did his work for H. H. Bancroft in the 1880s. The village of origin of each neophyte is given, but there are said to be numerous clerical errors. Both the Pinart copies and some of the original books were examined by Miss Stella R. Clemence for Dr. C. Hart Merriam. She constructed village lists from at least fourteen missions which have been recently published (1968, 1970). These lists are very valuable, although it was the primary purpose of Miss Clemence to put on record the names of the villages and their spelling variants.

Ten or fifteen years ago, I was permitted by the Church authorities to employ a competent assistant, Mr. Thomas W. Temple III, who transcribed the baptism and death books of some of the missions. He tabulated carefully the vital statistics pertaining to all gentile converts, including the name of the native rancheria of each. These copies, as far as they go, are probably as accurate as any we possess for the purpose of counting gentile baptisms.

Another set of documents which were examined and to some extent utilized by Miss Clemence consists of a series of censuses, ''padrones,'' or registers, pertaining to a number of the missions. Actually, each one enumerated the gentile neophytes as of a certain date who were living in the mission. The village of origin was always noted. It is clear that these lists are very useful for the study of names, but are of no value whatever for the determination of total gentiles baptized. They omit all gentiles who were baptized but died before the taking of the census, along with all those who were baptized after that date.

In a monograph on mission population (Cook, 1940), I employed a still different set of documents. These are a collection of transcripts, preserved at the Bancroft Library, which are copies of the annual reports of the missionaries to their superiors in Mexico. The originals were in the California Archive at San Francisco, but were destroyed by fire in 1906. The copies made for H. H. Bancroft show for each year and mission the existing number of neophytes, and the births and the deaths. A good many of the reports were missing. The vacancies were filled in by Bancroft's assistants, who made estimates as best they could. Fortunately, the missing items were not numerous and were widely scattered in place and time. It is clear that the entire set of data leaves much to be desired, but nevertheless it may be regarded as a fair approximation.

For number of total baptisms I have relied upon the tabulation by Father Zephyrin Engelhardt (1913, Vol. III, Appendix J, p. 653). He may be regarded as the most dependable of the serious writers on general mission history.

The first problem confronting us is to establish the number of gentile baptisms for each mission. The baptism books—as those used by Father Engelhardt, for example—record all persons baptized whether gentiles, mission-born Indians, or white people. Clearly the totals as shown by Engelhardt are in excess of the figure we want. The white persons are easy to recognize and may be excluded. The Indians are customarily distinguished according to whether or not they were born in the mission. Thus the children of neophytes may likewise be deleted. The remainder are heathen, who as children or adults, were converted from their native villages and brought under mission administration. Hence, starting with the baptism books, it is not difficult to get a value for gentile conversions.

Then come difficulties. Some are technical and inherent in the composition of the documents. The Bancroft transcripts show only total numbers for each year and mission. The baptisms had to be calculated from the record of deaths and the year-to-year differences in census population. The gentile baptisms then had to be derived by subtracting the number of *births* from that of the total *baptisms*. Needless to say a considerable error is unavoidable and the final result is only an approximation, although the order of magnitude is probably correct.

The copies by Temple are accurate and yield a reliable figure for gentile baptisms, because the mission births are either omitted from the copy or are designated as such. The Pinart copies appear to be reasonably faithful, at least insofar as pertains to the distinction between gentile and mission born, whatever may be their shortcomings in other respects. The Merriam lists are of dubious value for the present purpose. Miss Clemence was interested only in village names, and her statements concerning number of Indians converted from each village are unreliable. In some instances her arithmetic is at fault. For a few missions she compiled her list only from the ''padron'' or register, not the baptism book itself. Furthermore, she disregarded all place names of Spanish rather than Indian origin. Since many localities were known to the friars only by their Spanish names, the totals of Indians baptized are always too low.

Other difficulties arise when we have estimated the number of gentile baptisms and find that we are still not sure that the converts were of strictly local origin. Particularly in the northern missions, a great many Indians were brought from the central valley. These cannot be counted as part of the population derived from the coastal strip. There are two devices for effecting their exclusion. First, if the village or tribelet name is given it may be immediately recognized, and appropriate disposition made of the individual. Second, the time relations may be noted. Every mission in its early years drew upon the local or adjacent population. When these were exhausted, the friars went further afield. As far south as San Luis Obispo, the coastal conquest was completed by 1800 or 1805. There is then recognizable in the record for each mission a reduction or cessation of all gentile baptisms, which is followed within a few years by a new wave of conversions. These characteristically are foreigners, or Indians from outside the original mission area. The foreigners can readily be detected and excluded.

After we have computed the probable number of heathen converted within the territorial limits assigned to each mission, we are still confronted with the problem of estimating the aboriginal population from which these converts were drawn. Conversion did not occur simultaneously over the entire area. It was carried out by degrees until there were no remaining heathen. This process took as a rule from ten to thirty years, depending upon the stage of the whole program at which a given mission was initiated. At the same time certain general factors were operating to control the dynamics of conversion. Prominent among these was the demographic state of the native population at the point of departure for the mission system—that is, the year 1770.

All we know about aboriginal population in California indicates that the mid-eighteenth century was a time of equilibrium, that the birth and death rates were substantially equal, and that the total number of persons was more or less constant. With the arrival of the Spaniards the equilibrium in the coastal area was profoundly disturbed. Two processes were set in motion. The first was the withdrawal of natives as individuals from their native habitat to the mission establishments, where they were uniformly exposed to a much increased death rate, and probably a reduced birth rate. The second was the inevitable social and economic disruption of native living conditions, due to loss of many members and also to the spread of infectious disease from the missions to the remaining wild Indians.

If a population is in equilibrium so that the births just replace the deaths, and an external force initiates removals, the net number of persons will diminish. If we know the mathematical relation between the rate of loss and the time involved we can set up an equation to express the interaction of the variables. Thus, if the loss is proportional to the number present, or remaining, the function is exponential. However, in the present instance, due to the mechanics of conversion, we do not know the exact function. Furthermore, after missionization had begun, because of the second factor mentioned above, conversion operated upon not a residual equilibrium population, but upon one which was itself diminishing. The function hence becomes compound and the depletion of the aboriginal remnant proceeds faster than it would if conversion were the only causative factor. If it were the only factor, we could simply project the total conversions backward and get the initial population from which the converts were drawn. As matters stand, however, such a backward projection yields a value much smaller than that which actually expresses the aboriginal number. Our real problem is that of estimating the extent to which the initial population exceeds the sum of the conversions.

Since we cannot with safety apply rigid equations, it is necessary to resort to purely empirical devices. One of these is to make an outright assumption for the ratio of conversions to aboriginal population, or its reciprocal, population to conversions. For this purpose Merriam (1905) used the ratio 3:4 (or its reciprocal 1.33). Others have preferred 2:3 (reciprocal 1.5).

Some help is afforded by studies of restricted areas. One of these areas is Alameda and Contra Costa Counties (Cook, 1957), previously mentioned. The Fages-Crespi expedition in 1772 and the Anza-Font expedition in 1776 both circled the region: they moved along the shore of the bay from southern Alameda County around past the Carquinez Strait and back south through Dublin. They saw most of the villages but probably not all. The number of inhabitants reported was respectively 2,400 and 2,150. In the light of subsequent exploration and intercourse with the natives, it appears that these values are far too low for total population, and that 3,000 persons must be regarded as the minimum estimate. A somewhat higher figure, say 3,250, would not be inconsistent with the facts. The three missions—San Francisco, San Jose, and Santa Clara—baptized approximately 2,250 persons whose origin is stated as being in these counties. Hence the ratio of converts to population is 2,250:3,250 or 1:1.445, not far from 2:3.

A second area which can yield a meaningful figure is the Santa Barbara Channel. This stretch of coast, with unusually large and very numerous villages, has been studied by many investigators. Certainly the most exhaustive and careful work has been that of Brown (1967). His data may be used with the assurance that if they are not precisely accurate, nevertheless they are the best we are ever likely to have. Brown has examined all available mission records, and in his table 1 (1967:95) has shown the gentile baptisms for each of 26 towns located on the channel. In the body of his text (pp. 16-48) he catalogs these places and gives all known facts pertaining to their location and size, including the estimates of the first explorers, notably Portola, Crespi, and Costanso. The estimates are particularly clear and consistent for eleven of the towns. In our Table 1 we show (1) the average estimate of the explorers for each of these towns, taken from Brown's summary; (2) the total baptisms found by Brown in the mission books for each village; and (3) the ratio of population to baptisms in each instance. The average ratio is 2.37. In other words, the probable aboriginal

*Table 1.* BAPTISMS AND POPULATION IN ELEVEN
INDIAN VILLAGES, SANTA BARBARA CHANNEL

| Village[a] | Total baptisms[b] | Original population[c] | Ratio population/baptisms |
|---|---|---|---|
| Pedernales | 57 | 70 | 1.23 |
| Espada | 94 | 200 | 2.13 |
| Cojo | 163 | 210 | 1.29 |
| Bulito | 110 | 200 | 1.82 |
| Gaviota | 179 | 300 | 1.67 |
| Dos Pueblos | 360 | 1,100 | 3.65 |
| Mescaltitlan Island | 148 | 800 | 5.40 |
| San Joaquin | 198 | 600 | 3.03 |
| Carpinteria | 136 | 300 | 2.20 |
| Rincon | 130 | 300 | 2.31 |
| San Buenaventura | 292 | 400 | 1.37 |
| Mean ratio | | | 2.37 |

[a] Data from Chumash villages taken from Brown (1967).
[b] Total baptisms are from Brown, p. 95.
Original population is calculated as the average of the statements of Portola, Crespi, and Costanso, as given by Brown.

population is more than twice as great as would be indicated by the baptisms.

Brown furnishes further confirmation of this ratio in his table 3 (1967:98-99), where he lists for each of several villages both the number of converts born before 1771 and the percentage of these converts with respect to the estimated 1770 population. In this table he does not state this population in actual numbers. There are 17 places for which the percent of estimated 1770 population is given. The average is 25.5 percent. Otherwise expressed, the average ratio of aboriginal population to converts born *before* 1771 is 3.92. The difference between this value and that of 2.37, previously obtained, is referable to the omission, in Brown's table 3, of baptized gentiles who were born *after* 1771. If this fraction were added the ratio would come very close to 2.37. This very high ratio is discussed in detail in a subsequent paragraph.

The experience of Alameda and Contra Costa Counties was representative of the entire northern province. The climate, the vegetation, the food supply, the type and distribution of native settlements were all more or less similar from San Francisco to San Luis Obispo. The progress and effect of missionization were substantially alike throughout the territory. Hence there is no reason why the ratio of aboriginal population to gentile conversions found in the East Bay should not be applied generally. In order to avoid spurious accuracy we call the ratio not 1.445 but 1.5, and use this number as a multiplicative factor for deriving populations from number of conversions.

It is now necessary to examine with care the data relating to number of conversions. This task must be performed mission by mission, for each differed from the rest in at least minor respects. The results can not be embodied in a general table, for sources vary from case to case, and comment is required at numerous points throughout the compilation of figures. Nevertheless, the material is condensed wherever it is possible to do so.

SAN FRANCISCO DE ASIS

Engelhardt gives 6,899 for total baptisms.

The Bancroft Transcripts give 4,920 for total gentile baptisms. However, the Transcripts permit no differentiation according to locality. This differentiation is necessary with San Francisco records because many converts came from the region north of the bay, among the Coast Miwok, Pomo, and Patwin, as well as from nearer at hand Costanoan areas.

Merriam has two lists. The first (1968: 11-27) was taken by S. R. Clemence from the mission books of baptisms, and gives a total of 1,844 gentile baptisms. The second (1970: 49-53) "was compiled from an original Mission Register in possession of the Bancroft Library." It dates from 1780 to 1821, and according to the detailed list of Miss Clemence shows 1,237 baptisms. For some reason both these totals far understate the number of conversions.

This Mission Register, or "padron," I examined carefully some years ago, and found a total of 4,940 gentile baptisms recorded, very close to the number calculated from the Transcripts. Of these, 4,257 state the place of origin. See the accompanying detailed breakdown of rancherias, regarding nativity.

| | |
|---|---:|
| Western Costanoans (San Francisco and San Mateo Counties) | 1,087 |
| Eastern Costanoans (Alameda and Contra Costa Counties) | 985 |
| Coast Miwok, Pomo, Wappo, Patwin | 2,185 |
| Total | 4,257 |

In the Register, for the years 1796 to 1799 inclusive, no gentile baptisms are shown to have occurred, nor are there any shown by the Transcripts. For the years 1792 to 1795 inclusive, the Register shows baptisms but no rancherias. The baptisms amounted to 683, which, with 4,257, make up the total of 4,940. Since the Transcripts afford no clue, the origin of these 683 persons has to be estimated. There may have been a few from San Mateo County, let us say 53. Of the remaining 630 probably more came from the North Bay than from the East Bay. A fair guess is 420 and 210 respectively. (See accompanying table).

| | | |
|---|---|---|
| West Bay | 1,087 + 53 = | 1,140 |
| East Bay | 985 + 210 = | 1,195 |
| North Bay | 2,185 + 420 = | 2,605 |
| Total | | 4,940 |

The Pinart copy of the San Francisco baptism books is also relevant, despite its possible inaccuracy. This copy shows 1,125 baptisms from San Francisco and San Mateo Counties between 1777 and 1792, with none thereafter. From the East Bay are given 931 baptisms, to which may be added 287 from the Bolbones and other tribes which lived in eastern Contra Costa County or the adjacent delta. The total for Costanoans is then 2,343. There were 3,082 baptisms ascribed to North Bay and Suisun Bay groups, considerably more than were shown by the Register, a difference for which the reason is not clearly evident. We use the results from the Register (see Table 2), 2,335 conversions from the Costanoans, 2,605 from outside the area.

*Table 2.* BAPTISMS OF COSTANOAN AND SALINAN GENTILES IN TEN NORTHERN CALIFORNIA MISSIONS

| Mission | Local gentiles (Temple) | Local gentiles (Transcripts) | Local gentiles (other sources) | Gentiles from other areas | Total baptisms (Engel-hardt) |
|---|---|---|---|---|---|
| San Francisco | — | — | 2,335 | 2,605 | 6,899 |
| San Jose | — | 1,397 | 1,186 | 3,200 | 6,673 |
| Santa Clara | 4,240 | 4,257 | — | 1,840 | 8,536 |
| Santa Cruz | 1,220 | 1,130 | — | 503 | 2,439 |
| San Juan Bautista | 1,464 | 1,414 | — | 1,249 | 4,016 |
| San Carlos | 1,480 | 1,662 | — | 247 | 3,827 |
| La Soledad | 1,165 | 1,054 | — | 371 | 2,131 |
| San Antonio | 2,025 | 2,326 | — | 185 | 4,419 |
| San Miguel | 1,011 | 1,116 | — | 256 | 2,471 |
| San Luis Obispo | 1,361 | 1,263 | — | 29 | 2,644 |
| Total | 17,487 | | | 10,485 | 44,055 |
| Eight Missions, total | 13,966 | 14,222 | | | |

SAN JOSE

Engelhardt gives the total baptisms as 6,673.

We have the Bancroft Transcripts and also a Register. Merriam has no village list from this mission. In addition there is a copy by Pinart taken from the mission books.

The Register is highly defective. It shows only 2,084 gentiles baptized up to 1825, whereas the Transcripts give 5,177 up to 1832, and Pinart has 3,761. The census shows 510 mission born up to 1825, although the Transcripts and Engelhardt's data indicate three times that number.

The Pinart copy of the baptism record segregates village and tribelet names sufficiently to make an acceptable allocation of converts to the Costanoan territory. The number who were native to this area was 1,186. The Transcripts give for the period 1797-1807 inclusive 1,397 baptisms. Of these 1,186 could easily have been drawn from local villages. We therefore must use the value 1,186 as being Costanoan converts.

For the gentiles from the interior, the "Tulares," there is a wide discrepancy between Pinart and the Transcripts. The former gives 2,576, the latter 3,780. Both sources are likely at fault and we can do little more than take the average, approximately 3,200.

Engelhardt gives for total baptisms 8,536.

The Transcripts give 5,622 as total gentiles baptized, of which 4,257 were dated 1777 to 1808, inclusive, and may be regarded as local. From 1809 to 1832, 1,365 were baptized, mostly from the interior.

The copy of the baptism books made by Temple give by direct count 4,240 local gentiles, and 1,840 from the "Tulares," a total of 6,080 gentile baptisms. The discrepancy between 5,622 and 6,080 is considerable, and is referable almost entirely to the later conversions, for the estimates of local baptisms are very close to each other. Of the two sources, the Temple copy is of course the more reliable.

SANTA CRUZ

Engelhardt gives 2,439 for total baptisms.

The Transcripts give for 1791 to 1809 inclusive 1,130 local gentile baptisms; for the period 1810 to 1832 they show 420 gentiles, substantially all from the interior. The total is 1,550.

The Temple copy of the baptism books shows, by village 1,220 local baptisms and 503 from the interior, a total of 1,723. Merriam's list, from the Santa Cruz baptism books (1968: 38-42) gives 1,341 gentiles baptized from all areas. The number is clearly too small. We use the Temple copy.

SAN JUAN BAUTISTA

Engelhardt's total is 4,016 baptisms.

The Transcripts indicate that there were no gentile baptisms after 1805 until 1813, when they begin again and continue until 1834. Up to 1806 the number is 1,414, mostly, if not all, local. There are 1,249 from 1813 to 1834, all from the interior. The total is 2,663. The Temple copy of the baptism book stops at No. 1851, in the year 1808. The list up to 1807 shows 1,464 gentile baptisms, all local. We use this value from the Temple copy.

SAN CARLOS

Engelhardt's total is 3,827 baptisms.

The Temple copy shows 1,480 baptisms of local gentiles, with very few from the "Tulares."

The Transcripts between 1771 and 1800 give 1,662 baptisms, probably all local, and 247 between 1804 and 1832 from the interior, but this is no doubt an excessive value. Merriam's list (1968: 28-37) contains 1,426 gentile baptisms, almost all local. For this mission, the three estimates 1,480, 1,662, and 1,426, are quite consistent. We shall use the Temple copy, with 1,480 baptisms of local gentiles.

LA SOLEDAD

Engelhardt's total is 2,131 baptisms.

The Temple copy gives 1,165 local gentiles, with 371 from the interior valley. The total is 1,536.

The Transcripts give from 1791 to 1810 inclusive 1,054 gentiles, and from 1811 to 1832 inclusive 270. The total is 1,324. Merriam's list (1968: 48-62) has 1,187 total gentiles. We use Temple's value of 1,165.

SAN ANTONIO

Engelhardt's total is 4,419 baptisms.

The Temple copy gives 2,025 gentiles, all local as far as can be determined by the village names.

The Transcripts give from 1771 to 1808 inclusive 2,326 local baptisms, and from 1809 to 1832 inclusive 185, probably from the "Tulares." The total is 2,511. Merriam's list (1968: 63-89) gives nothing but names—no numbers of Indians.

SAN MIGUEL

Engelhardt's total is 2,471 baptisms.

The Temple copy of the baptism book shows 1,011 local gentiles, and 256 from the "Tulares." The total is 1,267.

The Transcripts have from 1797 to 1805 inclusive 1,116 local gentiles and, from 1806 to 1832 inclusive 324 whose names are of mixed origin but who may be regarded as coming from the interior valley.

SAN LUIS OBISPO

Engelhardt's total is 2,644 baptisms.

The Temple copy is of Vol. I only of the baptism books. It runs to

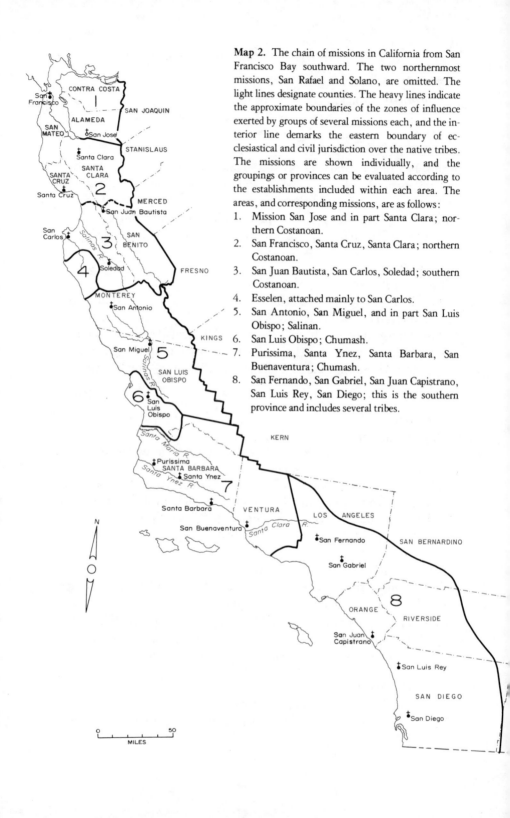

**Map 2.** The chain of missions in California from San Francisco Bay southward. The two northernmost missions, San Rafael and Solano, are omitted. The light lines designate counties. The heavy lines indicate the approximate boundaries of the zones of influence exerted by groups of several missions each, and the interior line demarks the eastern boundary of ecclesiastical and civil jurisdiction over the native tribes. The missions are shown individually, and the groupings or provinces can be evaluated according to the establishments included within each area. The areas, and corresponding missions, are as follows:

1. Mission San Jose and in part Santa Clara; northern Costanoan.
2. San Francisco, Santa Cruz, Santa Clara; northern Costanoan.
3. San Juan Bautista, San Carlos, Soledad; southern Costanoan.
4. Esselen, attached mainly to San Carlos.
5. San Antonio, San Miguel, and in part San Luis Obispo; Salinan.
6. San Luis Obispo; Chumash.
7. Purissima, Santa Ynez, Santa Barbara, San Buenaventura; Chumash.
8. San Fernando, San Gabriel, San Juan Capistrano, San Luis Rey, San Diego; this is the southern province and includes several tribes.

1821 and shows 1,361 local gentiles baptized, and 29 from the valley. The Transcripts from 1772 to 1805, inclusive, give 1,263 local gentiles and 69 from the valley. The total is 1,390. We use the Temple copy.

In Table 2 we have summarized the baptism and population data for the ten northern missions. The number of local gentiles baptized is shown according to Temple's copies (8 missions), according to the Bancroft Transcripts (9 missions), and according to other sources as explained previously (2 missions). Also given are Engelhardt's figures for total baptisms, and our best estimate for baptisms of gentiles from the interior valley and north of San Francisco Bay. For the total baptisms of local gentiles we have used other sources with San Francisco and San Jose, but Temple's values with the other eight missions. The total is 17,487.

It will be noted that there are eight missions for which there is an estimate of local gentile baptisms from both Temple's copies and from the Transcripts. The total from Temple's copies is 13,966 and from the Transcripts is 14,222. The difference is of the order of 1.83 percent, and indicates that the Transcripts, when several missions are involved, are reliable within a very small error.

If we now apply the ratio of total population to gentile baptisms which was found with Alameda and Contra Costa Counties, we get 17,487 x 1.5. This is 26,231, or in round numbers 26,000, as the probable aboriginal population of the first region of the mission strip.

Certain subsidiary matters merit brief attention. It has been stated that the area-density method cannot be employed with the coastal Indians because we have no basis for direct comparison with other regions such as the Sacramento and San Joaquin Valleys. However, the calculation of population which we have just derived permits an estimate of the overall density. The approximate area, as measured on the 1/1,000,000 map of California (see Map 2), was 10,890 square miles, for a population of 26,000. The density would be close to 2.4 persons per square mile, a value well within the range found for other areas.

Another method, which has not been utilized, depends upon the size and number of villages or other units of population. Kroeber (1925: 465, 548) shows two text-figure maps, on which he places 55 named locations. These he describes as ''villages as can in any way be identified.'' In truth they are probably tribelets, the principal village of which bore the assigned name. Six of them, Ausai-ma, Matsu-n, Wacharo-n, Paisi-n, Kalinta-ruk, and Huris-tak, appear repeatedly in the baptism books of San Carlos, San Juan Bautista, and Soledad. The average number of gentiles who were baptized from these places was 264. If the same number can be applied to all 55 locations on Kroeber's maps, the total would be 14,520, and if the factor 1.5 is used for correction, the aboriginal population would have been 21,800. If we add the area or region of Chalon, found in the Soledad baptism book 660 times, the average of seven localities becomes 321, and the aboriginal population 26,450. The similarity with the previous estimate is probably coincidental, but it does demonstrate that the order of magnitude cannot be too wide of the facts.

The second province which must be considered is the coast along the Santa Barbara Channel, the home of the Chumash. The boundaries which are described here are somewhat artificial. San Luis Obispo, with some Chumash, has been allocated to the northern province. Similarly it is convenient to consider San Fernando as one of the southern missions, although it drew numerous Chumash from the coast of western Los Angeles County. The middle area, therefore, is restricted essentially to Santa Barbara and Ventura Counties, with the Channel Islands included.

The Channel Chumash have been the subject of several comprehensive monographs, some of which deal extensively with aboriginal population. These may be mentioned briefly, but there can be no entrance upon a lengthy critique of methods and results. Kroeber (1925) thought 8,000-10,000 adequate. Cook (1943a) accepted Kroeber's figure. However, after a rather cursory consideration of the data (1964) he raised the estimate to 13,650 for all the Chumash. Subsequently Cook and Heizer (1965) reexamined the problem and arrived at a value of 20,400. Shortly thereafter Brown (1967) made an extremely thorough study of the Chumash towns. His primary conclusion is worth quoting: "The burden of this study has been to show the relative, and to suggest the absolute, reliability of these records which would indicate a population of perhaps 7,000 souls on the mainland channel shore in the third quarter of the eighteenth century. The further implication is a total population not over 15,000 for the Chumash-speaking area, including the islands and the sparsely populated hinterland. . . ." (1967: 79).

The various estimates thus run from 10,000 to 20,000. The easiest solution of the difficulty might be to take the median, 15,000. However, other considerations should be discussed.

Two types of data have been employed. One includes the reports of the 1769 expeditions with their detailed descriptions of village sizes, house numbers, head counts, and so on. The other has been the baptisms performed in the several missions. Kroeber (1925), Cook (1943), and Cook and Heizer (1965) relied principally upon the former source. Brown (1967) attempted to utilize the mission figures as well as the eighteenth century accounts and journals. The baptism books are still available, and if time and opportunity were favorable, it would be desirable to make a definitive count of all the gentile baptisms at the Channel missions. In view of the lack of this information we are constrained to fall back upon some rather unsatisfactory substitutes.

Brown gives a great deal of material derived from the baptism books, some of which has already been utilized for estimating population-baptism ratios. His table 1 (1967: 95) shows 3,361 baptisms in five Channel missions. If San Fernando is excluded, the remainder is 3,246. But these gentiles were from 26 coastal villages only.

Brown's Table 3 (1967: 98-99) gives four columns of numerical data for 38 villages, both coastal and interior. The *first* column gives the total mission converts from each village who were born before 1771. The *second* column shows the sex ratio. The *fourth* column gives the total mission converts born before 1771 expressed as a percentage of the *1770 estimated population.* These are the figures which we have used for calculating population-baptism ratios. The *third* column gives for each of the 38 villages the mission converts born before 1771 expressed as a percentage of the *total baptisms.* The mean percentage is 47.4. There were 2,324 converts born before 1771. Therefore there were 4,935 total baptisms in the 38 villages.

It is possible to check the reliability of these figures as stated by Brown. From his table 1, there were 3,361 baptisms from 26 villages, an average of 129 baptisms per village. From his table 3, the total baptisms are calculated as 4,935 with 38 villages. The average is 130 baptisms per village. The substantial identity indicates a real internal consistency.

What, now, was the number of baptisms by all the missions from all the villages? The 38 villages mentioned by Brown were of course the largest and the most important. On his map (1967: 18) he places 107 villages in Chumash territory, including the islands, 69 of which do not appear in the tables. We may consider that if the average number of baptisms from the 69 was about one-third the average number found for the larger 38, we have approximately 69 x 43, or 2,965. The total for the entire area would be 7,950. This is a very rough calculation. It would have been much simpler if Brown had merely stated his total for all gentile baptisms.

The Merriam lists are from La Purisima, Santa Ynez, and San Buenaventura (1970: 30-48, 54-58). Santa Barbara is lacking. For the three missions the total gentile baptisms are given as 3,219, far below Brown's figures, and clearly less than those which were actually record-ed. The Bancroft Transcripts do better, even though the values are calculated indirectly: La Purisma, 1,983; Santa Ynez, 768; Santa Barbara, 2,857; San Buenaventura, 2,301. The total is 7,909, quite close to the number apparently found by Brown.

Let us use provisionally Brown's total of 7,950 gentile baptisms. The final problem is to determine the ratio of baptisms to aboriginal population, or its reciprocal. The previous analysis of Brown's data in-dicated a ratio of 2.37:1 for eleven coastal towns. This value is much higher than any which we have discovered to the northward, and requires further comment.

Fully half the converts were recruited from the densely populated coastal strip, with its settlements of 1,000 or more. The probability of incidence and the severity of disease was magnified many times that among small and widely scattered interior villages (see discussion by Brown, 1967: 76). Moreover, the contact not only with Spaniards but also with foreigners of all descriptions was very close on the channel coast from the year 1769 onward. The relative rate of depletion must have been very great indeed among the Chumash.

There was also an unusual lag between the first discovery and the establishment of missions. The Portola expedition passed along the channel in 1769. San Buenaventura mission was not founded until 1782, Santa Barbara in 1786, Purisima in 1787, and Santa Ynez in 1804. Thus at least a dozen years elapsed during which the native population was subject to depletion before any conversions were attempted.

Brown estimates (1967:77) that the gross rate of decline in 13 years was about 30 percent, as was that in the next 14 years. The net reduc-tion of the non-missionized population on the mainland must have reached 50 percent. On the islands it may have been greater, in part because of the bad treatment suffered by the natives at the hands of Russian and other sea otter hunters.

We may therefore accept a factor of 2.4 for most of the regional population. The only exception would be the smaller, more protected villages in the interior of Santa Barbara and Ventura Counties. Here the ratio may have duplicated that found in the coast ranges further north, approximately 1.5. If so, we might reduce the ratio to 2.3. If the gentile baptisms are considered to have amounted to 7,950, the aboriginal population of the region would have reached nearly 18,300 souls.

In the work of Cook and Heizer (1965), the method was to measure the area of sites on maps of the archaeologist D. B. Rogers (1929), establish the slope of the graph of size against population, and then interpolate. The number of houses per site and the number of persons per house were also calculated. The final result, after correcting for possible overestimate of number of sites, was a population of 20,400 for the channel coast, not including the interior or the islands. If these are added, the total would reach 25,000.

Clearly the discrepancy between the results obtained from examination of sites and houses, and from computation based upon mission conversions is considerable. It is possible that Cook and Heizer overestimated the average number of houses per village and the average number of persons per house. Their figures are certainly too high for the interior villages and may also be excessive for the islands. On the other hand, although the total gentile baptisms in the channel missions may come close to 8,000, it is possible that the pre-conversion depletion in the populous coastal towns may have been greater than has here been assumed. Then the multiplicative factor exceeds 2.4 and might even attain 2.75. If so, the estimate of the aboriginal population would approach the 25,000 mark. We can say with some assurance that the population of this province attained a minimum of 15,000, and that the maximum could not have surpassed 25,000. As a compromise we shall use 18,500. It is very evident that in spite of Brown's admirable study the entire problem of aboriginal life among the Chumash needs an exhaustive reexamination, using clerical, documentary, archaeological, and ecological evidence.

As an additional note, it may be pointed out that population density figures have little value in the Chumash area, because of the extreme concentration of people on the coast and the relatively sparse occupation of the interior. Nevertheless, with an area of roughly 5,000 square miles, including the islands, a population of 18,500 means an overall density of 3.7 persons per square mile; 25,000 would give 5.0 persons per square mile. These figures are within the same range as are found for the thickly settled river and coastal tribes of northwest California, such as the Yurok and Wiyot. Thus, a density comparison shows nothing improbable in a Chumash population of somewhere between 15,000 and 25,000.

The third province of the mission strip which must be considered covers southern California from the western border of Los Angeles County to the Mexican boundary and from the ocean to he summits of the great mountain ranges (see Map 2). Here were located the five missions of San Fernando, San Gabriel, San Juan Capistrano, San Luis Rey, and San Diego. The limits of missionization are only vaguely defined, for all five missions pressed further and further inland for their converts throughout their entire existence. We have drawn a rather arbitrary line beginning with the Tehachapi Mountains, crossing to the San Gabriel Range north of Los Angeles, and continuing along the San Bernardino Mountains. Thence, the line runs across the San Gorgonio Pass to Mt. San Jacinto, and due south to the Mexican border. The area is approximately 10,500 square miles, and includes several native linguistic stocks, notably the Shoshonean divisions and the Yuman Diegueño. The peripheral groups, the Serrano and the Cahuilla, are represented in part.

For aboriginal population, the first serious estimate was that of Kroeber (1925: 893). His formulation appears in the accompanying table.

| | |
|---|---:|
| 1. Serrano, Vanyume, Kitanemuk, Alliklik | 3,500 |
| 2. Gabrieleño, Fernandeño, San Nicoleño | 5,000 |
| 3. Luiseño | 4,000 |
| 4. Juaneño | 1,000 |
| 5. Cupeño | 500 |
| 6. Cahuilla | 2,500 |
| 7. Diegueño, Kamia | 3,000 |
| Total | 19,500 |

It is doubtful whether all members of the outlying tribes were actually brought into the missions, or aboriginally lived in the mission area, as defined here. Thus at least 1,000 each might be deducted for the Serrano groups, for the Cahuilla, and for the Kamia. Kroeber's total would then reduce to 16,500. Nevertheless, his unaltered estimate was accepted by Cook (1943, 1964) as being the best obtainable.

There are few village or house counts in existence, except that of Kroeber. On his map (1925, plate 57, in pocket) he shows 136 names of native sites. If the villages averaged 100 persons apiece, the population would have been 13,600. But all the villages were not shown by Kroeber. An exhaustive study of the eighteenth-century Spanish documents would no doubt shed much light upon the number, size, and distribution of the more coastal settlements. There is much correspondence and several very informative reports from exploring expeditions conducted in the early years of the missions. These may be found in several archives and libraries, either in the original or on microfilm. Such a study is badly needed for southern California.

An alternative to the accounts of eyewitnesses would be examination of the mission records. Unfortunately, this task has been attempted only by S. R. Clemence, for C. Hart Merriam, and some of her lists from the southern missions resemble those from other areas in being numerically incomplete (1968: 93-175). The best value which I can obtain from a careful count of these lists is 11,784 as the total number of gentiles baptized. The Bancroft Transcripts may also be employed as a check and a comparison. According to this method of calculation, the total gentile baptisms reach 15,181.

A tabulation mission by mission is likewise instructive. Here are, for the five missions, the gentile baptisms as stated by the two sources, Merriam's lists, and the Bancroft Transcripts (see accompanying table).

| Mission | Baptisms by Merriam | Baptisms by Transcripts | Ratio Merriam : Transcripts |
|---|---|---|---|
| San Fernando | 1,023 | 1,715 | 0.597 |
| San Gabriel | 4,423 | 4,405 | 1.005 |
| San Juan Capistrano | 1,336 | 2,535 | 0.527 |
| San Luis Rey | 2,806 | 3,088 | 0.909 |
| San Diego | 2,196 | 3,428 | 0.639 |
| Total | 11,784 | 15,181 | 0.776 |

Clearly there are two missions for which the Merriam list and the Transcripts agree, or nearly so, San Gabriel and San Luis Rey. It follows that for these two the village numbers and sizes in the Merriam lists must be substantially reliable. The other three are of dubious value and are best left out of consideration.

With these two missions, as indeed with all those reported, the number of gentile baptisms is shown for each village, the name of which, despite spelling variants, indicated separate identity to S.R. Clemence. These villages may be classified according to the number of baptisms ascribed to each. Thus for San Gabriel and San Luis Rey we have the distribution by number of baptisms in the accompanying table.

| Number of Indians reported from village | Number of villages | Total number of baptisms |
|---|---|---|
| More than 100 | 24 | 4,169 |
| 50 - 100 | 22 | 1,618 |
| 25 - 49 | 19 | 667 |
| 10 - 24 | 25 | 369 |
| Less than 10 | 156 | 406 |
| Total | 246 | 7,229 |

Just how S. R. Clemence constructed these lists is unknown. It is extremely unlikely, however, that any rancheria can have consisted of less than 10 inhabitants. Very probably, also, few rancherias of permanence contained fewer than 25 souls. We would therefore be justified in allocating those baptisms recorded for the very small places to those of 10 persons or over, or those of 25 persons or over. When this is done, we get the following averages for probable rancheria size: for 90 villages of 10 or more persons, there are a total of 7,229 baptisms, or a mean of 80.3 gentile baptisms from each; for 65 villages of 25 or more inhabitants the mean is 111.3 persons per village. The range may be considered as established between 80 and 111 persons.

We have no grounds for making a categorical statement, but there is no evidence to the contrary when we assume that the territory embraced by the other three southern missions contained an equivalent number of villages of the same size as is found for San Gabriel and San Luis Rey. Then the number would be in proportion to the baptisms performed at them, or in other words proportional to the gross size of the missions. For ascertaining this value the best source is neither the Merriam lists nor the Bancroft Transcripts, but the total baptisms as given by Engelhardt (1913, Vol. III, p. 653). His total is 13,224 for San Gabriel and San Luis Rey, and 13,646 for San Fernando, San Juan Capistrano, and San Diego. Then by proportion, in the latter three missions, there would have been 93 villages of 10 or more souls, or 67 villages of 25 or more. The sums for all five missions would be respectively 183 and 132. These totals are entirely consistent with Kroeber's 136 sites and the assumption of an average of 100 inhabitants. If we use the figures derived from Merriam's lists, we have either 183 rancherias with an average of 80 persons, or 132 rancherias with an average of 111 persons. Both sets give a total for gentile baptisms of nearly 14,650.

The ratio of gentile baptisms to aboriginal population was taken as 2:3 for the northern province, or portion of the mission strip, and as 1:2.4 for the Santa Barbara Channel area. The causes for the high ratio on the Channel coast were not operative to the south. There conditions much resembled those in the north: smaller and more widely scattered villages, together with slimmer subsistence resources. Indeed, if we consider the semi-desert and mountain areas on the northern and eastern periphery, and their remoteness from the missions themselves, we may decide that the ratio was smaller than in the northern region. If so, it will be preferable to apply the ratio 3:4, or the multiplicative factor 1.33. Then we get very close to 19,500 as the aboriginal population. If we use the Transcript figure 15,181 for gentile baptisms we get approximately 20,200.

The various estimates may be compared. Kroeber's (1925) rather subjective figure, adjusted for non-missionized areas, was 16,500. Cook (1943) had 21,000 and (1964) 19,000. The Transcript value is 20,200, and that derived from Merriam's list is 19,500. The mean of all five attempts is 19,240. If Kroeber's early estimate is accepted without adjustment, the mean is 19,840. The best we can do, in round numbers, is a population of 20,000.

If 20,000 is taken as the population, and 10,500 square miles is the area of this province, the density is close to 1.9 persons per square mile. This value is consistent with those found elsewhere in California, and indicates that the population calculated is somewhere near the probable actuality. At least it has not been overestimated.

In conclusion, if we consider the entire mission area, we find the estimates that appear most probable at the present date, are, for the northern province, 26,000, for the central, or Channel province, 18,500, and for the southern province, 20,000. The total is 64,500. This is but a moderate increase over the estimate of 55,900 made in 1964.

## Conclusion

With the establishment of a definite value for aboriginal population in the Sacramento Valley and the mission area on the coast, it becomes possible to suggest a figure for the entire state. The basis would be the present essay, together with previous publications concerning other important areas. The areas and the calculated population are given in the accompanying table.

| | |
|---|---:|
| 1. Northwest coast; Oregon to San Francisco Bay (Cook, 1956) | 70,440 |
| 2. The Shasta, Achomawi, and Modoc (This chapter) | 9,600 |
| 3. The Sacramento Valley (This chapter) | 76,100 |
| 4. The San Joaquin Valley (Cook, 1955a) | 83,800 |
| 5. The northern mission area (This chapter) | 26,000 |
| 6. The central mission area (This chapter) | 18,500 |

7. The southern mission area
   (This chapter)                                    20,000
                                                   _____

   Total                                            304,440

The sum is 304,440. We add 5,560 to take account of the scattered Shoshonean people of the non-missionized portion of the Mojave and Colorado deserts, as well as of the Owens Valley. The final total may be put at 310,000.

This figure is at the upper limit of the population proposed by me several years ago (Cook, 1964). It is somewhat below Baumhoff's (1963) estimate of 350,000 and well above Merriam's (1905) value of 260,000. The total of 310,000 is certainly subject to scrutiny and revision in detail and might be altered up or down by perhaps 10 percent. The great volume of evidence, however, continues to support the thesis that the Indian population of California was originally of the order of 300,000 souls.

# II. THE INDIAN POPULATION
# OF CALIFORNIA, 1860-1970

Thirty years ago (1943b, 1943c), I tabulated all the data I could find which stated the population of the California Indian tribes north of Los Angeles, at a series of dates extending from prehistoric times to 1940. To the figures obtained from numerous documents I added several estimates of my own. Since that time new material has appeared and much of the older data deserves to be reevaluated in the light of fuller knowledge. Particularly deserving of reexamination is the period subsequent to the gold rush, that interval between the final disruption of native society and the modern demographic recovery.

In the earlier work I followed the example of the ethnographers and based all values for population upon tribal entities. This course was necessary when dealing with the aboriginal organization in a more or less undisturbed condition. However, as a result of missionization and, more profoundly, of the American mining-agricultural invasion, the pattern of linguistic and social grouping was so disordered that it carried little meaning after 1855. In both north and south the native aggregates came to be known by locality, rather than ethnic designation. The commonest manner of reference was according to mountain, valley, bay, reservation, county, or former mission. Therefore, in pursuing the trend of numbers, by far the most convenient approach is to use geographic and political rather than ethnographic units. Of these, the most conspicuous are the reservations, described in the annual Reports of the Commissioner of Indian Affairs (abbreviated here as BIA) and the counties, which were employed for Indians as subdivisions of the state by the Bureau of the Census.

The residual Indian population in California prior to the discovery of gold—in 1845 let us say —may be considered, perhaps liberally, as 150,000. By 1850, scarcely a year after the gold rush began, it had fallen to approximately 100,000. In another five years, by 1855, at the peak of mining activity, it was no more than 50,000. (For more data on the decade 1845-1855, see Cook 1943b, particularly Table 1, pages 40-48.) Seldom has a native race been subjected to such a catastrophic decimation. The responsible factors were mitigated after 1855, but they by no means disappeared. Consequently the decline in population persisted for several decades, although at a steadily diminishing rate.

At this point it is necessary to digress in order to discuss certain preliminary matters. The first relates to the organization and composition of the Indians who were settled on reservations. By no means all the natives were ever gathered into these institutions. At first they were no more than concentration camps into which as many Indians were herded as could be caught and transported. The living conditions were unimaginably bad, and quite naturally any native who was able absconded and found such shelter as he might in the wild. As a result, over many years, the reservations in California have contained only a minority of the aboriginal inhabitants and their descendants.

Furthermore, the number of residents who might be counted on a reservation fluctuated widely from year to year. During the period of establishment, prior to 1870, fugitivism was so common that it sometimes reached one hundred percent of the Indians. In later years there was a steady drift away from the reservation and toward an independent existence. This tendency was occasionally countered by some special effort to recover fugitives or recruit new members of the community.

Another source of confusion to the investigator, if not to the Indians themselves, was the propensity of the Bureau of Indian Affairs to close out moribund reservations and activate new ones, particularly in the south. As a result, especial care must be exercized to reconcile populations with places.

A second general question relates to the boundaries of the state of California, and the peripheral tribes. In considering aboriginal population, and the residue down to the mining era, I have consistently omitted many of these groups. It is not certain that this course should be followed past the establishment of California as a state. In the north no problem arises save in the case of the Modoc and some of the Pit Rivers (Achomawi). The Modoc occupied land in both California and Oregon. Kroeber (1926: 320) put the former number of the Modoc at 600 or 700 ''of whom perhaps half or less lived in what is now California''. Later (1957) he accepted about 255 Modoc who lived at the Klamath Reservation in Oregon as being of California origin, although he offered no demonstration whether these were descendents of California or Oregon Modoc. For the Pit Rivers, the case is quite clear: they must have been displaced from their former homes in

California. However, since the Reports of the Commissioner list these people consistently as belonging to the Oregon Reservation, and since their number is not large, they will be omitted, perhaps arbitrarily, from the totals of California Indians.

Further south, the Washo, Eastern Mono, and Paiute straddled the border of California and Nevada. However, residents of the two states are reasonably well distinguished. The California Washo are mentioned as having lived mainly in Alpine County. The other tribes are included with those reported from Bishop, Bridgeport, Independence, and the Owens Valley. Complete segregation is impossible. Nevertheless the Indians specifically allocated to Mono and Inyo Counties may be regarded as Californian. Others may be excluded. There will be little significant distortion of the facts.

On the Colorado River in prehistoric times lived the Mojave, the Halchidhoma, and the Yuma. They filled the bottom land which extended from the tip of Nevada to Baja California, and occupied both banks of the river. As Kroeber points out, it is very difficult to allocate them to either California or Arizona, the one to the exclusion of the other. Their homeland, along the river, was separated from the Cahuilla and the Diegueño to the west by many miles of almost uninhabitable desert, and their cultural affiliations seem to have been to the east rather than to the west. After 1850, when they had been joined by several score Chemehuevi, their centers of administration and their reservations were placed on the Arizona side of the river. For aboriginal population, Kroeber's estimate in the Handbook (1926: 883) comes as close as anyone reasonably can. He shows 6,500 for the Mojave, Halchidhoma, and Yuma. If 3,000 Yuma in Arizona are deducted, the balance is 3,500. In 1910 he suggests a net value of 950 for these tribes in California, a figure which corresponds with those given by the Indian Bureau of the period. In spite of these facts, for the sake of simplicity, and in order to avoid repeated attempts to make an equitable distribution of population between the two states, it will be preferable not to include these tribes among the California Indians, in either the aboriginal or the modern period.

We may now pick up the movement of Indian population in California at or shortly after 1860 and consider the number of natives who survived in this state during the years 1860 to 1865. According to C. Hart Merriam (1905: 599) the census of 1860 recorded the Indian population as 31,338. Merriam himself (p. 600) preferred a somewhat higher value, 35,000.

*Table 3.* NUMBER OF INDIANS AT CERTAIN RESERVATIONS,
ACCORDING TO REPORTS OF THE COMMISSIONER OF INDIAN AFFAIRS,
1867-1914

## PART I

| Year[1] | Hoopa | Lower Klamath | Round Valley | Tule River | Total of Hoopa, Round Valley, Tule River |
|---|---|---|---|---|---|
| 1867[2] | 623 | 625[3] | 1,389 | 725 | 2,737 |
| 1868[6] | 725 | 374[3] | 975 | 551 | 2,251 |
| 1869[7] | 975 | | 1,022 | 550 | 2,547 |
| 1870[8] | | | | | |
| 1871[9] | 800 | | 793 | 374 | 1,967 |
| 1872[10] | 725 | | 1,700 | 374 | 2,799 |
| 1873[11] | 725 | | 1,119 | 317 | 2,161 |
| 1874[12] | 666 | | 1,200 | 307 | 2,173 |
| 1875[13] | 716 | | 1,144 | 1,200[14] | 3,060 |
| 1876[15] | | | | | |
| 1877[16] | 427 | | 996 | 254 | 1,677 |
| 1878[17] | 427 | | 915 | 180 | 1,522 |
| 1879[19] | 415 | | 656 | 160 | 1,231 |
| 1880[20] | 414 | 1,125 | 534 | 160 | 1,108 |
| 1881[21] | 479 | | 589 | 163 | 1,231 |
| 1882[22] | 510 | | 645 | 159[23] | 1,314 |
| 1883[24] | 508 | | 633 | 143[23] | 1,284 |
| 1884[25] | 509 | | 599 | 143[23] | 1,251 |
| 1885[26] | 515 | | 600 | 135[23] | 1,250 |
| 1886[27] | 422 | | 608 | 141[23] | 1,171 |
| 1887[28] | 460 | 213 | 551 | 139[23] | 1,150 |
| 1888[29] | 463 | 213 | 535 | 145 | 1,143 |
| 1889[31] | 476 | | 531 | 147 | 1,154 |
| 1890[33] | 475 | | 534 | 161 | 1,170 |
| 1891[34] | 492 | | 564 | 161 | 1,217 |
| 1892[36] | 484 | 505 | 569 | 196 | 1,249 |
| 1893[37] | 486 | 505 | 546 | 172 | 1,204 |
| 1894[38] | 486 | 505 | 602 | 184 | 1,272 |
| 1895[39] | 492 | 673 | 623 | 184 | 1,299 |
| 1896 | | | | | |
| 1897[40] | 505 | 673 | 644 | | |
| 1898[41] | 510 | 673 | 621 | 175 | 1,306 |
| 1899[42] | 471 | 673 | 641 | 161 | 1,273 |

*Table 3 (continued)*

| Year[1] | Hoopa | Lower Klamath | Round Valley | Tule River | Total of Hoopa, Round Valley, Tule River |
|---|---|---|---|---|---|
| 1900[43] | 421 | 617 | 643 | 154 | 1,218 |
| 1901[44] | 417 | 560 | 637 | 146 | 1,200 |
| 1902[45] | 413 | 540 | 621 | 143 | 1,177 |
| 1903[46] | 412 | 530 | 625 | 143 | 1,110 |
| 1904[47] | 414 | 530 | 623 | | |
| 1905[49] | 412 | 745 | 615 | 154 | 1,181 |
| 1906[50] | 420 | 745 | 615 | 153 | 1,188 |
| 1907[52] | 424 | 745 | 620 | 154 | 1,198 |
| 1908 | | | | | |
| 1909[53] | 438 | 745 | 625 | 154 | 1,217 |
| 1910[54] | 436 | 745 | 607 | 156 | 1,199 |
| 1911[55] | 453 | 791 | 706 | 159 | 1,318 |
| 1912[56] | 1,269[57] | | 1,342 | 153 | |
| 1913[58] | 1,251 | | 1,528 | 151 | |
| 1914[59] | 1,345 | | 1,529 | 150 | |

## PART II

| Year | Mission | Digger | Fort Bidwell | Other Agencies | Non-agency |
|---|---|---|---|---|---|
| 1867 | 7,700[4] | | | | 14,900[5] |
| 1868 | 7,400[4] | | | | 14,900 |
| 1869 | 7,400[4] | | | | 12,000 |
| 1870 | | | | | 13,700 |
| 1871 | | | | | |
| 1872 | | | | | |
| 1873 | | | | | 20,000 |
| 1874 | | | | | 7,000 |
| 1875 | | | | | |
| 1876 | | | | | |
| 1877 | 4,400 | | | | 2,021 |
| 1878 | 4,400 | | | | 2,515[18] |
| 1879 | 3,000 | | | | 2,836[18] |
| 1880 | 3,000 | | | | |
| 1881 | 3,010 | | | | |
| 1882 | 3,010 | | | | 6,669 |

Table 3 (continued)

| Year | Mission | Digger | Fort Bidwell | Other Agencies | Non-agency |
|------|---------|--------|--------------|----------------|------------|
| 1883 | 3,010 | | | | 6,669 |
| 1884 | 2,400 | | | | 6,669 |
| 1885 | 3,070 | | | | 6,669 |
| 1886 | 3,096 | | | | 6,669 |
| 1887 | 3,112 | | | | |
| 1888 | 3,021[30] | | | | 6,456 |
| 1889 | 2,320[32] | | | | |
| 1890 | 2,895 | | | | 6,995 |
| 1891 | 2,812[35] | | | | 6,995 |
| 1892 | 2,797 | | | | 6,995 |
| 1893 | 2,726 | | | | 6,995 |
| 1894 | 2,766 | | | | 6,995 |
| 1895 | 2,893 | | | | 6,995 |
| 1896 | | | | | |
| 1897 | 2,966 | | | | 6,995 |
| 1898 | 2,966 | | | | 6,995 |
| 1899 | 2,954 | 30 | 700 | | |
| 1900 | 2,927 | 35 | 700 | | 5,300 |
| 1901 | 2,856 | 35 | 700 | | 9,371 |
| 1902 | 2,682 | 38 | 700 | | |
| 1903 | 2,855 | 35 | 700 | | 9,371 |
| 1904 | 2,823[48] | 36 | 700 | | 9.371 |
| 1905 | 2,751 | 36 | 700 | | 9,371 |
| 1906 | 2,675 | 38 | 700 | | 13,061[51] |
| 1907 | 2,602 | 37 | 700 | | 13,061 |
| 1908 | | | | | |
| 1909 | 2,628 | 39 | 700 | 649 | 13,061 |
| 1910 | 2,755 | 48 | 627 | 1,886 | 13,061 |
| 1911 | 2,984 | 43 | 632 | 3,710 | 5,150 |
| 1912 | 2,830 | 42 | 628 | 3,500 | 6,950 |
| 1913 | 2,788 | 49 | 651 | 2,355 | 6,950 |
| 1914 | 2,788 | 51 | 733 | 2,350 | 5,474 |

1. The reports of the Commissioner are always dated at the end of the fiscal year, June 30. Hence the report is usually designated by both years involved, e.g., 1866/1867. For convenience, however, sometimes only the last of the two years is mentioned—in the case cited, 1867.

2. These figures are from the Population Table, Doc. No. 170, BIA 1866/67. They differ somewhat from those given by the local agents in their reports.

3. These are designated "Smith River," a reservation which soon disappeared. G. Kingsbury, in his report, Doc. No. 20, says that there were 400 Indians.

4. Doc. No. 170 gives 3,300 Mission Indians plus 4,400 Cahuillas and other tribes. The total is taken here as 7,700. The data for 1868 and 1869 are similarly derived.

5. The non-agency Indians are designated Kings River and others, in the Population Table in Doc. No. 170. In Doc. No. 16, p. 94, Charles Maltby also excludes the Reservation and Mission Indians to get 14,900. The total is 25,962.

6. Population Table, Doc. No. 105, BIA, 1867/68.

7. Population Table, Doc. No. 33, BIA, 1868/69.

8. The total of the non-agency Indians as estimated by J. B. McIntosh, Doc. No. 21, p. 81, BIA, 1869/70.

9. Population Table, Doc. No. 123, BIA, 1870/71.

10. Population Table, Doc. No. 85, BIA, 1871/72. At Round Valley many Pomo were brought in from Mendocino County (Doc. No. 85, page 398). They soon absconded. Tule River is said to include remnants of the Tejon Reservation.

11. Population Table, Doc. No. 79, BIA, 1872/73.

12. Population Table, page 108, BIA, 1873/74.

13. Population Table, BIA, 1874/75.

14. Includes Kaweahs, Kings Rivers, etc., off the reservation but under the agency.

15. BIA report not available.

16. Table of Statistics, p. 288, BIA, 1876/77.

17. Table of Statistics, p. 280, BIA, 1877/78.

18. These are all in the north.

19. Table of Statistics, p. 228, BIA, 1878/79.

20. Table of Statistics, p. 238, BIA, 1879/80.

21. Table of Statistics, p. 272, BIA, 1880/81.

22. Table of Statistics, p. 328, BIA, 1881/82.

23. Plus 540 from Kings River.

24. Table of Statistics, p. 266, BIA, 1882/83.

25. Table of Statistics, p. 284, BIA, 1883/84.

26. Table of Statistics, p. 336, BIA, 1884/85.

27. Table of Statistics, p. 392, BIA, 1885/86.

28. Table of Statistics, p. 410, BIA, 1886/87.

29. Table of Statistics, p. 410, BIA, 1887/88.

30. Plus 150 Diegueños.

31. Table of Statistics, p. 496, BIA, 1888/89.

32. 1,118 Yuma are segregated from the Mission count. The Yuma are excluded hereafter from this table.

33. Table of Statistics, p. 448, BIA, 1889/90.

34. Table of Statistics, Vol. II, p. 72, BIA, 1890/91.

35. Mission agency is divided: on reservations 1,721, off reservations 924, desert Indians 167.

36. Table of Statistics, p. 784, BIA, 1891/92.

37. Table of Statistics, p. 694, BIA, 1892/93.

38. Table of Statistics, p. 568, BIA, 1893/94.

39. Table of Statistics, p. 564, BIA, 1894/95.
40. Table of Statistics, p. 115, BIA, 1896/97.
41. Table of Statistics, p. 598, BIA, 1897/98.
42. Table of Statistics, p. 562, BIA, 1898/99, Part I.
43. Table of Statistics, p. 638, BIA, 1899/1900.
44. Table of Statistics, p. 686, BIA, 1900/01.
45. Table of Statistics, p. 630, BIA, 1901/02.
46. Table of Statistics, p. 508, BIA, 1902/03.
47. Table of Statistics, p. 596, BIA, 1903/04.
48. On July 20, 1903, the Mission Agency was split into a northern half at San Jacinto, which included Tule River, and a southern half at Pala.
49. Table of Statistics, p. 516, BIA, 1904/05.
50. Table of Statistics, p. 481, BIA, 1905/06.
51. Taken from the report by C. E. Kelsey, March 21, 1906.
52. Table, Population of Indians, p. 177, BIA, 1906/07.
53. Table No. 48, Population of Indians, p. 143, BIA, 1908/09.
54. Table No. 7, Population of Indians, p. 60, BIA, 1909/10.
55. Table No. 2, Population of Indians, p. 55, BIA, 1910/11.
56. Table No. 2, Population of Indians, p. 74, BIA, 1911/12.
57. Hupa Valley, Klamath, and Lower Klamath are consolidated in Table No. 2, BIA, 1911/12.
58. Table No. 3, Population of Indians, p. 45, BIA, 1912/13.
59. Table No. 1, Population of Indians, p. 75, BIA, 1913/14.

*Table 4.* POPULATION OF COUNTIES, ACCORDING
TO KELSEY'S REPORT OF 1906 AND THE MEAN OF
THE CENSUSES OF 1890, 1900, 1910, AND 1920

| County | Kelsey's figure | Mean of censuses |
|---|---|---|
| Alameda | 43 | 48 |
| Alpine | 155 | 140 |
| Amador | 183 | 104 |
| Butte | 326 | 261 |
| Calaveras | 105 | 101 |
| Colusa | 132 | 170 |
| Del Norte | 263 | 376 |
| El Dorado | 258 | 142 |
| Fresno | 577 | 390 |
| Glenn | 62 | 27 |
| Humboldt | 753 | 1,647 |
| Inyo | 1,027 | 796 |
| Kern | 572 | 278 |
| Kings | 98 | 48 |
| Lake | 511 | 428 |

Table 4 (continued)

| County | Kelsey's figure | Mean of censuses |
|--------|----------------|------------------|
| Lassen | 378 | 364 |
| Madera | 780 | 404 |
| Mariposa | 232 | 153 |
| Mendocino | 840 | 1,040 |
| Modoc | 666 | 506 |
| Mono | 501 | 349 |
| Monterey | 77 | 30 |
| Nevada | 76 | 75 |
| Placer | 105 | 91 |
| Plumas | 479 | 383 |
| Shasta | 852 | 730 |
| Sierra | 18 | 40 |
| Siskiyou | 1,263 | 706 |
| Sonoma | 386 | 328 |
| Sutter | 7 | 13 |
| Tehama | 118 | 105 |
| Trinity | 246 | 188 |
| Tulare | 61 | 201 |
| Tuolumne | 128 | 132 |
| Yolo | 40 | 36 |
| Yuba | 53 | 28 |
| | | |
| 36 counties (above) | 12,183 | 10,858 |
| On reservations | 1,933 | — |
| 3 counties: San Francisco, Santa Clara, Solano | 0 | 52 |
| Not enumerated | 400 | — |
| 9 counties, in the south, census of 1900 | 184 | — |
| 9 counties in the south, mean of four censuses | — | 191 |
| Total | 14,700 | 11,101 |

These figures point to a major discrepancy in either the successive United States censuses, or in Merriam's reading of them. In his paper of 1905, Merriam quotes the censuses as finding the numbers of Indians in California which are shown below. Meanwhile the published census of 1880 (Vol. 1, part 2, table V, p. 382; Population by Race and by Counties, 1880, 1870, 1860) and that of 1910 (Thirteenth Census, abstract with Supplement for California, table No. 17, p. 596) give for the same dates the figures also shown in the accompanying table.

| Year | Merriam | Published census |
|------|---------|------------------|
| 1860 | 31,338  | 17,798           |
| 1870 | 29,025  | 7,241            |
| 1880 | 20,385  | 16,277           |
| 1890 | 16,624  | 16,624           |
| 1900 | 15,377  | 15,377           |

The figures for 1890 and 1900 are identical. Those for 1860, 1870, and 1880 are widely divergent. The census totals by county for 1870 are certainly most inadequate, and indicate very poor enumeration. Much the same must be said of the 1860 count. Indeed, these two tabulations may be discarded completely, both in the present context and as given for comparative purposes in Table 5. However, if the totals by county, as reproduced in the 1880 census, are entirely misleading, what can be said of the state values given by Merriam? Since he does not cite the volume or page of any published census we simply cannot decide definitively where the discrepancy lies. On the other hand, we know that the county lists printed in the 1880 census are wrong, and we know that Merriam was a careful investigator. Consequently we may provisionally accept his totals for the state in 1860 and 1870. Furthermore his values are in conformity with what we can tell of the Indian population from other sources. The numbers given by Merriam for the 1890 and 1900 censuses are those given also in the summary by counties of 1910 and hence are as correct as the census was. For 1880 the Merriam figure is greater than that of the county total by some 4,000. Here, again, was undoubtedly faulty enumeration, and perhaps faulty tabulation. Merriam's figure may be accepted.

Apart from the United States censuses for 1860 and 1870, and from Merriam's estimates, we have scattered information from the Bureau of Indian Affairs. The Report of the Commissioner for 1861-1862, in its several documents, gives considerable detail with reference to Indians on and off the reservations. Document No. 62 in this report was written by George M. Hanson. He mentions the agency at Smith River (Del Norte County) as containing 2,000 Indians plus several hundred more at Fort Humboldt, say 2,500 in all. On page 310 he says that Round Valley Reservation had held about 2,000 ''previous to a late stampede.'' The time is more exactly expressed on page 314, where he says that this reservation had 2,000 ''last fall,'' that is in 1861. The Mendocino Reservation, which soon disappeared, had about 1,400 Indians, also ''before a recent stampede'' (p. 313). In the fall of 1861, it had counted 1,600 to 1,700 captives. The only other reservation in this area was Nome Lackee, which also was moribund. Document No. 74 of BIA 1861-1862, an unsigned statement of population, credits this reserve with 3,941 persons. However, in his report for 1860-1861 (Document No. 56, p. 147), G. M. Hanson says that although Nome Lackee formerly had 2,000 to 3,000 Indians, it now contained only 200 persons. By the end of 1862 it was defunct. The population statement mentioned (Document No. 74, BIA 1861–1862) must have reference to an earlier date.

*Table 5.* POPULATION OF COUNTIES ACCORDING TO THE DECENNIAL CENSUSES. (The figures for 1905 are inserted from the report of C.E. Kelsey, 1971, pp. 1-3. The figures in parentheses are the values given by Kelsey as the census population of 9 counties. The census sources are given in the notes to this table.)

## PART I

| County | 1860 | 1870 | 1880 | 1890 | 1900 | 1905 | 1910 |
|---|---|---|---|---|---|---|---|
| Alameda | 131 | 111 | 103 | 25 | 71 | 43 | 41 |
| Alpine | — | — | — | 224 | 142 | 155 | 94 |
| Amador | 22 | — | 272 | 58 | 130 | 183 | 143 |
| Butte | 121 | 40 | 522 | 319 | 201 | 326 | 208 |
| Calaveras | 1 | 18 | 169 | 77 | 100 | 105 | 161 |
| Colusa | 75 | 424 | 353 | 277 | 121 | 132 | 169 |
| Contra Costa | 114 | 9 | 47 | 3 | 8 | — | 3 |

Table 5 *(continued)*

| County | 1860 | 1870 | 1880 | 1890 | 1900 | 1905 | 1910 |
|---|---|---|---|---|---|---|---|
| Del Norte | 266 | 784 | 411 | 376 | 269 | 263 | 337 |
| El Dorado | 8 | 6 | 193 | 136 | 138 | 258 | 177 |
| Fresno | 3,294 | 2,635 | 794 | 347 | 520 | 577 | 313 |
| Glenn | — | — | — | — | 24 | 62 | 32 |
| Humboldt | 153 | 76 | 1,935 | 1,379 | 1,728 | 753 | 1,652 |
| Imperial | — | — | — | — | — | — | 282 |
| Inyo | — | 311 | 637 | 850 | 940 | 1,027 | 792 |
| Kern | — | 585 | 332 | 337 | 344 | 572 | 220 |
| Kings | — | — | — | — | 51 | 98 | 32 |
| Lake | — | 23 | 774 | 556 | 428 | 511 | 433 |
| Lassen | — | 1 | 330 | 335 | 381 | 378 | 410 |
| Los Angeles | 2,014 | 219 | 316 | 144 | 69 | — | 97 |
| Madera | — | — | — | — | 401 | 780 | 419 |
| Marin | 210 | 126 | 162 | 31 | 25 | (25) | 26 |
| Mariposa | 7 | 34 | 184 | 152 | 173 | 232 | 192 |
| Mendocino | 1,054 | 542 | 1,265 | 581 | 1,353 | 840 | 1,170 |
| Merced | 4 | 37 | 7 | 30 | 4 | (25) | — |
| Modoc (Klamath) | 46 | 61 | 404 | 499 | 503 | 666 | 546 |
| Mono | — | 2 | 35 | 368 | 389 | 446 | 386 |
| Monterey | 411 | 201 | 222 | 58 | 26 | 77 | 29 |
| Napa | 1 | 66 | 64 | 15 | 18 | — | 6 |
| Nevada | 5 | 8 | 101 | 159 | 48 | 76 | 52 |
| Orange | — | — | — | 5 | — | — | 21 |
| Placer | 7 | 2 | 91 | 73 | 74 | 105 | 102 |
| Plumas | 108 | 5 | 538 | 374 | 444 | 479 | 380 |
| Riverside | — | — | — | — | 809 | — | 1,590 |
| Sacramento | 251 | 34 | 14 | 40 | 24 | (50) | 62 |
| San Benito | — | — | 81 | 41 | 36 | (40) | — |
| San Bernardino | 3,028 | — | 658 | 399 | 572 | — | 573 |
| San Diego | 3,067 | 28 | 1,702 | 478 | 2,197 | — | 1,516 |
| San Francisco | 41 | 54 | 45 | 31 | 15 | 0 | 46 |
| San Joaquin | 4 | 5 | 31 | 2 | 1 | (30) | 8 |
| San Luis Obispo | 149 | 137 | 153 | 47 | 1 | (70) | 14 |
| San Mateo | 52 | 8 | 8 | 6 | 1 | (15) | 1 |
| Santa Barbara | 365 | 153 | 88 | 73 | 72 | — | 45 |
| Santa Clara | 157 | 12 | 73 | 19 | 9 | 0 | 16 |
| Santa Cruz | 218 | 2 | 131 | 10 | 67 | (60) | 15 |
| Shasta | 8 | 26 | 1,037 | 693 | 862 | 852 | 756 |
| Sierra | — | — | 12 | 10 | 31 | 18 | 54 |
| Siskiyou | 51 | 50 | 493 | 710 | 480 | 1,263 | 1,009 |
| Solano | 21 | 3 | 21 | 11 | 2 | 0 | 1 |
| Sonoma | 144 | 85 | 339 | 297 | 316 | 386 | 340 |

Table 5 *(Continued)*

| County | 1860 | 1870 | 1880 | 1890 | 1900 | 1905 | 1910 |
|---|---|---|---|---|---|---|---|
| Stanislaus | 6 | — | 27 | 12 | 25 | (25) | 30 |
| Sutter | 10 | — | 13 | 1 | 20 | 7 | 18 |
| Tehama | 656 | 54 | 167 | 101 | 99 | 118 | 94 |
| Trinity | 100 | 140 | 261 | 193 | 234 | 246 | 227 |
| Tulare | 1,340 | 4 | 118 | 178 | 175 | 61 | 204 |
| Tuolumne | 6 | 3 | 347 | 218 | 149 | 128 | 186 |
| Ventura | — | — | 80 | 91 | 5 | — | 3 |
| Yolo | — | 117 | 47 | 41 | 28 | 40 | 32 |
| Yuba | 72 | — | 67 | 27 | 24 | 53 | 16 |
| Total as stated in the census | 17,738 | 7,241 | 16,277 | 16,624 | 15,377 | — | 16,371 |

## PART II

| County | 1920 | 1930 | 1940 | 1950 | 1960 | 1970 |
|---|---|---|---|---|---|---|
| Alameda | 56 | 182 | 196 | 510 | 1,688 | 5,688 |
| Alpine | 102 | 104 | 110 | 82 | 179 | 97 |
| Amador | 83 | 125 | 169 | 152 | 115 | 160 |
| Butte | 225 | 277 | 261 | 207 | 421 | 890 |
| Calaveras | 65 | 125 | 89 | 94 | 113 | 171 |
| Colusa | 112 | 107 | 143 | 172 | 147 | 132 |
| Contra Costa | 137 | 30 | 25 | 247 | 447 | 1,701 |
| Del Norte | 524 | 499 | 466 | 484 | 691 | 727 |
| El Dorado | 115 | 144 | 85 | 110 | 88 | 230 |
| Fresno | 380 | 652 | 689 | 726 | 1,083 | 2,144 |
| Glenn | 24 | 31 | 63 | 39 | 89 | 188 |
| Humboldt | 1,829 | 2,174 | 1,940 | 1,825 | 2,608 | 3,055 |
| Imperial | 1,185 | 796 | 736 | 741 | 830 | 889 |
| Inyo | 632 | 736 | 943 | 799 | 1,036 | 1,170 |
| Kern | 208 | 369 | 296 | 316 | 676 | 2,039 |
| Kings | 63 | 162 | 147 | 126 | 176 | 357 |
| Lake | 294 | 377 | 362 | 368 | 433 | 323 |
| Lassen | 331 | 308 | 189 | 223 | 228 | 349 |
| Los Angeles | 281 | 997 | 1,378 | 1,671 | 8,109 | 24,509 |
| Madera | 392 | 520 | 264 | 414 | 420 | 748 |
| Marin | 34 | 119 | 82 | 82 | 153 | 382 |
| Mariposa | 94 | 141 | 185 | 186 | 111 | 201 |
| Mendocino | 1,056 | 1,154 | 1,143 | 1,252 | 1,215 | 1,433 |
| Merced | 7 | 40 | 258 | 44 | 199 | 356 |
| Modoc | 475 | 561 | 311 | 297 | 273 | 173 |
| Mono | 252 | 293 | 314 | 264 | 124 | 190 |

Table 5 *(continued)*

| County | 1920 | 1930 | 1940 | 1950 | 1960 | 1970 |
|---|---|---|---|---|---|---|
| Monterey | 7 | 32 | 89 | 128 | 695 | 1,139 |
| Napa | 2 | 16 | 28 | 43 | 118 | 215 |
| Nevada | 40 | 33 | 42 | 54 | 50 | 112 |
| Orange | 990 | 125 | 66 | 134 | 730 | 3,920 |
| Placer | 115 | 146 | 129 | 188 | 244 | 413 |
| Plumas | 332 | 251 | 235 | 218 | 240 | 305 |
| Riverside | 1,958 | 1,327 | 1,701 | 1,211 | 1,702 | 2,922 |
| Sacramento | 53 | 186 | 246 | 325 | 802 | 2,670 |
| San Benito | — | 3 | 6 | 11 | 25 | 54 |
| San Bernardino | 1,029 | 468 | 478 | 846 | 1,864 | 3,456 |
| San Diego | 1,352 | 1,722 | 1,650 | 1,693 | 3,293 | 5,880 |
| San Francisco | 45 | 151 | 224 | 331 | 1,068 | 2,900 |
| San Joaquin | 9 | 62 | 71 | 160 | 363 | 1,218 |
| San Luis Obispo | 13 | 20 | 16 | 22 | 98 | 517 |
| San Mateo | 3 | 42 | 18 | 54 | 319 | 1,340 |
| Santa Barbara | 50 | 44 | 122 | 41 | 306 | 1,008 |
| Santa Clara | 4 | 45 | 74 | 144 | 705 | 4,048 |
| Santa Cruz | 45 | 12 | 12 | 17 | 144 | 360 |
| Shasta | 610 | 687 | 611 | 525 | 793 | 1,321 |
| Sierra | 65 | 78 | 45 | 41 | 70 | 39 |
| Siskiyou | 624 | 964 | 636 | 589 | 592 | 968 |
| Solano | 7 | 18 | 27 | 84 | 208 | 1,048 |
| Sonoma | 357 | 545 | 383 | 585 | 949 | 1,623 |
| Stanislaus | 41 | 37 | 16 | 90 | 224 | 686 |
| Sutter | 12 | 12 | 8 | 39 | 27 | 209 |
| Tehama | 125 | 125 | 76 | 130 | 183 | 306 |
| Trinity | 99 | 280 | 106 | 69 | 172 | 287 |
| Tulare | 246 | 351 | 175 | 402 | 705 | 1,368 |
| Tuolumne | 73 | 153 | 181 | 110 | 134 | 548 |
| Ventura | 10 | 14 | 25 | 62 | 203 | 1,150 |
| Yolo | 43 | 54 | 232 | 78 | 244 | 476 |
| Yuba | 46 | 86 | 103 | 81 | 122 | 210 |
| Total as stated in the census | 17,360 | 19,212 | 18,675 | 19,947 | 39,014 | 91,018 |

The sources of the census figures are as follows:

1860. The Population of the United States in 1860; compiled from the original returns of the eighth census. State of California, Table No. 1, pp. 26-27. Washington, 1864.

1870. Ninth Census of the United States, 1870. Statistics of Population. Tables I-VIII, inclusive. Table II, California. Washington, 1872.

1860, 1870, 1880. Census of 1880, Vol. I, part 2, Table V (p. 382), Population, by Race and by Counties: 1880, 1870, 1860. California.

1880, 1890. Report on Population of the United States at the Eleventh Census, 1890, Vol. I, Part I, 1895. California, Indian Population by Counties.

1890, 1900. Twelfth Census of the United States, taken in the year 1900. Census reports, Vol. I, Population, Part I, Table No. 19, p. 531.

1910. Thirteenth Census of the United States, taken in the year 1910. Abstract of the Census . . . with Supplement for California, Table No. 17, p. 596.

1900, 1910, 1920. Fourteenth Census. State Compendium, California, 1924, Table No. 7, pp. 109-110.

1930, 1940. Sixteenth Census of the United States: 1940. Population, Vol. II, Characteristics of the Population, Part I. California. Table No. 25, pp. 567-568.

1950. Seventeenth Decennial Census of the United States. Census of Population: 1950. Vol. II. Characteristics of the Population, Part 5, California. Table No. 47, p. 179.

1960. Eighteenth Decennial Census of the United States: 1960. Vol. I. General Population Characteristics. California. Table No. 28, pp. 195-199.

1970. Nineteenth Decennial Census of the United States: 1970. General Population Characteristics, California. Table 34.

These citations illustrate clearly how unstable was the occupancy of the reservations at this period, and how subject they were to wholesale desertion by way of the ''stampede.'' Nevertheless, it is apparent that Northwestern California, in 1862, must have contained at least 6,000 Indians, who, at one time or another, were gathered upon the existing reservations, Smith River, Round Valley, and Mendocino. To be sure, most of these Indians escaped, but they were still at large over the countryside. Not included by the reporting agents were the Hupa, Karok, and Yurok on the Klamath and Trinity Rivers (unless some of them were at Smith River), and the Shasta, Pit Rivers, and other tribes in northern and northeastern California. Likewise neglected were the remnants of the Indians living in the central part of the State, the valley and foothills from Red Bluff to Fresno. At least 10,000 must be allowed for these people. When 6,000 are added for the northwestern area, the total becomes 16,000.

To the southward, J. H. P. Wentworth reported (BIA 1861-1862, Document No. 67) that in California from the Tehachapi south, there were at least 10,000 Indians who either were derived from the missions or who formed the Cahuilla and the smaller desert tribes. In addition, he says there were 1,370 now at Tejon Reservation, and, according to the census of 1860 there were 1,500 in Owens Valley. Document No. 74, entitled "Statement of Population . . . etc." states that at the Fresno Reserve (including Tule River) there were 2,436. Wentworth, who was the agent in charge of the southern district, concluded: "In my department there are at least sixteen thousand Indians." If we combine the northern and southern districts we get a total of 32,000 as the Indian population in 1862.

The next evidence of value supplied by Indian Service officials is the report of Charles Maltby in the Commissioner's Report for 1864-1865, Document No. 14. He lists six reservations—Round Valley plus Mendocino, Hoopa, Humboldt Bay, Smith River, and Tule River—which held a total of 6,910 Indians. He then makes two estimates (pp. 115-116). The first is of the non-reservation Indians in the north, and west of the Sacramento River, who amounted to 13,500 souls. The second estimate is of those in the southern part of the state and east of the Sacramento River, 16,500. The total, after adding the 6,910 reservation Indians, is 36,910. The geographical boundaries are poorly defined and it is not clear whether Maltby included the reservation Indians in the south. On the other hand, it is probable from the context that he was trying to estimate the Indian population of the state as a whole.

A final statement for the period is the summary table of population on page 589 of the 1864-1865 report. This table gives the total for the state as 33,810 Indians. We now have five totals as shown in the accompanying table.

| 1860 | Census according to Merriam | 31,338 |
| 1860 | Merriam's estimate | 35,000 |
| 1862 | Hanson and Wentworth (BIA) | 32,000 |
| 1865 | Maltby's estimate (BIA) | 36,910 |
| 1865 | Table of population (BIA) | 33,810 |

It is possible that all these estimates are too low and that all counts failed to include many Indians who had fled the approach of the white man. However, convincing evidence is lacking. It is also undoubtedly true that the native population was still declining during the interval 1860-1865. Hence we may accept Merriam's figure of 35,000 for 1860, and use the BIA total of 33,810 for 1865.

For the period 1869-1871, the census of 1870, according to Merriam, gave 29,025. Merriam's own estimate was 30,000. The reports from the reservations are erratic. The totals for the northern group, embracing Hoopa, Round Valley, and Tule River, vary from 2,737 in 1867 to 1,967 in 1871. In general there is a decline, but the figures are of marginal significance. In 1872 the total jumped again to 2,799, but this increase, apart from the incorporation of the Tejon Reservation with Tule River, is explained in BIA, 1871-1872, Document No. 85, as due to the addition of many Pomo. These Indians had been rounded up in Mendocino County and were settled on the reservation at Round Valley. By 1880 they had all gone back home.

There are one or two comprehensive statements by agents at this time. J. B. McIntosh (BIA, 1869-1870, Document No. 21, p. 81) counted 13,700 to 14,200 non-reservation Indians in various, but not all, parts of the state. He estimated 16,000 "on and off" the reservations, but thought a full count would yield "over 20,000." B. C. Whiting (BIA, 1870-1871, Document No. 19, p. 329) said that the Commissioner of the Census Bureau gave him an advance report that the 1870 census found 31,000 Indians in California. The published census report, as repeated by Merriam, gave only 29,000. The total by counties, as taken from the 1880 recapitulation, and shown here in Table 5, was only 7,241. Merriam's figure of 30,000 may be accepted as a fair approximation for 1870.

By 1880 the reservations had been stabilized administratively and no further change in organization occurred for a number of decades. Hence we might attempt to assess the Indian population at this date. The sources are, as customary, the United States censuses and the Reports of the Commissioner of Indian Affairs. Mention has been made previously of the inadequacy displayed by the Census Bureau, but further comment will be in order.

Official policy regarding enumeration of Indians has fluctuated from decade to decade, with the result that the accuracy of the counts has varied enormously. The condition has been well described recently in a publication of the Bureau of the Census, a supplement to the Statistical Abstract (1960). On page 3 we read this paragraph:

The census of 1860 was the first in which Indians were distinguished from other classes in the population. Prior to 1890 enumeration of Indians was limited to Indians living in the general population of the various states; Indians in Indian territory and on Indian reservations were excluded. In 1910 a special effort was made to secure a complete enumeration of persons with any perceptible amount of Indian ancestry. This probably resulted in the enumeration as Indians of a considerable number of persons who would have been reported as white in earlier censuses. There were no special efforts in 1920, and the returns showed a much smaller number of Indians than in 1910. Again in 1930 emphasis was placed on securing a complete count of Indians, with the result that the returns probably overstated the decennial increase in the number of Indians.

On the local level, also, there have been difficulties. Some of these were described by Helen Hunt Jackson. In her ''Report on the Condition and Needs of the Mission Indians of California'' (1888), she made the following remarks concerning the census of 1880:

This estimate [of the 1880 census] falls considerably short of the real numbers, as there are no doubt in hiding, so to speak, in remote and inaccessible spots, many individuals, families, or even villages; some on reservations . . . some on land not reserved, and some upon lands included within the boundaries of confirmed Mexican grants. Considerable numbers of these Indians are also to be found on the outskirts of the white settlements, as at San Bernardino, Riverside, and Redlands, and the colonies of the San Gabriel Valley, where they live like gypsies in brush huts, here today, gone tomorrow . . . .

In the Commissioner's Report for 1899—1900 (p. 208), L. A. Wright criticized the 1900 census after he himself had made a special effort to count the Mission Agency Indians. He said that ''the census as taken by the enumerators of the Mission Indians is perfectly unreliable and worthless, some reservations not being visited at all.'' He also wrote that ''many positively refused to answer the questions of the census agent.'' In terse language Agent Wright put his finger on the three primary defects of all the Federal censuses: First, the paid enumerators were too lazy or too incompetent to hunt out and visit all the known enclaves of Indian residents. Second, a great many Indians were sequestered in remote spots unknown even to reservation agents. Third, there was almost universal opposition to being interviewed by anyone with even a remote official association. Hence even though bureaucratic policy might favor obtaining a full count, it was almost impossible to secure one in the field.

As a consequence of these deficiencies, the Reports of the Federal Bureau of the Census concerning the California Indians, even up to recent years, must be regarded as ''perfectly unreliable,'' although they are not entirely ''worthless.'' In the half century from 1870 to 1920, they must be treated as severe underestimates of the true population. Some of the irregularities may be followed through the figures given for individual counties. In Table 5 are shown the values for Indian population by county as presented in the officially published, consecutive, decennial censuses. The data for 1860 and 1870 have already been discarded as completely erroneous. From 1880 to 1950 the totals are relatively consistent, and range from 15,000 to 20,000. Meanwhile from the table it is evident that the separate county figures fluctuate widely, if not wildly. The variability cannot be referred to random movement in birth and death, or in migration, on the part of the actual population. Instead, it must be due to inaccurate counting throughout the state. If such is the case, we must be skeptical of the totals as well as of the individual figures.

The Reports of the Commissioner indicate that there was a decrease in the number of reservation Indians between 1875 and 1882. Thus it may be noted, as in Table 3, that the enrollment at Hoopa Valley fell from 716 in 1875 to 427 in 1877; at Round Valley from 1,144 in 1875 to 996 in 1877 and 534 in 1880; at Tule River from 307 in 1874 to 254 in 1877 and 160 in 1879. In 1880 the total at the three reservations was 1,108, a value which was very little exceeded for the next twenty-five years. This reduction may be ascribed in part to disease and poor living conditions, in part to losses through fugitivism. In any event, by 1880 the *reservations* had reached their lowest level of prosperity.

That a great number of Indians were living apart from the reservations, and in fact quite independently of all government supervision, was consistently recognized by the reporting of the "non-agency" population. The magnitude of this group, however, as late as 1906, was determined principally by the census records rather than through personal investigation by Indian Bureau personnel. On the other hand, in their annual reports, the agents frequently commented upon the large number of Indians who were beyond their jursidiction.

Humboldt, Del Norte, and Trinity Counties contained the Hoopa Valley Reservation, which averaged 445 Indians from 1877 to 1882 inclusive. In addition there were the Yurok and Karok on the Klamath River, who were later organized as the Lower Klamath Reservation. In 1880 (BIA, 1879-1880, p. 238) they amounted to 1,125 persons. The total given for the three counties by the 1880 census was 2,607, not including the Hoopa Valley Reservation. This figure may be accepted without further discussion. The total is 3,052.

Round Valley is in Mendocino County. It averaged 606 Indians from

1879 to 1882, but by no means included all the Indians in the county. For the latter, the list of the 1880 census shows 1,265, but even this value is not adequate. H. B. Sheldon (BIA, 1877-1878, p. 11), the agent at Round Valley, stated that "according to reports" within a distance of 20 to 250 miles there were 1,500 Indians. The next year he raised his estimate to 2,000-2,500, plus more than 100 on or near the reservation "who belong to their tribes." This distance mentioned and the region involved imply that Sheldon was thinking of the northern Coast Ranges in Mendocino, Lake, Sonoma, and Napa Counties. The 1880 list, which Sheldon cites, gives a total Indian population of 2,579 for the four counties. Hence Sheldon's upper value of 2,500 is probably a close approximation. The total, with Round Valley, would be 3,100.

In the north and northeast there was at that time no reservation or other agency such as a school. Hence we can cite only the county list of the 1880 census. The counties involved may be taken as Siskiyou, Shasta, Modoc, Lassen, Plumas, and Tehama, and their total Indian population is 2,969. The strip from Butte to Madera counties is rarely mentioned by the agents of the Indian Bureau. Yet we know that it harbored a host of Indians. Most of them lived in remote mountain valleys or on foothill ranches, ignored alike by the Indian Bureau and the census takers. The 1880 census for the ten counties of Butte, Yuba, Sutter, Nevada, Placer, El Dorado, Amador, Calaveras, Tuolumne, and Mariposa, gives 1,959 persons, to which may be added the valley counties of Colusa, Yolo, Sacramento, San Joaquin, Stanislaus, and Merced, with 482. The total, 2441, is certainly an underestimate.

Fresno (including Madera), Tulare (with Kings), and western Kern Counties contained the Tule River Reservation, together with a large residue of the valley Yokuts and foothill western Mono, who were widely scattered and not under the control of an agent. Tule River, in 1880, had close to 160 inhabitants. However, the peripheral territory was better populated. As early as 1877, C. G. Belknap (BIA, 1876-1877, p. 42) mentioned 250 Kings River Indians, 90 miles north of Tule River. In 1881, the number on Kings River is stated at 540 (BIA, 1880-1881, p. 272), a number which is carried over in reports for several years. The same agent, Belknap, later claimed (BIA, 1883-1884, p. 17) that within a radius of 75 miles from Tule River, there were 600 to 700 Indians. In 1885 (BIA, 1884-1885, p. 12) he put the 600-700 Indians within the bounds of the four adjoining counties.

Since the reservation is in Tulare County, this means Fresno, Madera, Kings, and Kern in addition to Tulare. The 1880 county list gives a total of 1,244 Indians for Fresno, Tulare, and Kern. The others are not listed. With Tule River Reservation the sum is approximately 1,400.

Throughout this period the reports of the Commissioner make no mention of Indians who might be living in the region bordering San Francisco Bay, or who were in the coastal counties from San Francisco to Santa Barbara. These Indians were principally descendants of mission neophytes, and were indifferent or even hostile to the agencies of the Federal Government. Our only clue to their number is the county list. The total found for the census of 1880 from the counties of San Francisco, Alameda, Contra Costa, Santa Clara, San Mateo, Santa Cruz, Monterey, San Luis Obispo, and Santa Barbara was 951, a surprisingly large population for an area which was supposed to contain no Indians at all.

If we turn now to the southern half of the state, we note first the Indians under the jurisdiction of the Mission Agency. The population reported in 1877 and 1878 (see Table 3) was 4,400. Then in 1879, it fell to 3,000, near which figure it remained for three decades. In the tables of population in the reports for 1880-1881 (p. 272) and for 1881-1882 (p. 10) there is a division by tribes in which it is stated that there were 381 Serranos, 778 Coahuila, 1,120 San Luis Rey, and 731 Diegueños. The county lists give values only for Ventura, Los Angeles, San Bernardino, and San Diego Counties. Orange and Riverside Counties were not yet in existence. The total Indian population is 2,756.

It is very difficult to accept 3,000 as representing all the Indians in southern California in 1880, with the exception of the Colorado River tribes, but such a procedure is not necessary. It was noted previously, in a quotation from the recent (1961) publication entitled "Historical Statistics of the United States," that prior to 1890 the census records did not include reservation Indians. If this statement is true, and there is no reason to doubt its veracity, we may simply conclude that the Mission Agency reported 3,000 reservation Indians, whereas the census of 1880 showed only those not attached to a reservation. The Indian population of the region would then be the sum of the two reports, in round numbers 5,750. This figure is minimal, because although the agency estimate for the reservations is probably substantially correct, the census was no doubt defective.

One final area must be considered, those portions of California which were inhabited by the Shoshonean groups commonly designated the Paiute. They ranged over much of Nevada but were also settled in what are now Mono and Inyo Counties. To these may be added those Washo who lived in Alpine County, across the line from Minden and Gardnerville. The county list of 1880 shows no Indians in Alpine County, 35 in Mono County, and 637 in Inyo County, a gross underestimate. The list for 1890 (as published in the census of 1910, Supplement for California) gives for the three counties respectively, 224, 368, and 850, for a total of 1,442. The reports of the Commissioner in the period 1910-1915 show about 500 Indians in the Bishop area, 900 at or near Independence, and perhaps 100 in Alpine County. There can have been no fewer Indians in these counties in 1880 than there were in 1890 or 1910. Thus it will not exaggerate the facts to ascribe a population of 1,500 to the Alpine-Bridgeport-Owens Valley region. The sum of all the areas described for north and south, now are shown in the accompanying table.

| | |
|---|---|
| Northwest (Hoopa Res.) | 3,050 |
| Mendocino (Round Valley Res.) | 3,100 |
| North and northeast | 2,970 |
| Foothill strip | 2,440 |
| Fresno (Tule River Res.) | 1,400 |
| Central coastal counties | 950 |
| Southern mission area | 5,750 |
| Alpine, Mono, and Inyo Counties | 1,500 |
| Total | 21,160 |

This is as far as official recording will carry us. The result is probably too low due to failure to include many Indians who were, in effect, fugitives. How many are involved no one can say with assurance. However, Merriam felt that it exceeded 2,000. An approximation to this figure is reasonable and will be accepted. The final total becomes 23,160, or, in even terms, 23,000. It represents, if valid, a severe reduction from the 30,000 postulated for 1870.

During the twenty-five or thirty years subsequent to 1880, there occurred very little change in the count of Indians on the reservations.

The aggregate recorded may have increased slightly with the establish-ment of the tiny ''Digger'' reserve at Jackson, in Amador County, and the opening of the Fort Bidwell School in Modoc County. Repeated reorganization of the reservations in the south seems to have had little effect upon the total number of Indians. There is small gain in following the details of enrollment and the various and fluctuating guesses with respect to the non-reservation component. We may pass immediately to the period of 1900-1910.

Apart from the annual statements of reservation agents and the decennial censuses, we have one document which is valuable for evaluation of the Indian population at the turn of the century. This is the report of Special Agent C. E. Kelsey on the non-reservation Indians in 1905-1906 (Kelsey, 1971). The editorial background will be found in the Introduction to the 1971 printing, edited by Prof. Robert F. Heizer. Kelsey went personally into a series of counties and enumerated the Indians living there. He recorded the names and family relationships but not the age or degree of blood. We can therefore ascertain the number of Indians who did not live on a reservation, but who lived in each county covered by Kelsey.

The most critical question which must be asked concerning the Kelsey report is whether he was able to find all the Indians in the 36 counties which he entered. It is clear from the context of the report, as well as from the serious attention which was given it by the Bureau of Indian Affairs, that Kelsey made a conscientious effort during nine months to locate every person who claimed Indian descent. We can also lend complete credit to his reliability as a witness. His com-pilation, therefore, cannot err on the side of exaggeration and unquestionably records non-reservation Indians who were alive in 1905-1906. On the other hand, we do not know from the published account exactly how Kelsey worked; whether he got his information first hand, which would have meant interviewing some 3,700 heads of families, or whether he took a series of local counts, each one being provided by some knowledgeable person in a community. Each method would leave room for gaps and omissions. Also passed by might have been scattered or isolated individuals who avoided Kelsey, or whom he was unable to reach. For these reasons, his totals must be regarded as minimal, with the possibility present that the true number was con-siderably greater. However, let us examine the Kelsey record as it stands.

The discussion by Kroeber (1957) is relevant here. Kroeber calculated Kelsey's non-reservation total as 13,361, and from other sources got 6,536 for the reservations. Since my reading of Kelsey differs from Kroeber's, and since, in this essay, the Colorado River Indians are omitted from the California reservation total, it will be necessary to reconsider the data in detail.

For each of 33 counties *without* reservations Kelsey reported the Indians with and without lands, the full bloods and the mixed bloods; also for three counties *with* reservations he made the same report for the Indians *not* on reservations. Three additional counties, San Francisco, Santa Clara, and Solano, reported no Indian settlements, and are considered to have contained no Indians. Beyond these 39 counties are nine others which, Kelsey says, "could not be visited on account of the special agent being called to Washington, and the figures are from the census." As listed against the county names on page 3 of the published version of Kelsey's report, these figures add up to 80 heads of families and 340 persons. However, the Thirteenth Census, Abstract with Supplement for California, 1910, table No. 17, page 596, shows 184 Indians as living in 1900 in the nine counties of Merced, Sacramento, San Joaquin, San Luis Obispo, San Mateo, Santa Cruz, Stanislaus, Marin, and San Benito. Where Kelsey got 340 is something of a mystery, particularly since he does not mention his source.

These 340 persons are reported in two other places. They occur listed under the appropriate names in the main list of counties visited (pp. 1 and 2), and are added in to get the total of 7,928 Indians who were without land. They also appear in the final "Summary" on page 3 under the heading "Not visited (count for 9 counties taken from 1900 census)." Here they are added a second time in the column of "Number of persons."

Another difficulty attends the persons who were not enumerated. On page 2, following Yuba County, we read the caption "Estimated as not enumerated," with 400 persons. On page 3 it is stated: "It is estimated that 400 Indians have failed of enumeration," with 400 repeated in the column headed "Number." But in the final summary we read "Estimated as missing by Kelsey," with the figure 60. This follows the item of "Not visited," with 340 persons.

In view of these discrepancies it may be desirable to recalculate Kelsey's entire count. If we start with the 36 counties which Kelsey visited and in which he found Indians, we get for the non-reservation natives 12,183, including those who lived on Forest Reserves. The latter component, incidentally, totals 1,306—not 1,206, as given by Kelsey on page 3. We allow no inhabitants for the three San Francisco Bay counties, nor for Napa and Contra Costa Counties, which are not even mentioned by Kelsey. We add 184 for the nine counties, the population of which must be derived from the 1900 census, and get 12,367. Since it is stated clearly in two places that the estimate of Indians not enumerated was 400, this amount must be included, and the total of non-reservation Indians becomes 12,767.

For the reservations we may follow Kroeber's example and use the figures given in the reports of 1905 and 1906. With the Hoopa Reservation Kroeber prefers the figure 420, from the report of 1906. The Klamath River "extension" was allocated 600 persons by the agent, Frank Kyselka, but the official table of population (BIA, 1905-1906, p. 481) gives 745. At Round Valley there were 615 and at Tule River 153. The total is 1,933. The aggregate for the entire area is 14,700.

The southern part of the state was not visited by Kelsey. Consequently we must depend upon the census returns and the reports of the Commissioner. In 1900 (Thirteenth Census, Abstract, table No. 17, p. 586) there were, in Santa Barbara, Ventura, Los Angeles, San Bernardino, Riverside, and San Diego Counties, 3,724 Indians. Orange and Imperial Counties are not reported. In 1910, all eight counties had an Indian population of 4,527. The increase appears to be due primarily to the inclusion of Imperial County, which contained large numbers of Yuma. However, since Kelsey worked with the census of 1900, we shall use the figures of that year, 3,724. Meanwhile, the reports of the Indian Commissioner show for 1905 and 1906 respectively 2,751 and 2,675 individuals under the Mission Agency. Since these estimates certainly failed to include all Indians living in the eight counties, the census list provides a better value.

An indirect approach is through comparison, in the north, of census reports with Kelsey's count of 48 counties. Here, in order to smooth out the random variation in the individual county values from census to census, we take the mean for each county in 1890, 1900, 1910, and 1920. These means are shown in Table 4. The total, including the three counties where Kelsey found no Indians, is 11,101. Meanwhile, we have determined Kelsey's total for the same area to be 14,700. The ratio of the Kelsey count to the census count is therefore 1.324.

If this ratio is applied to the total of the southern counties for 1900, that is 3,724 persons, the result is very close to 4,950. In other words if Kelsey had counted the south in the same way as in the north, and if the Mission Agency, but not the Colorado River reservations, are included, the number of Indians might have approached this value. This conclusion rests upon pure assumption, but there is nothing inherently improbable contained within it. If it be allowed, the total Indian population of the state will come to 19,650.

Kroeber (1957: 220), who includes nearly 2,000 from the Colorado River, allows 2,751 for the Mission Agency, but omits all non-reservation Indians in the southern counties. Our omission of the Yuma and Mojave might be balanced substantially by the inclusion of non-reservation Indians. If so, the total obtained here would be expected nearly to equal Kroeber's 19,897, as it does. Kroeber's statement that "the true figure was in the neighborhood of 20,000" covers the situation quite adequately.

There are grounds for the belief that this estimate is still too low. We may mention the entire omission of Napa and Contra Costa Counties, for which later censuses reported several dozen Indians. Furthermore, San Francisco, Santa Clara, and Solano Counties, where Kelsey found no one, and to which the 1900 census allocated only 52 Indians, were found to contain over 200 in 1930. In Modoc County, Kelsey found 666 non-reservation Indians. At the same time the Commissioner of Indian Affairs (1905-1906, Table of Population, p. 481) reported 200 Paiute and 500 Pit Rivers at Fort Bidwell School. Whether these were counted by Kelsey as non-reservation, or omitted as belonging to a reservation, cannot be determined now. In any event, the number of Indians in Modoc County was underestimated by Kelsey. Along the upper Kern River and its affluents, the former home of the Tubatulabal, Kelsey counted approximately 160 persons. This number is much below the probable total surviving in 1905. Nevertheless, in spite of these doubtful counts there is little concrete evidence upon which to base a really large increase in Kelsey's estimate, and it is better to leave the total at a relatively low value than to undertake unwarranted enlargement. Therefore, we may increase the aggregate by somewhat more than 1,000 and consider that the state contained at least 21,000 Indians in 1910.

In preceding discussions the native population was taken as approximately 35,000 in 1860, and, following Merriam, 30,000 in 1870. A further decline brought the population to a level at somewhere near 23,000 in 1880. If the value was at or above 21,000 in 1906 it is probable that the decline had reached its lowest point somewhere between the two dates. Since neither the estimate for 1880 nor for 1906 can be claimed as exact, it is preferable to consider the period 1890-1900 as representing the minimum, with a population above 20,000 but below 25,000. Kroeber thought much the same (1957: 220). He said: "The decrease in the final years of the nineteenth century had slowed beyond its estimate; and this decrease had been converted into the beginning of a slow increase some years before 1905-1906." A decline, culminating in the range of 21,000-25,000 would have been entirely consistent with the difficult task of adjustment which, even in the absence of actual warfare or epidemic disease, confronted the Indian race in California after 1860. However, in the 1890s the trend began to reverse itself and the Indians ever since have been on the increase.

This increase during the decades 1950-1970 has been enormous, so great, indeed, as to border on the incredible. At the same time some degree of rise has been evident since close to 1900. In detail we may follow the reports of the commissioner, which give the reservation, or agency population, the several decennial national censuses, and the general enrollments carried out for fiscal purposes by the Bureau of Indian Affairs.

The Reports of the Commissioner of Indian Affairs, since 1914, only a few of which I have seen, give the number of reservation Indians and the number under the supervision of school districts. Non-agency Indians are estimated, but these estimates are manifestly too low. For example (see Table 3) in 1906 and through 1910 the non-reservation component is given as Kelsey's total (13,061). In 1911 the figure suddenly drops to 5,150, although in 1912 it rises to 6,950. Even in the 1940s the estimates of unenrolled Indians do not exceed the range of 12,900 (in 1943) to 13,400 (in 1942). Such changes are obviously absurd and render the BIA reports virtually useless, except for the local population of certain reservations. Meanwhile the decennial censuses become more and more reliable.

The distribution of the Indian population by county in California is shown in Table 5 for each census year from 1860 to 1970. It has been previously emphasized that the variation for each county from census to census is very great, and that as a consequence the lists for 1860 and 1870 must be discarded. It is also difficult to follow the figures in a single county, even after 1900. For instance, Merced County shows, decade by decade, from 1920 to 1970, a population of 7, 40, 258, 44, 199, and 356 Indians. There may have been an increase, but its numerical significance is very dubious.

The existence of these discrepancies makes it desirable, instead of working with individual counties, to observe the trend of the censuses in their entirety. The figures are shown as the totals in Table 5, and are repeated in Table 6. It will be noted that the recorded Indian population of the state appeared to remain almost constant from 1880 to 1920. It then rose approximately twenty percent through 1950. However, in 1960 it had doubled and in 1970 had more than quintupled its value of 1950. In order to show the increase in units of percentage, we may take the mean of the four censuses from 1890 to 1920, inclusive, and call this mean 100 percent. Then the subsequent populations are represented by the values shown in Table 6. The final figure, in 1970, is close to 550 percent of the 1890-1920 mean. The increase in gross numbers is very great. Yet even more surprising is the fact that all this increase occurred in twenty years, from 1950 to 1970.

*Table 6.* INDIAN POPULATION OF CALIFORNIA:
TOTALS FROM TABLE 5, WITH THESE TOTALS
EXPRESSED AS PERCENTAGES OF THE MEAN OF
1890-1920

| Census | Indian population | Percent of mean of 1890-1920 (16,433 equals 100 percent) |
|--------|-------------------|----------------------------------------------------------|
| 1880   | 16,277            |                                                          |
| 1890   | 16,624            |                                                          |
| 1900   | 15,377            |                                                          |
| 1910   | 16,371            |                                                          |
| 1920   | 17,360            |                                                          |
| 1930   | 19,212            | 116.91                                                   |
| 1940   | 18,675            | 113.64                                                   |
| 1950   | 19,947            | 121.38                                                   |
| 1960   | 39,014            | 237.41                                                   |
| 1970   | 91,018            | 553.87                                                   |

The census increases are supported by the results of three Great Rolls, or enrollments, conducted by the Bureau of Indian Affairs, with termination dates in 1928, 1950, and 1970. In the late 1920s Congress appropriated funds with which to compensate the California Indians for the loss of their lands, according to the terms of the Treaty of Guadalupe Hidalgo, signed at the termination of the war with Mexico in 1848. It was necessary to establish the identity of those who were lineal descendents of the Indians inhabiting California at that time. No others could qualify. The information required for application was name, sex, age, tribal affiliation, degree of Indian blood, family relationship, and post office address. The applications are now on file in the National Archives at Washington, but a typed copy of the roll is at the Bureau of Indian Affairs, which maintains an office in Sacramento, California.

The final cut-off date for the receipt of applications was May 25, 1928, at which time 21,981 persons had been accepted. However, provision was made for late applications. These names are kept in a Supplemental Roll, and total 1,604, such that the total number of Indians included is 23,585.

In the early 1950s, in connection with the California Indians Claims Cases (Dockets 31-37), a new roll was undertaken, with a cut-off date at May 24, 1950. This list is alphabetical by person (the 1928 list is alphabetical by families). It shows the previous listing number, if any, the sex, age, address, and tribal affiliation, but not the degree of blood. There are 36,094 names on the list.

The third roll was undertaken in order to provide compensation for the descendants of California Indians in accordance with the act of Congress in 1964 which implemented the decision of the commissioners in the Claims Cases. The legal cut-off for filing applications was on September 21, 1968. However, the deadline was extended such that the last entry on the Date of Birth list was August 30, 1970, and the final actual cut-off was on September 21, 1970. According to information received at the local office of the Bureau of Indian Affairs, there were in all 69,911 applications approved for payment of compensation. In addition, 6,402 applications were received but were rejected, primarily on the ground that descent from California Indians of 1848 had not been legally proved. It is therefore probable that the number of bona fide descendants would exceed 69,911, the number now recorded on the roll. A comparison of the censuses and enrollments since 1920 is given in the accompanying table.

| | Census | | Enrollment |
|---|---|---|---|
| 1920 | 17,360 | | |
| 1930 | 19,212 | 1928 | 23,585 |
| 1940 | 18,675 | | |
| 1950 | 19,947 | 1950 | 36,094 |
| 1960 | 39,014 | | |
| 1970 | 91,018 | 1970 | 69,911 |

Certain points are immediately clear. The census population has increased enormously since 1920, and especially since 1950. The enrollment population has likewise increased greatly since 1928. The enrollment exceeded the census in 1928 and 1950, but fell below it in 1970.

What has been the cause of this precipitous rise in number of California Indians during the past fifty years? A series of possibilities may be considered.

*Natural Increase.* If the known California Indian population may be regarded as having reached its minimum of 21,000, and as being in a state of temporary equilibrium at or about the year 1900, its rate of increase thereafter will have been low at first, but will have become greater as time went on. Such an accelerating rate of increase would produce a pattern which showed a rising population, with the relative new increment becoming larger during each interval of time. A convenient unit for calculation is the *percent* by which the population rose from one decennial census to another.

This increment for the United States as a whole between 1900 and 1970 averaged an approximately constant 16 percent of each census. Then, if the California Indians had followed the general course of the North American population, they would have increased 16 percent of the 1900 value by 1910, 16 percent of the 1910 value by 1920, and so on. The final result in 1970 would have been roughly 59,000. But we can be sure that the California Indian population did not increase in this manner. It is almost a certainty that the decennial increment began at zero in or near 1900 and has reached a maximum to date in the decade 1960-1970.

*Table 7.* FOUR MODELS OF POSSIBLE INCREASE IN
THE INDIAN POPULATION OF CALIFORNIA, 1900-1970

| Year | *Percent* | *X* *Population* | *Percent* | *A* *Population* |
|------|---------|------------|---------|------------|
| 1900 | 16 | 21,000 | 2.5 | 21,000 |
| 1910 | 16 | 24,360 | 7.5 | 21,525 |
| 1920 | 16 | 28,257 | 12.5 | 23,140 |
| 1930 | 16 | 32,778 | 17.5 | 26,033 |
| 1940 | 16 | 38,022 | 22.5 | 30,589 |
| 1950 | 16 | 44,105 | 27.5 | 37,472 |
| 1960 | 16 | 51,162 | 32.5 | 47,777 |
| 1970 |   | 59,348 |   | 63,782 |

| Year | *Percent* | *B* *Population* | *Percent* | *C* *Population* |
|------|---------|------------|---------|------------|
| 1900 | 2 | 21,000 | 2 | 21,000 |
| 1910 | 4 | 21,420 | 5 | 21,420 |
| 1920 | 7 | 22,279 | 9 | 22,491 |
| 1930 | 11 | 23,838 | 14 | 24,515 |
| 1940 | 16 | 26,460 | 20 | 27,947 |
| 1950 | 22 | 30,393 | 27 | 33,536 |
| 1960 | 29 | 37,079 | 35 | 42,591 |
| 1970 |   | 47,832 |   | 57,948 |

NOTE: All models assume a population of 21,000 in 1900.
Model X assumes an increase in each decade of 16 percent of
the population in the initial year of that decade. Each of the other
models assumes an increase indicated by the mean percentage
given for each initial year of the decade.

We do not know, and have no numerical evidence for determining,
just what magnitude has been attained by this entity. On the other
hand, we can reasonably believe that the rate of increase among the Indians has not exceeded the recent value of approximately twenty-five
percent per decade reached by the non-white population of the United
States, nor the value of close to 38 percent found in Mexico for the
period 1960-1970 (IX Censo General, Resumen, 1970, p. XVII, and
VIII Censo General, Resumen General, 1962, p. XXII) We might set
the extreme limit at 35 percent from 1960 to 1970. A few simple cases

will illustrate what may have happened (see Table 7).

Case A. We start with 21,000 in 1900 and assume the rate of increase at that year to be zero, and in 1910 to be 5 percent per decade. The average increase would then be 2.5 percent. The progression we assume to be linear, 7.5 percent in 1910-1920, 12.5 percent in 1920-1930, up to 32.5 percent in 1960-1970. The terminal population in 1970 is 63,782.

Case B. The initial assumptions are as in Case A. However, the increase in the first decade is taken as 2 percent, that in the second decade 4 percent, followed by percentages increasing by arbitrary amounts: 7, 11, 16, 22, and finally 29 percent. The final population is 47,832.

Case C. The method is the same as in Case B, except that the percentage increase per decade rises faster: 2, 5, 9, 14, 20, 27, and 35 percent. The final population is 57,948.

The rates of increase may be manipulated at will and numerous models may be constructed. However, if none of them show an increase from 1960 to 1970 of more than the permissible 30-35 percent of the 1960 population, it will be very difficult to obtain a terminal population in excess of 60,000. Yet the apparent census increase for 1950-1960 is close to 95 percent, and for 1960-1970 is above 135 percent, both values manifestly impossible if excess of births over deaths is the sole cause of the rise in population. It is clear, therefore, that in order to account for a 1970 population of 90,000 by census and 70,000 by BIA enrollment, other factors must be invoked.

*Immigration.* During and after the Second World War, migration from inland states to California assumed great proportions. Of those entering, many have been American Indians from the reservations of the Dakotas, Oklahoma, and the southwest. How many there have been it is not easy to determine, for in order to do so it would be necessary to study the statements of individuals regarding birthplace. However, it is clear that such persons will be included in the census reports of 1960 and 1970 as Indians and hence will help to swell the total of Indians who, according to the census, were living in California on these dates. At the same time the Great Rolls of the Bureau of Indian Affairs will not contain their names because they are not descendants of Indians native to California in 1848, and therefore do not qualify for Federal financial assistance. The numbers involved may be estimated by the difference in the two types of enumeration.

The Roll of 1928 showed 23,585 names, including the Supplemental Roll, whereas the census of 1930 gave an Indian population of 19,212. Thus the census was still failing to record many Indians of California origin, and the number of Indian immigrants must have been so small as to be negligible. The 1950 Roll contained 36,094 names; the census of 1950 had 19,947 and that of 1960 had 39,014. The number reported in the latter census thus equaled or exceeded the level of enrollment. The change within a decade was probably due in part to the rising influx from other states. The process is more clearly seen in the Roll of 1970. This Roll contains approximately 70,000 names, but the census of 1970 shows 91,000 Indians. Despite increased effectiveness on the part of the census takers, the difference of 21,000 persons must be referable mainly to the presence of immigrants who are Indian but not Californian. This question, together with that of the distribution of the difference between the two counts, is discussed further in Chapter Six,

*Economic Advantage.* A third source of apparent increase in the California Indian population during the past few decades is of a quite different nature. It has been noted that after the disruption of native life following the invasion of the Americans, many Indians withdrew from political and social intercourse with the whites. One manifestation of this propensity was the avoidance of census enumeration. Another was a consistent refusal to cooperate in any way with officials of every persuasion. When the first Roll was formed in the mid-1920s, many Indians at first declined to participate. But as time went on, and it became evident that certain economic advantages could be obtained by enrollment, more and more Indians came out of retirement, so to speak, answered the questions, and submitted their applications. In this manner many more persons were recorded than had ever been found by the census takers. The growing familiarity with bureaucratic procedure and the increasing prospects of material gain induced an even greater proportion of the Indian population to participate in the 1950 enrollment. By 1970 word had spread to the most secluded corners of the state, and all but a few California Indians had been persuaded of the usefulness of applying for a monetary stipend.

The net effect has been to augment not only the absolute but the relative numbers of the Indian population. The economic factor has influenced the size of enrollments as they have progressed from 1928 to 1970, and at the same time has indirectly affected the proportion who were included in the census. It is impossible to obtain a precise value for this increment, but its magnitude must have been of real significance. It may well account for the rapid rise in population shown by the enrollments, over and above the rise due to natural increase.

*Social situation.* The reluctance of the Indian population to participate in any activity such as a census has also been in large measure dissipated by the change in social atmosphere which has taken place during the postwar period. The disappearance of the old hostility and the recognition of the rights of the Indian as a citizen have relieved the tension to a considerable extent and have made it easier for all parties to come together on a reasonable basis. As a result the Indian has less motive for passive resistance to rolls and censuses.

*Genetic dilution.* A final factor, perhaps not widely recognized or advertised, is the steady and rapid dilution of the Indian blood by means of crossing with other races. From the earliest days of the missions intermarriage was common between Indians and Spaniards or Mexicans. With Americans, the unions were at first principally forced and extralegal. However, there has been much intermixture of one sort or another. Since a child of mixed parentage, under the existing social system, has always been regarded as Indian, the result has been to incorporate all those with even a quarter or less of Indian blood into the Indian stratum. This process has not increased significantly the Indian gene pool, but has created a large number of individuals who qualify as and are counted as Indian. Hence the increase in population of "Indians" is much greater than would be anticipated if only pure bloods had been produced.

# III. AGE DISTRIBUTION AMONG THE CALIFORNIA INDIANS

The vital statistics of the Indian population in California must be drawn from the most heterogeneous sources. They vary greatly in their completeness and reliability, and can be described only as extremely spotty in both quantity and quality. To assemble them and to organize them in some sort of logical order is a task of no small magnitude.

Concerning births, deaths, and marriages, careful records were kept during the active period of the missions. Since 1830 and to the present day there have been few published summaries or statements of any kind. It is true that individual certificates of birth and death have been filed since approximately 1900 and are maintained in the Bureau of Vital Statistics at Sacramento and in the recorders' offices of the several counties. However, these are buried among the records of the general population. An additional but not very satisfactory source is provided by the occasional reports of physicians and agents who were in charge of reservations. To some extent these form a clue to survivorship among a limited segment of the Indian community.

Family and household composition can be studied in the Roll of 1928, which is organized according to blood and marital relationship, and also on some of the local reservation censuses. The Kelsey count of non-reservation Indians in 1905-1906 is also very helpful. On the other hand, the mission records are unsuitable and the Rolls of 1950 and 1970 are arranged alphabetically by surname. The United States censuses on the original returns undoubtedly showed family organization, but these records are difficult to obtain, if they exist at all.

There remains the age composition of the living population. This parameter is a good criterion of population status because the relative proportion of young and old can become an index to the general order of natality and mortality. Concerning age there are data spread over most of the history of the Indian population, although the gaps are wide and the reliability of the figures is not always as high as might be desired.

The aging pattern of a living population can be expressed in various ways. The simplest, most direct, and most suitable for such minority groups as the Indians, is the distribution of individuals according to age. If the group is of adequate size and the enumeration is sophisticated, classification may be attempted according to single year.

Usually, however, five-year periods are more appropriate, or even ten-year intervals.

The formulation of the data may follow the tabular method, or it may depend upon graphic presentation. If the latter method is used, and if the data are accurate, the result is a smooth curve. Otherwise block diagrams are commonly employed, for by this device deviations from an even trend are easily depicted. However, for two reasons I prefer the tabular method when Indian populations are involved. In the first place, the age intervals must necessarily be so wide that any graphic representation will be extremely crude. In the second place, graphs of such irregular character are less valuable for comparative purposes than standard tabulations which may be readily set against each other. Moreover, the latter are selected magnitudes which best illustrate the broad features of the population.

Of these tabulations, the first group consists of three categories into which any population may be divided—the young, the middle-aged, and the old. The young reach from birth to puberty, with the terminal age taken for both sexes at 14 years. The middle-aged component then runs from 15 to the age at which most reproductive and economic activity ceases. By convention this is at the age of 65 years. The oldest group therefore extends from 65 onward as long as life endures. A second type of partition is indicated when the data are grossly defective in the youngest range, from birth through 4 years. This situation often arises, as with archaeological material, with mission baptism records, and even with modern censuses and other enumerations. In such cases, although the elimination of the children constitutes a serious loss, nevertheless the age composition of the adult population is frequently more stable and more suitable for comparisons than one which includes an inadequate, or falsely reported number of young children. Accordingly three periods are taken in the later phases of life: 75 and older, 65 and older, and 50 and older. Each is referred to the adult population as a basis.

The units of expression can, of course, be absolute: the actual number of persons in each category, including the total population. There is no question, however, that relative units are preferable, if only because these alone permit comparisons between populations of widely differing size. The most convenient unit is the percentage, which is obtained merely by dividing the number in the age category by the total under consideration, whether the whole population or the adult element thereof.

A further magnitude, the median, is useful for assessing the age status of a population. This is merely the mid-point of age. It tells nothing concerning the disposition of ages above or below this number. It does tell, however, the aggregate of young and of relatively old. Thus a median of 30 years, as in the United States today, indicates a heavy preponderance of those in the later age groups, whereas one of 16 years testifies to a very youthful population indeed.

Contingent upon the above considerations, I have arranged the presentation of age composition of the California Indian population in the form of tables which show the percent in the whole population who are in specified age groups. The groups usually include the years 0-4, 0-9, 0-14, 50 and over, 65 and over, 75 and over, but some of the categories may be omitted. The percentages in the adult population refer to some or all of the groups 50 and over, 65 and over, 75 and over. In most instances there is also given the median, for what it may be worth.

The age status of the aboriginal, or pre-contact Indian population, can be evaluated only by the methods of physical anthropology, when these are applied to skeletal material excavated at the many archaeological sites in California. In the Lowie Museum of Anthropology at the University of California, Berkeley, there has been preserved a series of several hundred skeletons, in part only skulls, which have been removed from numerous habitation mounds in the northern part of the state. Some years ago I asked the late Prof. T.D. McCown about the age distribution of these. In reply he kindly tabulated for me the ages of 547 skeletons, exclusive of 32 fetuses. Regarding his methods he wrote me, under date of October 25, 1946: "Age can be assessed pretty accurately during the first twelve years of life on the basis of tooth eruption; up to twenty the general guide is the union of the epiphyses; from twenty-one to forty suture closure is the best guide. After forty it becomes increasingly difficult, and above sixty it is extremely difficult to assess age. In terms of reliability, therefore, the best data is for age groups of thirty five or younger." From the tabulation we derive the results shown in the accompanying table.

| | |
|---|---|
| Total number is 547 | 100 percent |
| Group 0-4 years is 41 | 7.50 percent |
| Group 0-14 is 79 | 14.45 percent |
| Group over 50 years is 17 | 3.11 percent |
| Group over 65 is 0 | 0.00 percent |

Two features of the tabulation are immediately apparent, the very small number of children, and the very small number of the aged. The two categories are low in number for different reasons. The reported child skeletons probably do not represent the true proportion because (1) many infants were not buried in the sites excavated, (2) young bone deteriorates and disappears more rapidly than that of older persons, particularly in the Central California climate, and (3) it is unavoidable that excavators should miss many of these fragile skeletons, either through inadvertence or deliberation.

That the number of older persons represented in this collection is extremely small is not due to any technical factor. They simply were not there; only 3 percent over 50, none over 65 years of age. Even if the younger component is eliminated by omitting all individuals under 15 years, the remaining adult group contains only 3.63 percent who died at an age of over 50 years.

This curtailment of life at a very early age is a universal characteristic of primitive populations, or indeed any population which exists under a high birth rate and high death rate regime. The entire phenomenon has been thoroughly discussed in two recent works (Rosset 1964 and Acsadi and Nemeskeri 1970) and need not be considered in detail here. It should be noted, however, that the University of California series shows an unusual lack of skeletons from persons over 50 years old, for with most aboriginal peoples at least 10 percent, and often more, live past the mid-century mark. The cause of the extremely poor showing of the California natives may rest in the type of material which was available for excavation, or in the techniques employed for treatment. In any event, the value of 3 percent alive over 50 years must be regarded as excessively and suspiciously small.

In spite of the possibility of defective data at both ends of the age spectrum, it is clear that the aboriginal Indian population lived on the average only a few years. Apart from the generally reduced survivorship which characterizes all primitive populations, it is difficult to explain this demographic peculiarity in the case of California. The climate was salubrious, the food supply was adequate, and no epidemic disease, so far as we are aware, afflicted the natives before the coming of the white man. For further enlightenment we must await more thorough studies of the ancient inhabitants whose skeletons still survive, both in the ground and in the museum. In the meantime it will be instructive to look at the age composition of the same natives as they came under the influence of the white man the first time, in the Spanish missions.

The missionary fathers kept very careful records concerning the number of their neophytes, as well as of births, baptisms, marriages, and deaths. In addition to the books in which these events were recorded for every Christian convert, the totals were submitted annually by each missionary to the Father President and through him to the central Church authority in Mexico. It is possible to use both these sources in order to obtain data concerning the age of the persons who constituted the mission community.

Most of the annual reports, or copies of them, were preserved in the archives of the Church, in San Francisco, but were destroyed in the earthquake and fire of 1906. In the meantime, however, H. H. Bancroft had transcribed and tabulated the figures which they contained. These Bancroft Transcripts, as they may be designated, formed the basis of a monograph (Cook, 1940) published just before the Second World War, and to which reference may be made for details of sources, and discussion of many aspects of mission demography.

The Bancroft Transcripts give for each mission annually, from its foundation to secularization in 1833, the population, the baptisms, marriages, and deaths. The age of the neophytes is mentioned in only two categories, adults and children. Even an abridged tabulation according to five or ten-year periods thus becomes impossible. The only recourse is to establish the ratio of children to adults, or, preferably, the percent of the children in the entire population. This may be done if we remember that subsequent to 1793, the fathers used the age of 10 years as separating the two categories, and that, for reports prior to 1793, an adjustment can be made so as to bring the number of children into conformity with the 0-9 year system (see Cook 1940 for details of the method).

It is now possible to calculate the percent of children in the population of each mission for every year of its existence. If this is done, more than 900 numbers are obtained. These may be combined and arranged for many areas and time periods, and the result usually falls between 15 and 25 percent. Nevertheless, this method is subject to certain objections. In the first place, the individual annual mission values display a very wide variability, owing to inaccurate counting or transcription, and to rapid changes in the missions themselves, brought about by mass conversions, fugitivism, epidemics, and a host of random factors. In the second place, the 21 missions differed widely in size. As a result, a percentage from a large mission is averaged with one from a small mission without reference to the actual number of persons.

A better method for consolidation is to obtain the total population of a group of missions, or if desired, all the missions for a single year and then determine the percent of children in the total. If a period longer than one year, such as a decade, is to be considered, the annual percentages may be averaged without serious error and the status of the mission population as a whole may be evaluated, rather than that of single establishments. This procedure was followed, with all missions collectively, and the means for successive decades were given in Table 4, page 38 of the monograph previously mentioned (Cook 1940). However, a reexamination of the data from the Bancroft Transcripts indicates that a division of the mission region into two portions is of significance.

The five southern missions may be segregated from the remainder of the twenty one. The group includes San Fernando, San Gabriel, San Juan Capistrano, San Luis Rey, and San Diego. Then the percent of children may be calculated in the annual reports of these missions and may be set opposite the values for the collective total of the other sixteen. Cross comparisons are difficult with so many figures, but become clearer when averages are obtained for approximate decades and for approximate thirds of the entire mission period. These numbers are shown here in Table 8.

*Table 8.* PERCENT OF CHILDREN 0-9 YEARS
OLD IN TWO GROUPS OF MISSIONS

| Period[a] | A. 5 missions, south | B. 16 missions, center and north |
|---|---|---|
| 1771-1781 | 20.9 | 25.0 |
| 1782-1792 | 23.5 | 26.6 |
| 1793-1802 | 23.9 | 22.5 |
| 1803-1812 | 24.8 | 16.4 |
| 1813-1822 | 24.1 | 16.2 |
| 1823-1833 | 25.6 | 15.8 |
| 1771-1794 | 22.2 | 25.9 |
| 1795-1814 | 24.4 | 18.3 |
| 1815-1833 | 25.1 | 16.0 |

[a] The periods are inclusive years for which the percentage values from the annual reports are averaged.

The trend is clear both for decades and for approximate twenty-year intervals. In the south the relative number of children increased steadily from roughly 22 percent to 25 percent of the total mission population. In the center and north it fell from an initial maximum of nearly 25 percent to a final value of 15 percent. Most of the decline occurred during the period from 1793 to 1812. The difference between the two regions may be ascribed in varying degree to certain causes (see also discussion in Cook 1940: 41). One of these was the initial conversion to Christianity of heathen children to the exclusion of older persons. This policy was followed most intensively in the north. Another cause, and perhaps the most important, was the tremendous mortality, particularly among children, which was observed in the northern missions during the epidemics of 1800-1810. The southern missions, whether for climatic or administrative reasons were much healthier and escaped the worst consequences of measles, influenza, tuberculosis, and other introduced maladies. The slow rise in proportion of children in this area may be ascribed to the general prosperity of its missions and the fact that the natives were able to adapt to the new life with relative ease.

In the north the high initial value of the percentage of children must have been referable to rapid preferential conversion of heathen children. There then followed extremely heavy losses due to epidemics and to a failure to react favorably to the mission system. A further influence was exerted by the disturbance attending importation of many new gentiles subsequent to 1805. They were brought in wholesale from the San Joaquin Valley, were poorly assimilated, and contributed to a high infant mortality. Here is an excellent example of influence exerted upon composition of the population by a prolonged period of bad health and social disturbance. These ills were in great measure escaped by the Mission converts in the south.

From the range of percentages between 15 and 25, little can be deduced with respect to the overall status of the mission Indians. Nor, in view of the great alteration in mode of life and physical environment which accompanied transfer to the missions, can we make a precise estimate of what might have been the aboriginal percentage of the population who were under 10 years of age. The nearest we can come is to calculate the average percent for the first three years of each mission which was established clearly. There are eleven which were founded prior to 1790. The averages for the first three years are: 22.0,

21.3, 31.8, 26.6, 24.4, 29.7, 24.3, 17.7, 24.3, 23.1, 14.8. The means of the eleven missions is 23.6. This tells us only that the aboriginal population may have contained from 20 to 25 percent of children under 10 years of age. At the same time it makes very clear that the value found for young children in the California archeological material is undoubtedly a wild underestimate.

Two other documents, found in manuscript form in the Bancroft Library, are helpful at this juncture. They are local mission censuses, taken at San Francisco Solano in 1826 and at San Luis Obispo in 1794, and are described minutely in the work previously mentioned (Cook 1940: 35-36). Since the age of each neophyte was given, it is easy to construct the five-year age groups. The summary of age percentages will be found here in Table 9. It must be admitted that two small counts taken at missions widely separated in space and time do not constitute a very solid sample of the whole mission system as it existed over several decades. Nevertheless, these two lists are of singular importance because they provide the only clear illustration we possess of the entire age range in the missions. Before discussing them further it will be desirable to mention the third primary source of mission demography, the baptism and burial books.

*Table 9.* SPECIFIED AGE GROUPS AS A PROPORTION OF THE TOTAL POPULATION (PART I) AND OF THE ADULT POPULATION OF 15 YEARS AND OVER (PART II)

PART I

| *Entity* | *0-4* | *0-9* | *0-14* | *50 and over* | *65 and over* | *75 and over* |
|---|---|---|---|---|---|---|
| Missions[a] | | | | | | |
| San Luis Obispo, census, 1794 | 8.22 | 23.05 | 36.50 | 9.03 | 3.10 | 0.94 |
| Solano, census, 1826 | 14.16 | 26.26 | 33.18 | 11.16 | 2.83 | 0.00 |
| Local gentiles, 9 missions, baptisms | 26.70 | 39.51 | 46.73 | 12.05 | 3.60 | 1.19 |

*Table 9 (continued)*

| Entity | 0-4 | 0-9 | 0-14 | 50 and over | 65 and over | 75 and over |
|---|---|---|---|---|---|---|
| Tulare gentiles, 9 missions, baptisms | 9.59 | 19.68 | 30.59 | 11.31 | 2.53 | 0.78 |
| Monterey, town, 1833[b] | 19.24 | 33.33 | 47.30 | 5.64 | 1.49 | 0.33 |
| California Indians | | | | | | |
| U.S. census, 1860[c] | 10.47 | 20.25 | 30.71 | 7.41 | 3.46 | 1.82 |
| U.S. census, 1870[d] | 11.26 | 20.80 | 31.65 | 6.84 | 1.49 | 0.36 |
| U.S. census, 1910[e] | 11.47 | 20.36 | 34.30 | 17.98 | 8.16 | 4.03 |
| Agency Roll, 1928[f] | 13.91 | 25.95 | 37.12 | 16.74 | 6.50 | 2.56 |
| Agency Roll, 1950[g] | 16.62 | 29.53 | 40.12 | 14.05 | 4.98 | 1.87 |
| Agency Roll, 1970[h] | 15.19 | 30.72 | 44.65 | 10.97 | 3.86 | 1.42 |

## PART II

| Entity | 50 and over | 65 and over | 75 and over | Median | Total population |
|---|---|---|---|---|---|
| Missions | | | | | |
| San Luis Obispo, census, 1794 | 14.52 | 4.88 | 1.49 | 22.32 | 742 |
| Solano, census, 1826 | 16.70 | 4.24 | 0.00 | 23.44 | 636 |
| Local gentiles, 9 missions, baptisms | 22.61 | 6.75 | 2.23 | 16.67 | 18,009 |
| Tulare gentiles, 9 missions, baptisms | 16.13 | 3.64 | 1.12 | 22.82 | 3,086 |
| Monterey, town, 1833 | 10.68 | 2.83 | 0.65 | 16.25 | 603 |

Table 9 *(continued)*

| Entity | 50 and over | 65 and over | 75 and over | Median | Total population |
|---|---|---|---|---|---|
| California Indians | | | | | |
| U.S. census, 1860 | 10.70 | 5.00 | 2.62 | 22.71 | 17,738 |
| U.S. census, 1870 | 10.00 | 2.16 | 0.52 | 23.90 | 7,241 |
| U.S. census, 1910 | 27.35 | 12.42 | 6.13 | 23.16 | 16,347 |
| Agency Roll, 1928 | 26.60 | 10.34 | 4.08 | 20.77 | 20,379 |
| Agency Roll, 1950 | 23.47 | 8.32 | 3.13 | 20.54 | 35,012 |
| Agency Roll, 1970 | 19.81 | 6.97 | 2.57 | 16.34 | 75,664 |

[a] These are manuscript sources—see discussion in text.

[b] From the archive of Monterey County, Salinas, Vol. 7, pp. 673 and ff.

[c] The Population of the United States in 1860, compiled from the Original Returns of the Eighth Census by Joseph C. G. Kennedy, Superintendent of the Census. Washington, 1864. State of California, Table No. 1, pp. 26-27.

[d] Ninth Census, Volume II. The Vital Statistics of the United States . . . etc. Compiled from the Original Returns of the Ninth Census by Francis A. Walker, Superintendent of Census. Washington, 1872. Table XXX, pp. 662 and ff. Ages of the Civilized Indians, 1870. California.

[e] Thirteenth Census of the United States, taken in the year 1910. Abstract of the Census . . . with Supplement for California. Bureau of the Census, Washington, 1913. Table 3, p. 587.

[f] The printed Roll is contained in two large volumes at the Office of the Bureau of Indians Affairs at Sacramento, California. It is arranged alphabetically by families and includes the age and birthdate of every individual.

[g] The printed Roll for 1950 is also at Sacramento, in six volumes. It is arranged alphabetically by individual names and contains the birthdate, but not the age, of every person.

[h] The 1970 Roll was computerized. Several print-outs exist, of which the most important is that which is arranged according to the alphabetical list of names. Another runs according to the date of birth. All these documents are on file at the Office of the Bureau of Indian Affairs at Sacramento.

In a previous section of this study I have described the transcript of the baptism and burial books of several missions that were made for me by Mr. Thomas W. Temple. The copies of the baptism books omit the record for those persons born in the mission or under its direct supervision. On the other hand, they show for each Christianized pagan the date, the age of the individual, and the rancheria or tribal entity from which he came. Thus the age distribution of the converted heathen can be obtained.

We were not able to examine all the books. Some have been lost. With the rest, time and other factors intervened. We have therefore the gentile baptisms for nine missions: Santa Clara, Santa Cruz, San Juan Bautista, San Carlos, Soledad, San Antonio, San Miguel, San Luis Obispo, and San Gabriel. Obviously the geographic distribution is biased in favor of the north; there are no channel missions and only one from the south. Hence any regional differences will be totally obscured.

The converts fall into two distinct classes. Every mission started its work of Christianization with those gentiles who lived in the immediate vicinity and spread gradually outward until it had incorporated all the heathen within a comfortable distance, usually one or two days journey, depending upon terrain, population, and similar considerations. These Indians we may call *local* gentiles, for they were within the circle of influence of the mission. Their complete conversion consumed approximately 30 years, or, if a range is preferable, 20 to 40 years. At the end of this period the mission was obliged to exist with the descendants of the original neophytes, or to seek new converts a relatively long distance away. In the north this need was satisfied, after about 1805, by the tribes who lived in the interior valley, and who were said by the Spaniards to have inhabited the "Tulares." These Tulare gentiles were secured for conversion in groups, often as a consequence of a formal military expedition. They were taken under circumstances quite unlike those obtaining with the local gentiles, and their entire career in the missions was set apart by their origin and their reaction to mission life.

The two groups of gentiles, in the baptism books abstracted by Mr. Temple, can be clearly distinguished by (1) the name of the rancheria from which they came, and (2) the period in mission history during which they were converted. The local gentiles appear first as neophytes and as a rule disappear before the Tulare gentiles and are recorded in the baptism books. The total number which can be counted in our transcript of these books is approximately 17,800 local Indians and 3,100 from the Tulares.

A summary of the age composition of these two groups is found in Table 9. Most notable is the fact that both sets of natives show very few persons of advanced years, whereas the local gentiles have far more in the younger age brackets—about three times as many in the category of 0-4 years. This discrepancy deserves further examination.

In the expeditions which produced the converts from the interior valley, it was the desire of the missionaries to get as many children as possible. At the same time the children and the old people were the most vulnerable to persuasion and seizure, for the young and mature adults could most easily escape. It was therefore probable that the proportions indicated in Table 9 do not misrepresent the relative number of persons at each end of the age scale who were actually part of the population. If so it means that the tribes which were oriented toward the west of the valley and the delta, and which consequently were first encountered by the Spanish invaders, had already been exposed for several years to demographic strain and to severe depletion before the missionaries were able to reach them for conversion. This strain and depletion could have been caused by repeated incursions, both official and private, of which we know very little, and by the spread of epidemic diseases from the missions and presidios of the coast to the neighboring interior.

With respect to the youthful component of the local population, it has been suggested that the relative number of such persons was deliberately increased by the preferential selection of children during the early years of mission existence. To what extent this factor was of significance is subject to discussion.

*Table 10.* SPECIFIED AGE GROUPS AS A PROPORTION OF (A) THE TOTAL POPULATION AND OF (B) THE ADULT POPULATION OF 15 YEARS AND OVER; ALSO BAPTISMS OF LOCAL GENTILES

| | | *A* | | *B* | |
| | | | | *65 and* | *Gentiles* |
| *Mission* | *Date* | *0-4* | *0-14* | *over* | *baptized* |
|---|---|---|---|---|---|
| Santa Clara | 1777-1781 | 46.00 | 75.70 | 2.99 | 276 |
| | 1782-1786 | 64.40 | 84.50 | 5.89 | 547 |
| | 1787-1791 | 54.65 | 77.10 | 7.62 | 917 |
| | 1792-1796 | 26.25 | 38.90 | 6.06 | 1,135 |
| | 1797-1801 | 25.50 | 43.05 | 3.84 | 502 |
| | 1802-1806 | 12.90 | 32.35 | 8.05 | 504 |
| | 1807-1812 | 12.70 | 23.93 | 8.80 | 284 |
| San Gabriel | 1772-1776 | 16.10 | 47.20 | 0.00 | 267 |
| | 1777-1781 | 33.30 | 69.00 | 1.82 | 347 |

*Table 10 (continued)*

| | | A | | B | |
| | | | | 65 and | Gentiles |
| Mission | Date | 0-4 | 0-14 | over | baptized |
|---|---|---|---|---|---|
| San Gabriel | 1782-1786 | 28.86 | 55.70 | 3.22 | 350 |
| | 1787-1791 | 39.40 | 56.45 | 5.04 | 500 |
| | 1792-1796 | 49.52 | 58.45 | 2.23 | 214 |
| | 1797-1801 | 36.24 | 45.00 | 12.18 | 149 |
| | 1802-1806 | 18.45 | 29.30 | 8.58 | 461 |
| | 1807-1811 | 32.88 | 51.90 | 2.06 | 706 |
| | 1812-1816 | 28.21 | 38.00 | 7.66 | 358 |
| San Luis Obispo | 1773-1777 | 17.04 | 42.55 | 2.96 | 235 |
| | 1778-1782 | 12.92 | 50.20 | 2.88 | 209 |
| | 1783-1787 | 13.33 | 38.45 | 8.11 | 60 |
| | 1788-1792 | 15.24 | 39.83 | 16.89 | 256 |
| | 1793-1797 | 11.69 | 27.90 | 10.80 | 154 |
| | 1798-1802 | 9.40 | 27.70 | 11.22 | 148 |
| San Antonio | 1771-1775 | 32.42 | 64.60 | 5.17 | 327 |
| | 1776-1780 | 24.88 | 38.30 | 10.24 | 269 |
| | 1781-1785 | 24.45 | 41.23 | 8.57 | 417 |
| | 1786-1790 | 29.00 | 46.13 | 18.27 | 193 |
| | 1791-1795 | 32.00 | 47.00 | 22.65 | 100 |
| | 1796-1800 | 30.23 | 41.30 | 15.82 | 172 |
| | 1801-1805 | 17.45 | 33.78 | 7.14 | 465 |
| San Carlos | 1771-1775 | 20.47 | 57.00 | 2.07 | 337 |
| | 1776-1780 | 20.00 | 31.04 | 0.00 | 145 |
| | 1781-1785 | 21.41 | 47.50 | 6.02 | 411 |
| | 1786-1790 | 27.67 | 49.65 | 7.50 | 159 |
| | 1791-1795 | 20.16 | 40.72 | 4.00 | 253 |
| | 1796-1800 | 40.40 | 53.85 | 12.50 | 52 |
| Santa Cruz | 1791-1795 | 17.29 | 50.20 | 5.79 | 590 |
| | 1796-1800 | 20.72 | 54.70 | 2.59 | 256 |
| | 1801-1805 | 10.60 | 40.40 | 2.54 | 198 |
| | 1806-1809 | 17.92 | 27.18 | 1.59 | 173 |
| San Juan Bautista | 1797-1801 | 28.11 | 55.20 | 3.67 | 729 |
| | 1802-1807 | 15.05 | 33.08 | 5.63 | 744 |
| Soledad | 1792-1796 | 29.66 | 55.20 | 3.08 | 290 |
| | 1797-1801 | 16.45 | 37.45 | 2.83 | 395 |
| | 1802-1806 | 13.18 | 32.55 | 3.32 | 402 |
| San Miguel | 1797-1801 | 21.85 | 47.30 | 8.21 | 531 |
| | 1802-1806 | 6.96 | 15.25 | 12.52 | 518 |

An analysis of the individual missions shows immediately that certain ones, notably Santa Clara, for some years after their foundation, baptized predominantly very young persons. This characteristic of conversion can be seen clearly in the summary contained in Table 10, with respect to the missions San Luis Obispo, Soledad, San Antonio, San Juan Bautista, and San Miguel. On the other hand, in some of the missions, for example San Gabriel and San Carlos, the baptisms of children remained roughly constant for years. Although the data are erratic, they imply that the mode of conversion of the local gentiles depended upon individual mission policy, upon the condition of the nearby Indian population at the time when each mission was founded, and upon the stage in history of the entire province. For instance, the difference between Santa Clara on the one hand and San Gabriel and San Carlos on the other, is very marked, yet all three of these missions were founded at almost the same time and among relatively undisturbed gentile populations. By way of contrast, the four later missions were forced to draw their neophytes from native tribes which had already been subjected for several years to economic disruption and introduced disease. Here the missionaries appear to have quickly exhausted the reservoir of youthful converts and within a few years were gathering in the remnants, who consisted of middle-aged and older persons.

On the whole the consolidated value for all the missions (see Table 9) of 26.7 percent baptized under 5 years of age seems too high a value for the intact aboriginal population, as does 46.7 percent for those under 15 years. The much lower percentages found in the two mission censuses of San Luis Obispo and Solano are suggestive, although these documents cannot be directly compared with the baptism records because the censuses refer to the resident population of the missions, rather than to the extra-mission, native condition.

Similar considerations apply to the populations reported in the Bancroft Transcripts. These records show a range of 15 to 25 percent for the proportion of children between 0 and 9 years of age. The comparable figure for the baptism books is close to 40 percent. When the first three years of eleven early missions are averaged, the mean of children under 10 years is 23.6 percent, and the maximum for any single mission is 31.8 percent. These values must be close to those which would be obtained from the baptism records, because during the first three years of existence a mission baptized almost exclusively gentiles. Yet they are significantly lower than the figures obtained from baptism books themselves.

If the proportion of children under 15 years which actually was present in the aboriginal Indian population was lower than that shown by the gentile baptism records (Table 9), we might reduce the latter proportion. A conservative factor would be three-quarters of the stated value. Hence for the groups 0-4, 0-9, and 0-14 years the revised figures would be, in round numbers, 20, 30, and 35 percent. A more radical adjustment would use a factor of two-thirds and make the corresponding percentages 18, 26, and 31. At all events it must be regarded as probable that these values indicate generally the ranges which characterized the youthful groups in the aboriginal condition.

As was previously explained, the proportion of the aged can be expressed in two forms. The first is as the percent of those exceeding a certain age in the entire population. This value will of course be influenced by the number of children, for the greater the number of children the smaller will be the relative number of persons in the older age groups. This factor can be eliminated by using the adult instead of the total population as a base, and by computing the percent of aged among those 15 years or older. In Table 9 the result by both methods is given; in Table 10 only the adult value is shown.

The values of the aged are extremely low by both methods with the mission censuses as well as the baptisms. For the group over 65 years the four cases shown in Table 9 give a range of 2.5 to 3.6 percent in the total population and for that over 75 years of age a range of 0.0 to 1.2 percent. When based upon the adult population the level is correspondingly low. These values are almost of the same order as was found in the skeletal material from ancient habitation sites.

In summary, it may be stated that the mission data, despite its great variability and its many exceptional cases, indicates for the native population in 1770-1780 a relatively large proportion of infants and young children, together with a much depressed survivorship past the age of 50. This type of distribution must therefore be recognized as the starting point for all later changes in the composition of the California Indian population.

In recent years there has come to be distinguished what is known as the demographic transition, a phenomenon which has manifested itself in all the technologically more advanced countries and which has started to appear in those parts of the world generally considered only partially developed. The transition, in brief, starts with the condition which obtained throughout the world prior to the eighteenth century, and in which the birth and death rates both were high. As a result the age distribution showed a great proportion of persons in the younger groups and a very small proportion in the older. An example of this condition is seen in Table 9 with the town of Monterey, California, in 1833, when its inhabitants were exclusively Spanish or Mexican. Contingent upon various factors, in Western Europe and the United States, the effective birth rate and the death rate both fell, the latter more rapidly. The final state, produced by low natality as well as mortality, displays an age distribution characterized by a small proportion of young persons and a relatively high level of the aged. For example, in the United States, according to the census of 1860, the white population contained approximately 40 percent in the age group 0-4 years, and 9.6 percent over 50 years. In 1967 (see Statistical Yearbook for 1968, table 8, p. 10) the corresponding percentages were respectively 9 and 25.

It is clear that the California Indian population, when the white man first arrived, was in the pre-transition state. This fact is supported by both the archaeological and the mission figures. However, it is also apparent that the Indian did not move immediately to an intra- or post-transition state. During the conventional transition, in its early phases the death rate is falling and the birth rate is stationary. The older component of the population increases and the younger falls but slightly. Toward the end of the transition the older component reaches a high level and the younger sinks to a new low. The Indian pattern, as seen in the two mission censuses and in the baptism record of the Tulare gentiles, shows none of these conditions. In fact, there is clearly a reduction of the younger component coupled with a retention of the low level of aged.

An explanation of this pattern may be sought in the gross movement of population. In the usual case the birth rate exceeds the falling death rate and the total population increases. With the California Indians the birth rate remained stationary or fell, while the death rate rose and the population decreased very rapidly. The killing of the very young and the very old reduced the *relative* proportions at both ends of the age sequence, with a concomitant increase in the proportion of young and mature but not aged adults. As long as the death rate remained high, with the birth rate remaining virtually unchanged, and the population diminished, this type of distribution could be anticipated. But if and when recovery began, with a falling death rate, perhaps a rising birth rate, and a stabilizing or increasing of the population, a pre-transition type of distribution would be restored. Later this population might go through the entire cycle and emerge in a post-transition condition.

After the missions were secularized in 1834, the recording of vital statistics relating to Indians ceased. During the following decades the natives underwent the population collapse attendant upon the invasion of the Americans and the mining activities of the 1850s. Subsequent to the restoration of somewhat stable conditions, the federal government, through the Bureau of Indian Affairs, began to count the Indians who were living at the reservations, although no serious attempt was made to determine closely the number of those who were living independently in the community. Not until the Kelsey Report of 1906 could the magnitude of this component even be estimated.

With respect to the age composition of the Indian population, our only information is contained in the United States censuses of 1860, 1870 and 1910, together with a series of local counts on certain of the reservations. The data are found in Table 9. The enumeration methods employed with the two earlier federal censuses were crude in the extreme. Furthermore, the native society was so demoralized and the relations with the whites so utterly confused that it is remarkable to find any rational tabulation at all of population characteristics. The total numbers reported—17,738 who gave their ages in 1860, and 7,241 in 1870—are extremely low. Actually, therefore, the census reports must be regarded as providing relatively large samples, rather than a full count of individuals. Whether these samples were random is subject to doubt, because only the more accessible Indians were included. Nevertheless, there is no clear bias present with regard to age distribution, and we may regard the census data as reproducing the age status of the population with acceptable fidelity.

Inspection of the proportions shown in Table 9 for the various age groups indicates that the age structure of the Indian population prior to 1880 resembled most closely that of the Tulare gentiles in the mission days. The relative number of both children and old people is very low, and the pattern conforms to that expected of a population which is in the midst of a sharp decline, and which is being subjected to a severe demographic strain.

By 1910 the situation had changed. There was a small increase in the proportion of children, and considerable increase in the relative number of aged persons. The conclusion would be that the decline in total population had come to a halt, and that the death rate had been drastically reduced in the mature and elderly age groups. This improvement in survivorship among the aged can have been due only to the general betterment in health conditions which was in process everywhere during the latter part of the nineteenth century.

For the period between the Civil War and the First World War we have two further sets of data which bear upon age distribution, and which, although of secondary importance, are of interest. Both are derived from the activity of reservation agents. The first is a group of counts made by the agents locally; the second is a series of estimates of children who were prospective students in the elementary schools.

The agency counts were seen by me in 1940 at the Hoopa (Eureka), Nevada (Stewart), and Mission (Riverside) agencies, and the age data were at that time transcribed. Table 11 gives a summary in terms of the proportion of persons in each of the age groups which have been employed consistently in this study. The dates range from 1887 to 1920.

*Table 11.* LOCAL CENSUSES FROM THREE AGENCIES—EUREKA (HOOPA), RIVERSIDE (MISSION), AND STEWART, NEVADA (WASHO AND PAIUTE)— SHOWING SPECIFIED AGE GROUPS AS A PROPORTION OF (PART I) THE TOTAL POPULATION AND OF (PART II) THE ADULT POPULATION OF 15 YEARS AND OVER

PART I

| Local census and year | 0-4 | 0-9 | 0-14 | 50 and over | 65 and over | 75 and over |
|---|---|---|---|---|---|---|
| Eureka agency | | | | | | |
| 1887 | 15.00 | 24.14 | 32.82 | 18.70 | 7.39 | 0.87 |
| 1897 | 12.86 | 22.44 | 32.47 | 17.96 | 7.56 | 1.63 |
| 1910 | 13.23 | 23.63 | 36.00 | 19.07 | 6.54 | 3.13 |
| 1920 | 12.55 | 25.20 | 36.85 | 18.03 | 7.07 | 2.65 |
| Riverside agency | | | | | | |
| 1902 | 7.89 | 18.77 | 31.10 | 17.55 | 7.89 | 4.59 |
| 1920 | 9.22 | 18.60 | 28.48 | 19.60 | 7.89 | 3.66 |
| Stewart agency | | | | | | |
| 1902 | 9.41 | 20.96 | 29.70 | 20.86 | 10.14 | 5.07 |
| 1920 | 8.42 | 18.31 | 26.87 | 19.94 | 8.28 | 3.41 |

*Table 11 (continued)*

PART II

| Local census and year | 50 and over | 65 and over | 75 and over | Median | Total population |
|---|---|---|---|---|---|
| Eureka agency | | | | | |
| 1887 | 27.84 | 11.00 | 1.29 | 22.57 | 460 |
| 1897 | 27.00 | 11.34 | 2.45 | 23.74 | 490 |
| 1910 | 29.80 | 10.21 | 4.89 | 23.37 | 703 |
| 1920 | 28.58 | 11.20 | 4.20 | 22.25 | 1,131 |
| Riverside agency | | | | | |
| 1902 | 25.50 | 11.46 | 6.67 | 25.17 | 2,546 |
| 1920 | 27.37 | 11.02 | 5.11 | 26.89 | 3,007 |
| Stewart agency | | | | | |
| 1902 | 29.63 | 14.42 | 7.21 | 27.19 | 1,084 |
| 1920 | 25.40 | 10.55 | 4.35 | 27.53 | 3,456 |

Despite small differences the results from the three agencies are very similar. Moreover, they resemble in all essential respects the proportions found for the same age groups in the federal census of 1910, particularly with respect to the large relative number of persons over the age of 50 years. It is again clear that at least the reservation Indians in California were living longer than their aboriginal ancestors, even though the replacement through new births may not have been significantly improved.

The data concerning school children are scattered through the file of reports of the Commissioner of Indian Affairs. For the period of 1880 to 1920, they occur in two series. The first consists of casual statements by reservation agents, chiefly those at Hoopa and Round Valley. They are incorporated with the annual reports and may or may not be present in any particular year. I have found and tabulated 29 of these, between 1887 and 1909 (see Table 12). The second series is found in the BIA reports for 1910-1911, 1911-1912, and 1912-1913. In each is shown the proportion of children in 15 to 18 reservations or agencies. The three sets are shown separately in Table 12.

*Table 12.* PERCENT OF CHILDREN OF
"SCHOOL AGE" ON RESERVATIONS,
1887-1920

| Date | *Agency, reservation, or rancheria* | *Percent of children* |
|------|-------------------------------------|------------------------|
| 1887/88 | Hoopa | 21.0 |
| | Round Valley | 14.2 |
| 1888/89 | Round Valley | 12.1 |
| 1889/90 | Hoopa | 22.7 |
| | Round Valley | 15.9 |
| 1890/91 | Round Valley | 13.9 |
| 1891/92 | Round Valley | 14.9 |
| 1892/93 | Round Valley | 13.4 |
| 1894/95 | Hoopa | 23.2 |
| 1895/96 | Hoopa | 24.0 |
| 1897/98 | Hoopa | 23.4 |
| | Mission | 27.5 |
| 1898/99 | Hoopa | 21.7 |
| 1899/00 | Hoopa | 21.7 |
| 1900/01 | Hoopa | 19.2 |
| 1901/02 | Mission | 21.6 |
| | Round Valley | 18.7 |
| 1902/03 | Mission | 21.5 |
| | Round Valley | 23.0 |
| 1903/04 | Hoopa | 17.6 |
| | Mission | 21.9 |
| 1904/05 | Yuma | 17.0 |
| | Hoopa | 20.4 |
| | Mojave | 19.5 |
| 1905/06 | Hoopa | 21.2 |
| | Mission | 18.4 |
| 1906/07 | Hoopa | 17.0 |
| | Mission | 21.9 |
| 1908/09 | Pala | 22.3 |
| | | Mean 19.7 |

SOURCES: The several Reports of the Commissioner, together with the federal census of
1910 and the local agency censuses indicated by
date.

*Table 12 (continued)*

| Date | Agency, reservation, or rancheria | Percent of children |
|---|---|---|
| 1910/11 | Colorado River | 31.5 |
| | Cahuilla | 24.2 |
| | Campo | 26.5 |
| | Digger | 34.9 |
| | Fort Bidwell | 31.3 |
| | Fort Yuma | 26.7 |
| | Hoopa | 16.7 |
| | La Jolla | 24.8 |
| | Malki | 26.5 |
| | Martinez | 30.9 |
| | Mesa Grande | 25.0 |
| | Pala | 25.9 |
| | Pechanga | 31.0 |
| | Rincon | 27.3 |
| | Round Valley | 28.8 |
| | Soboba | 24.4 |
| | Upper Lake | 24.1 |
| | Volcan | 18.3 |
| | Mean | 26.6 |
| 1911/12 | Colorado River | 25.5 |
| | Fort Mojave | 26.1 |
| | Bishop | 24.0 |
| | Campo | 25.5 |
| | Digger | 33.3 |
| | Fort Bidwell | 32.0 |
| | Fort Yuma | 19.8 |
| | Hoopa | 33.1 |
| | Malki | 24.3 |
| | Martinez | 32.6 |
| | Pala | 24.6 |
| | Pechanga | 15.8 |
| | Round Valley | 26.6 |
| | Soboba | 19.4 |
| | Volcan | 30.6 |
| | Klamath, Ore. | 31.7 |
| | Mean | 26.6 |

*Table 12 (continued)*

| Date | Agency, reservation, or rancheria | Percent of children |
|------|-----------------------------------|---------------------|
| 1912/13 | Colorado River | 29.4 |
| | Fort Mojave | 27.6 |
| | Bishop | 20.0 |
| | Campo | 22.6 |
| | Digger | 28.6 |
| | Fort Bidwell | 30.4 |
| | Fort Yuma | 26.8 |
| | Hoopa | 32.8 |
| | Malki | 22.7 |
| | Pala | 25.0 |
| | Pechanga | 14.1 |
| | Round Valley | 28.1 |
| | Soboba | 22.6 |
| | Volcan | 30.6 |
| | Klamath, Ore. | 31.5 |
| | Mean | 26.2 |
| 1910 | Federal census | 22.86 |
| 1887 | Hoopa | 17.83 |
| 1897 | Hoopa | 20.60 |
| 1910 | Hoopa | 22.77 |
| 1920 | Hoopa | 24.32 |
| 1902 | Mission (Riverside) | 23.22 |
| 1920 | Mission (Riverside) | 19.25 |
| 1902 | Stewart, Nev. (Paiute) | 20.20 |
| 1920 | Stewart, Nev. (Paiute) | 18.45 |

NOTE: For the years 1887 to 1909, "school age" is stated as being from 6 to 15 years inclusive. For the years 1911, 1912, and 1913, an age span for "school age" is not stated, but it probably exceeds the limits of 6 to 15 years. For the nine censuses shown at the bottom of the table (beginning with the federal census of 1910), the age limits are set at 5 to 14 years inclusive.

The children are those who normally would attend school, from the primary grades perhaps through high school. They are frequently listed as being of ''school age,'' but in several places they are specified as being of age 6-15 years. Thus a ten-year span is indicated which, in general, coincides with school age. The limits, however, are not always clearly defined, and the second series (1910-1913) may have been somewhat more inclusive than the first.

The first series, with 29 cases, yields a mean for school children of 19.7 percent of the population. The three annual reports in the second series show, for 18, 16, and 15 reservations or tribes, respectively 26.6, 26.6, and 26.2 percent. Certainly the second series gives a higher proportion of children. For the difference various reasons may be assigned: (1) the second series included a wider range of ages, as suggested above; (2) the relative number of children really did increase between the period of 1887-1909 and that of 1910-1913; and (3) the first series is taken mainly from the north, the second from the south, and there may have been a regional difference in the relative number of children.

A further comparison of interest is between the school children of the reservations and the same age group as reported in the agency and the national censuses. The former are uniformly stated as falling within the interval 6-15 years. The censuses have been tabulated with age groups 0-4, 5-9, 10-14, 15-19. However, the interval 5-14 is very close to that of 6-15, so close that the error introduced by making the substitution is less than that inherent in the censuses, and consequently there will be caused no serious complication if the decade 5-14 is compared directly with that one year older. The figures are in Table 12.

The 1910 federal census and the eight agency censuses show, within quite narrow limits, that the age group 5-14, and, *pari passu*, the group 6-15, constituted from 20 to 22 percent of the Indian population. This value comes quite close to the first series discussed above. It is definitely below the second series, and lends credence to the idea that at the low point of Indian population the age group 5-14 (or 6-15) constituted a little more than 20 percent of the population. It may be added that the 1920 census of Indians in California showed no change from the census of 1910 (22.9 percent in the age group 5-14). The high values in the 1910-1913 reports of the BIA must therefore be referable to cause (1) rather than to any other, and, in sum, there is little indication of any increase in the relative number of children throughout the period from 1880 to 1920.

From 1910 the age distribution of the California Indians as a complete population may be followed only through the Rolls of 1928, 1950, and 1970. The Bureau of the Census has published no age data for the Indians of the state in any of its reports during the past sixty years, although these native people have been thrown together with Orientals as "other races." Perhaps ultimately the Bureau will segregate the Indians with respect to age in the detailed reports of some census, but no such publication has as yet appeared.

All three Rolls compiled by the Indian Service are thorough, and as far as the agency personnel could make them, complete. They do, however, from the statistical point of view, embody certain disturbing features which are particularly manifest when age composition is being considered.

The first failing, if it is one, is the restriction of the Rolls to the descendants of Indians living in California in 1848, a restriction made necessary by historical and legal considerations. Thus migrants from many other portions of the country, many of whom live in California, are excluded, and the Rolls must be regarded as representing a special type of native, who, in the aggregate to be sure, constitutes a major sample of the Indians presently inhabiting the state.

A second difficulty derives from the inclusion of the Yuma, who, hitherto in this essay, have been excluded from the total Indian population of California. In compiling the list for age distribution, members of this tribe were omitted in the case of the 1928 and the 1950 Rolls. Hence the sample was reduced by over 1,000 names in 1928 and 664 in 1950. In the 1970 Roll the tribal affiliation of some of the peripheral tribes who splintered from the main body of the California Indians, notably the Paiute, Washo, and Yuma, is omitted. Since several tribes are involved it is impossible to exclude the Yuma alone and retain the others. Consequently it was decided to retain them all. A few out-of-state Indians may be included, but their age characteristics will not deviate significantly from those of enrollees as a whole.

The 1970 Roll is plagued by further discrepancy. The official figure for applications approved is 69,911, with 6,402 applications rejected.

The computer print-out which is arranged alphabetically by name contains 69,911 entries. Nevertheless, the computer print-out which is organized according to date of birth contains over 75,000 names. I can only assume that this print-out includes applications which were rejected, or which for other reasons are not to be found in the official total.

A third difficulty concerns the cut-off date for enrollment. In 1928 this occurred on May 21, 1928, with 21,981 names. In order to calculate the age distribution accurately it would be necessary to determine the number of persons born between May 21 of each year and the same date in the following year. This procedure is impossible, hence some error is unavoidable. In practice all those listed as born between January 1 and May 21 in 1928 were deleted and the annual births employed were taken from January 1 to December 31, 1927, as 0 years of age, and similarly for all prior years. The number of omissions was 211, or slightly over one percent of the total. The same method was used with the 1950 Roll, the cut-off date of which was May 24, 1950. The zero year of age was used for those born in 1949, one year of age for those born in 1948, and so forth. The omissions amounted to 418, or approximately 1.2 percent of the total.

The 1970 Roll presents a somewhat different situation. The legal cut-off date was September 1, 1968. To omit those born January 1 to September 21 would have removed over one-half of the births during that year. On the other hand, the births for the remainder of the year are unknown. A further complication arises from the fact that the deadline was extended to September 1, 1970, and therefore infants born during the intervening two years could qualify for compensation. The numbers involved here are of interest (see accompanying table).

| | |
|---|---:|
| Names with birth date 1968 (Jan. 1 to Sept. 21) | 1,503 |
| Names with birth date 1969 | 233 |
| Names with birth date 1970 (Jan. 1 to Sept. 21) | 3 |

Obviously the registration in 1969 and 1970 was drastically curtailed, and by no means represents the actual number of births which occurred. In order to effect some sort of adjustment, the year 1968 was used but the total number of births was taken as a calculated value. The assumption was that the *rate* of addition of births was constant throughout the year. Then, if there were 1,503 born in the seven and two-thirds months from January 1 to September 21, there would have been 850 born in the four and one-third remaining months, and the total would have been 2,353 born in 1968. This is then used as zero years of age.

The proportions found in the customary age groups are given in Table 9. Two characteristics of the Indian population since 1910 are clearly displayed. The proportion of young people increased and that of old people diminished. The latter phenomenon is observed with both total population and adults alone.

It was previously pointed out that the Indian population aboriginally and in the early missions appeared to illustrate the condition antecedent to the demographic transition, a high birth rate and a high death rate, which yields a population with a high proportion of the younger component and relatively few in the later age groups. During the century of upheaval from 1800 to 1900, the indigenous inhabitants underwent a profound decline, which was manifested in a reduced reproductivity and an increased mortality, accompanied by a relative reduction of both younger and older elements. When this process was brought to an end somewhere near 1900, a recovery began. The age distribution of the Rolls of 1928, 1950, and 1970 show clearly that at least up to the middle of the twentieth century the recovery took the form of a reversion to the aboriginal condition, which was featured by a high birth rate. This rise in replacement potential is seen clearly in the increase in proportion of age groups 0-4, 0-9, and 0-14 in Table 9. This rise must have begun at or near 1910 and was still in progress in 1970. The general improvement in diet and health which affected all segments of the American population during the present century would have prevented an increase of mortality among the aged. The reduction of relative numbers in the group over 50 years must, therefore, be attributed mainly to the sharp rise in the number of the young.

The white population of the United States during the past one hundred years, despite rather wide fluctuations, has moved from the early to the later phases of the demographic transition, such that at present the relative number of young is low and that of old is very high. It is noteworthy that the California Indian in recuperating from a severe demographic blow, has taken at least an initial course which simulates the early rather than the later aspects of the demographic revolution. If the trend follows the pattern which has characterized other races and peoples, there will be a shift in future generations which will bring the Indian into line with other and more conservative segments of the population.

# IV. VITAL STATISTICS

In the preceding essay an examination was made into the age distribution of the living California Indian population throughout its known history. The material used for that study was drawn almost entirely from censuses and other enumerations, and is severely limited in quantity. There exists in addition a large but quite diffuse body of data which pertains to the vital events, birth and death, instead of the mass of individuals who make up the population at a given moment. To this field of information attention must now be directed.

At the outset it must be clearly understood that the sources of numbers and figures are incomplete and are scattered through documents which were compiled during the past two hundred years. So variable in quality are they, and so full of omissions and errors, that no uninterrupted and consistent series of indices or constants can be derived from them. Consequently we are obliged to use whatever information happens to be at hand and, apart from a consideration of aggregate population, to present only a fragmented picture of the demographic development of the Indian people.

Many of these documentary sources have already been discussed and need no further elaboration. Some of them have not yet been described in this essay. We may mention all six of them briefly.

1. For the Mission period, the Bancroft Transcripts are the most useful compilation of data which refers to births, deaths, and population level. These tabulations were employed extensively in the writing of a monograph which treated of population trends in the missions (Cook 1940). The primary conclusions contained in that article will only be summarized here. Another compilation which has been very valuable for certain purposes is the death records in the burial books of the seven missions which were transcribed for me by Mr. Thomas W. Temple, and which have been described in a previous context. They will be mentioned again.

2. After the destruction of the missions no vital records of any kind were kept in California until after the Civil War. During the 1860s and the 1870s the newly organized State Department of Public Health initiated a program whereby the births and deaths which occurred among the general public were reported by municipal agencies and by many physicians. As early as 1880 the annual reports of the Bureau of Vital Statistics became sufficiently complete to warrant their use for following natality and mortality trends in the population at large.

There was, however, no attempt to record vital events among the Indians as a separate category until after the end of the century. In the meantime, nevertheless, some of the reservation agents reported births and deaths among their groups. These figures are included in many, although by no means all, of the annual reports of the agents to the Commissioner of Indian Affairs in Washington.

3. The United States censuses, which began effectively for the California Indians in 1880, show total population, as previously mentioned. There are also included tables of mortality for the census years 1870, 1880, 1890, and 1900. From these information may be extracted concerning the Indians of the United States as a whole, and in a few instances of the state of California alone. The data are as accurate as might be expected in consideration of the time and circumstances. Subsequent to 1900 the national censuses have provided few statistics pertaining to the California Indians, apart from aggregate number of persons.

4. In the first years of the present century the state of California began the official registration of births and deaths, followed somewhat later by marriages. Certain information was required including matters pertaining to parentage, race or color, age, and, in the case of death, cause. There was considerable confusion in some instances with reference to race, and it is probable that in the early years of registration many persons of Indian descent were classed as white.

The records are available today in two forms. The first consists of microfilm of the actual birth or death certificates, film which is kept on file at the Bureau of Vital Statistics in Sacramento. It is therefore possible to scan the series of certificates and select those which record the birth or decease of Indians. In view of the enormous range of material—many millions of certificates—it has been necessary to examine only a sample. A group of counties was chosen, seventeen in the north, three in the south, in which the reported Indian population was substantial, but in which the total population was not excessive. For this reason the large entities, particularly San Francisco and Los Angeles Counties, were omitted. Further detail concerning examination procedure is given in a subsequent discussion.

The second source of information concerning the natality and mortality characteristics of all races in California is the file of annual, or at one period biennial, reports of the Bureau of Vital Statistics, which tabulate a great deal of the data contained in the certificates themselves.

Reports were first issued in the early 1870s, long before the introduction of the registration method, and have continued ever since. They vary widely with respect to both content and format, but in general give the numerical values for births, deaths, marriages, and other events in the lives of the total population and selected ethnic, social, and geographic portions thereof. Unfortunately, for extensive stretches of years, the Indian component is either omitted or is lumped gratuitously with "other races" or with "non-white." With this exception, the trend of the Indian demographic behavior can be followed throughout the twentieth century.

5. The Office of the Indian Probate Hearings Branch, Bureau of Indian Affairs, Sacramento, contains a file of reports of hearings conducted after the demise of Indians who possessed property derived from the Federal Government. These reports provide data concerning the decedents, particularly age at death and number of children. For certain special purposes, therefore, they are very valuable.

6. The Central California Agency of the Bureau of Indian Affairs possesses copies (typewritten or as computer print-outs) of the Great Rolls of 1928, 1950, and 1970. Although these Rolls actually are censuses of the California Indians at the dates mentioned, they contain a vast store of facts relative to the demographic condition of the people enrolled.

### Crude Birth and Death Rates

Perhaps the least exact method for assessing the reproductive potential and the viability of a population is by calculating the relative number of individuals who are born and who die within a given period of time. Nevertheless this must be the first and probably the only approach when the available data are inadequate to support a more refined procedure. Such is the case with the California Indians.

The crude birth rate is usually taken as the number of births per year per thousand persons of all ages and both sexes. The crude death rate is analogous. It is obvious that in order to find these magnitudes one must know the number of births and/or deaths and the average total population which existed during the interval selected. It is equally clear that to operate with the births and deaths without knowledge of total population is like trying to analyze sound in a vacuum. Yet this is the situation which confronts the student of Indian demography. Censuses and counts are frequently lacking or are woefully inadequate. A poor substitute, but a necessary one, is to take the simple ratio of births to deaths and disregard the total number of living people. In this way one may at least derive a notion of the relative strength of reproduction and of mortality within the group, and may make valid, even if rather sketchy, comparisons among populations and at different times with the same population.

The state of affairs in the California missions was explained in the monograph previously mentioned (Cook 1940). In this environment, which differed widely from the aboriginal, or natural habitat, the data as transmitted with sufficient reliability through the Bancroft Transcripts, show that the natives underwent severe attrition. The birth and death rates, calculated according to the methods described in the 1940 article, have been condensed into ten-year means and have been summarized, Table 13. The birth rate was high by modern standards, for it appears to have ranged between 30 and 50 births per thousand per year. Meanwhile the crude death rate was extremely high, from 70 to 90 deaths per thousand per year. The birth-death ratio was of course less than unity. The significance of these values has been discussed elsewhere, but it must be emphasized here that conditions were extreme in the missions from the standpoint of health and do not represent the aboriginal relation between depletion and replacement of population.

*Table 13.* BIRTH AND DEATH RATES IN THE
CALIFORNIA MISSIONS

| Period[a] | Mean birth rate per 1,000 | Mean death rate per 1,000 | Ratio: birth rate/ death rate |
|---|---|---|---|
| 1771-1780 | 49.0 | 75.0 | 0.654 |
| 1781-1790 | 36.9 | 69.6 | 0.530 |
| 1791-1800 | 43.4 | 80.9 | 0.525 |
| 1801-1810 | 35.9 | 90.0 | 0.399 |
| 1811-1820 | 37.5 | 76.3 | 0.492 |
| 1821-1830 | 33.1 | 77.4 | 0.428 |
| 1771-1830 | 39.3 | 78.2 | 0.503 |

[a] Each value is the mean rate for all the missions during the ten year period indicated.

The next block of figures which portrays the birth-death status of the Indians is found in the reports to the Commissioner of Indian Affairs by the several agents in charge of reservations between the years 1882 and 1914. In many of these reports, too numerous to cite in detail, the agent stated the population of the reservation together with the total of births and deaths. These numbers are probably relatively accurate, since the people were under close control and vital events would be uniformly known to the agent in charge. On the other hand, considerable variability would be introduced by the small numbers of individuals who resided on each reservation. This variability is reflected in the birth and death rates shown in Table 14.

*Table 14.* CONDENSED SUMMARY OF BIRTH AND DEATH RATES
ON CERTAIN RESERVATIONS, 1882-1914

| Mean rates | Birth rate and Standard Deviation | Death rate and Standard Deviation | Ratio: birth rate/ death rate |
|---|---|---|---|
| Mean, all reservations 1882-1907 (36 cases) | 28.3 ±10.5 | 29.4 ±16.5 | 0.963 |
| Mean, all reservations 1911-1914 (24 cases) | 26.1 ±10.6 | 30.7 ±16.5 | 0.850 |
| Mean, all reservations 1882-1914 (60 cases) | 27.4 ±13.1 | 29.9 ±13.1 | 0.916 |

SOURCE: Figures derived from reports of agents to the Commissioner of Indian Affairs; dates are for years ending on June 30.

For this table the annual individual crude birth and death rates were calculated for the reservations and other entities which reported the requisite figures. During the period 1882 to 1907 there were 36 such reports, from Hoopa Reservation, from Round Valley, and from the

Mission Agency, which included numerous small reservations. During the four years from 1911 to 1914, inclusive, there were 24 reports from six entities—Hoopa, Round Valley, Tule River, the Mission Agency, Fort Bidwell, and the Paiute in the Bishop-Independence district. In Table 14 the mean rates for the 36 earlier, the 24 later, and the total of 60 reports, or cases, are shown, together with the Standard Deviations and the appropriate birth-death ratios.

Since it is clear from the magnitude of the Standard Deviations of the combined rates that the variability of the individual values is great, the differences among the six means shown in the table must be quite without statistical significance. It follows that the natality and mortality exhibited during this period of 30 years by the reservation Indians was held consistently at the level of 26 to 31 births or deaths per year per thousand people, and that the birth-death ratio remained on the average just below unity. In other words, deaths exceeded births by a small amount, roughly 10 percent. This condition may be contrasted with that found in the missions one hundred years earlier, where deaths amounted to nearly double the births. Although the Indians here reported were in a state of semi-confinement, yet their pattern of vitality had improved far beyond the earlier condition. If it is true that the decades between 1880 and 1910 witnessed the low point of Indian population, it might be expected that subsequent years would show an increasing birth-death ratio and a further broad improvement in both birth and death rates.

Our best source, imperfect though it may be, for the period since 1900 is the set of figures contained in the reports of the Bureau of Vital Statistics of the California Department of Public Health. In an unbroken series through these volumes are values for the births and deaths of the total population of the State. The corresponding numbers of Indians who were born or who died are present in many volumes but in by no means all. What can be extracted has been summarized in Table 15. Here are the figures which I can find or calculate for the birth-death ratio of the total population (for purposes of comparison), and for the births, deaths, and birth-death ratios of the Indian population.

A survey of this table discloses immediately that the registration facilities were very inadequate during the first years in which the system was being applied. From 1906 to 1911 the ratios for the total population were below 1.0. It is not probable that in these years the death rate exceeded the birth rate. Rather it is likely that all the births were not brought to the attention of the health authorities, whereas the deaths could not be concealed. With respect to the Indians, until 1919 the annual number of listed births averaged close to 30. The censuses were reporting about 16,500 Indians in the state at this time: the birth rate would have been 1.8 per thousand persons, a preposterous value. This condition persisted until the number of births jumped from 25 in 1919 to 123 in 1920 and 188 in 1921. Meanwhile the deaths climbed, but much more slowly. Figures for Indian births are then lacking in the Bureau reports until 1926, when there were 221, with 283 deaths and a ratio of 0.781. Thenceforward the trend has been steady and quite consistent, even with some long gaps in the record from 1945 to 1960. The deaths have remained relatively constant, despite a known profound increase in absolute numbers of Indians, whereas the births have climbed from 221 in 1927 to 1,868 in 1970. The corresponding increase in birth-death ratio has far outstripped that found for the total population and is, indeed, extraordinary by any standard. With all races there has been a great reduction in death rate, which accounts for most of the rise in the birth-death ratio of the total population. However, the figures in Table 15, certainly subsequent to 1926, when birth registration seems to have become more or less accurate, demonstrate an increase in the Indian birth rate to a level much exceeding that characteristic of the population at large.

*Table 15.* BIRTHS, DEATHS, AND BIRTH/DEATH RATIOS FOR THE INDIAN POPULATION OF CALIFORNIA, WITH BIRTH/DEATH RATIOS FOR THE TOTAL POPULATION

| Year | Total Population Birth-death ratio | Indian Population | | |
|------|------|------|------|------|
| | | Births | Deaths | Birth-death ratio |
| 1906 | 0.716 | 10 | 117 | 0.085 |
| 1907 | 0.784 | 22 | 120 | 0.183 |
| 1908 | 0.881 | 19 | 126 | 0.151 |
| 1909 | 0.998 | 34 | 130 | 0.261 |
| 1910 | 0.993 | 17 | 156 | 0.109 |
| 1911 | 1.024 | 23 | 162 | 0.142 |
| 1912 | 1.072 | 29 | 169 | 0.172 |

*Table 15 (continued)*

| Year | Total Population<br>Birth-death<br>ratio | Indian Population | | |
|------|------|------|------|------|
| | | Births | Deaths | Birth-death<br>ratio |
| 1913 | 1.137 | 49 | 183 | 0.268 |
| 1914 | 1.226 | 51 | 170 | 0.300 |
| 1915 | 1.233 | 38 | 139 | 0.273 |
| 1916 | 1.270 | 21 | 179 | 0.117 |
| 1917 | 1.240 | 62 | 166 | 0.373 |
| 1918 | — | — | — | — |
| 1919 | 1.229 | 25 | 216 | 0.116 |
| 1920 | 1.425 | 123 | 242 | 0.508 |
| 1921 | 1.529 | 188 | 219 | 0.859 |
| 1922 | 1.439 | — | — | — |
| 1923 | 1.474 | — | — | — |
| 1924 | 1.531 | — | 252 | — |
| 1925 | 1.507 | — | 255 | — |
| 1926 | 1.401 | 221 | 283 | 0.781 |
| 1927 | 1.372 | 236 | 267 | 0.884 |
| 1928 | 1.263 | 315 | 346 | 0.911 |
| 1929 | 1.248 | 314 | 368 | 0.854 |
| 1930 | 1.277 | 329 | 418 | 0.788 |
| 1931 | 1.208 | 329 | 308 | 1.068 |
| 1932 | 1.155 | 336 | 334 | 1.006 |
| 1933 | 1.107 | 376 | 314 | 1,197 |
| 1934 | 1.151 | 362 | 320 | 1.131 |
| 1935 | 1.106 | 401 | 344 | 1.166 |
| 1936 | 1.112 | 429 | 353 | 1.215 |
| 1937 | 1.174 | 436 | 455 | 0.958 |
| 1938 | 1.336 | 451 | 312 | 1.444 |
| 1939 | 1.345 | 563 | 355 | 1.585 |
| 1940 | 1.391 | 451 | 387 | 1.165 |
| 1941 | 1.531 | 404 | 303 | 1.334 |
| 1942 | 1.801 | — | 325 | — |
| 1943 | 1.932 | 561 | 316 | 1.775 |
| 1944 | 1.931 | 652 | 318 | 2.050 |
| 1945 | 1.967 | — | — | — |
| 1946 | 2.284 | — | — | — |
| 1947 | 2.534 | — | — | — |
| 1948 | 2.434 | — | — | — |
| 1949 | 2.443 | — | — | — |

*(Table 15 (continued)*

| Year | Total Population | Indian Population | | |
|------|------------------|-------|--------|------------|
| | Birth-death ratio | Births | Deaths | Birth-death ratio |
| 1950 | 2.481 | 848 | 322 | 2.634 |
| 1951 | 2.510 | — | 331 | — |
| 1952 | 2.598 | — | — | — |
| 1953 | 2.712 | 889 | — | — |
| 1954 | 2.800 | — | — | — |
| 1955 | 2.738 | 1,120 | — | — |
| 1956 | 2.786 | 1,282 | — | — |
| 1957 | 2.830 | — | — | — |
| 1958 | 2.781 | — | — | — |
| 1959 | 2.795 | — | — | — |
| 1960 | 2.747 | 1,738 | 301 | 5.775 |
| 1961 | 2.777 | 1,756 | 296 | 5.940 |
| 1962 | 2.680 | 1,695 | — | — |
| 1963 | 2.578 | 1,841 | 292 | 6.310 |
| 1964 | 2.486 | 1,826 | 281 | 6.498 |
| 1965 | 2.327 | 1,861 | 305 | 6.102 |
| 1966 | 2.146 | 1,735 | 309 | 5.615 |
| 1967 | 2.149 | 1,705 | 300 | 5.683 |
| 1968 | 2.112 | 1,687 | 273 | 6.180 |
| 1969 | 2.127 | 1,799 | 297 | 6.060 |
| 1970 | 2.180 | 1,868 | 321 | 5.819 |

SOURCE: Annual Reports of the Bureau of Vital Statistics, California State Department of Public Health.

The data provided by the national censuses perhaps confuse the issue more than they clarify it. In Table 16 we show the birth and death rates of the total population of the state for the census years from 1910 to 1970 as given in the Statistical Supplement to the Report of the Bureau of Vital Statistics for 1970, table 3, page 14. The fall in death rate is very clear. The birth rate rose to a maximum in 1960 but fell again in 1970. The figures for the Indian population are derived from the births and deaths given by the Reports of the Bureau of Vital Statistics for census years, and the populations shown in the corresponding censuses.

*Table 16.* BIRTH AND DEATH RATES OF THE TOTAL AND THE
INDIAN POPULATION OF CALIFORNIA IN THE CENSUS YEARS
FROM 1910 TO 1970

| | Total population | | Indian population | | |
|---|---|---|---|---|---|
| Year | Birth rate | Death rate | Population | Birth rate | Death rate |
| 1910 | 13.5 | 13.6 | 16,371 | 1.0 | 9.5 |
| 1920 | 19.6 | 13.8 | 17,360 | 7.1 | 13.9 |
| 1930 | 14.9 | 11.7 | 19,212 | 17.1 | 21.7 |
| 1940 | 16.2 | 11.6 | 18,675 | 24.1 | 20.7 |
| 1950 | 23.1 | 9.3 | 19,947 | 42.5 | 16.1 |
| 1960 | 23.7 | 8.6 | 39,014 | 44.5 | 7.7 |
| 1970 | 18.2 | 8.3 | 91,018 | 20.5 | 3.5 |

SOURCE: The rates for the total population are taken from the Statistical Supplement to the Annual Report of 1970 of the Bureau of Vital Statistics, p. 14, table 3.
The rates for the Indian population are calculated from the births and deaths shown
in the annual reports for the census years of the Bureau of Vital Statistics and the
populations given by the corresponding national censuses.

It is evident that both the birth and death rates in 1910 and 1920 are
much too low, an error referable to the incomplete registration carried
out among the Indians of the state. However, it is also apparent that
the populations as published in the censuses for 1930, 1940, and 1950
are defective. This difficulty has been touched upon in a previous context, but the fact that 17,000 to 19,000 Indians could not possibly
have represented the entire number of Indians in California during
these years is demonstrated here by the bulge in both birth and death
rates in 1940, 1950, and even until 1960. This complete uncertainty
concerning the censuses renders entirely futile any attempt to ascertain
precise trends in Indian birth and death rates by the use of census
populations. The best we can say is that there has been an overall
movement upward of the birth rate and downward of the death rate.
How the Indian compared with the white population can not be determined with the figures contained in the United States censuses. Meanwhile the birth-death ratios, if one wished to calculate them, fall into
the same pattern as is exhibited by the annual values given in Table 15.

## Other Measures of Reproductivity

Apart from crude birth rate there are certain other indices whereby the reproductive potential of a sub-population can be tested. One of them is the so-called fertility ratio, the ratio of children to reproductive females. Usually the number of children under five years old is taken as the basis, together with females between 15 and 44, or 15 and 45 years of age. In order to simplify the calculation the former age limits are used here: 15 to 44 years inclusive.

In Table 17 are presented the values of the fertility ratio as calculated from the documents which are available for the California Indians. These include several local censuses from the Mission and Carson Agencies, which were taken in 1902, 1920, and 1940. Then come the national censuses of 1910 through 1970. Here are shown the ratios for the total white population throughout this period. It is recognized, to be sure, that the total white population has always contained many immigrants, and that the age distribution of the foreign born shows an extreme paucity of children. Hence the ratios given here are somewhat too low. However, the error probably is not of serious dimensions. There are also given the ratios for Indians in 1910 and 1920, after which date the Bureau of the Census ceased to record the age distribution of this race. Finally we have the ratios as calculated from the three Rolls inscribed by the Bureau of Indian Affairs in 1928, 1950, and 1970, all of which give the age and sex of the applicants.

From the table it is clear that the fertility ratios of the Indians, and hence the relative production of children, despite a great deal of variability, have increased steadily from the earliest records, dated in 1902. Meanwhile, the ratios for the white race, derived from the census tables, have undergone significant fluctuation but have not materially altered in seventy years. A further conclusion is that the relative number of children in the Indian population has always exceeded that in the non-Indian fraction, in recent years by a factor of almost double.

Aside from the fertility ratio, the absolute number of children born to each female of a group may be indicative of reproductive performance, if not of potential. There are a few scattered data in the Reports of the Bureau of Vital Statistics which bear upon this matter. In particular there are two tables, one in 1921, the other in 1964, which give the number of children ever had for women who were, during the year, brought to child-bed. The first appears in the Report

*Table 17.* FERTILITY RATIOS IN CALIFORNIA, EXPRESSED AS
NUMBER OF CHILDREN 0-4 YEARS OLD PER 1,000 FEMALES
OF THE AGE OF 15-44 YEARS

| Source and date | Total white population, California | Total Indian population, California |
|---|---|---|
| Mission Agency | | |
| 1902 | | 367 |
| 1922 | | 447 |
| 1940 | | 506 |
| | | |
| Carson Agency | | |
| (Nevada) | | |
| 1902 | | 412 |
| 1920 | | 348 |
| 1940 | | 477 |
| | | |
| National Censuses | | |
| 1900 | 370 | |
| 1910 | 349 | 533 |
| 1920 | 343 | 552 |
| 1930 | 300 | |
| 1940 | 274 | |
| 1950 | 456 | |
| 1960 | 543 | |
| 1970 | 383 | |
| | | |
| Roll of 1928 | | 623 |
| | | |
| Roll of 1950 | | 813 |
| | | |
| Roll of 1970 | | 745 |

for 1920-1921 (volume 27), as table 7, page 41, and is entitled
"Births of Mother and Number of Previous Issue." There are shown
for several races the number of previous births which had occurred to
each woman, including those who had never before given birth. The
number of issue is carried up to 9 plus. The second table appears in the

Report for 1964, page 40, table 11, and is entitled "Live Births by Previous Live Births, Age of Mother and Race, California, 1964." The format resembles that of the previous table except that for each race the females are segregated by age, and that the number of previous births is carried only to 3 plus. In order to achieve uniformity I have recast the figures for all ages of both white and Indian women so as to make the two tables correspond in structure. This means that the number and percent of births are given as far as 3 plus for each race. The resulting values are in Table 18.

From this table two facts become evident. First, at both dates the Indian women produced on the average more children per family than did the white women, a difference which was more conspicuous in 1964 than in 1921. Second, the Indians increased their fecundity between 1921 and 1964. This feature is demonstrated by the fall in the number of women who had had no previous children from 38.3 percent in 1921 to 24.5 percent in 1964, and by the simultaneous increase in those who had produced 3 or more children from 24.0 percent in 1921 to 37.8 percent in 1964.

*Table 18.* PREVIOUS LIVE BIRTHS OF INDIAN AND WHITE
FEMALES WHO HAD CHILDREN DURING 1921 AND 1964

### YEAR 1921

| Number and percent of women | Number of children in previous issue | | | |
| --- | --- | --- | --- | --- |
| | 0 | 1 | 2 | 3 and more |
| Number of white women | 24,975 | 15,476 | 9,457 | 15,675 |
| Number of Indian women | 72 | 29 | 22 | 65 |
| Percent of white women | 38.0 | 23.6 | 14.4 | 24.0 |
| Percent of Indian women | 38.3 | 15.4 | 11.7 | 34.6 |

*Table 18 (continued)*

## YEAR 1964

| | Number of children in previous issue | | | |
|---|---|---|---|---|
| *Number and percent of women* | *0* | *1* | *2* | *3 and more* |
| Number of white women | 102,610 | 84,985 | 60,237 | 80,676 |
| Number of Indian women | 448 | 373 | 315 | 690 |
| Percent of white women | 34.2 | 25.8 | 18.3 | 21.7 |
| Percent of Indian women | 24.5 | 20.4 | 17.3 | 37.8 |

SOURCE: Bureau of Vital Statistics, Report of 1920-1921, Table No. 7, p. 191; and Report of 1964, Table No. 11, p. 40.

Further evidence concerning the changes in Indian fertility during the past several decades is obtained from the case records in the Office of the Indian Probate Hearings Branch, Bureau of Indian Affairs, Sacramento. Here will be found the documents relating to probate of estate of every Indian in northern California and western Nevada who had died within the past 80 years and had been in the possession of property derived from federal sources. Most of these documents show the age of the decedent and the number of his or her children, the latter information naturally being of primary importance to the inheritance examiner. It will be noted that we are here dealing with a selected group of Indians, those who owned land, cash, or commodities which required legal intervention in order to be passed on to the heirs. In other words these people were in general at the upper level of the economic structure. However, whether their demographic features differed from those of the Indian community at large is subject to debate.

In this file are the records of more than 2,200 females who died at an age greater than 40 years. They have been arranged according to the decade of their birth. The first interval is 1810-1819, the second is

1820-1829, and so on until the decade 1920-1929. Any woman born after the latter date would not have been over 40 years of age by 1970. The average number of children had by the females born in each decade has been placed in Table 19. It is evident that the mean number of children produced by a woman born in the years 1810 to 1839 was greater than two but not as great as three. The reproductive period of these females would have extended from 1825 to 1880, or would have coincided with the worst of the demographic upheaval caused by the entrance of the Americans. The next five decades show an increase to a maximum mean of 4.16 children for the women born 1880-1889, whose active reproductive period would have occurred from 1900 to 1930. At this time stabilization appears to have been achieved with perhaps a small decline up to 1970.

*Table 19.* NUMBER OF CHILDREN BORNE BY WOMEN
WHO DIED AFTER THE AGE OF 40 YEARS

| Decade of birth | Number of women | Number of children | Mean number of children per mother |
|---|---|---|---|
| 1810-1819 | 17 | 46 | 2.71 |
| 1820-1829 | 62 | 148 | 2.39 |
| 1830-1839 | 143 | 406 | 2.84 |
| 1840-1849 | 213 | 737 | 3.46 |
| 1850-1859 | 304 | 1,144 | 3.76 |
| 1860-1869 | 366 | 1,516 | 4.14 |
| 1870-1879 | 328 | 1,347 | 4.11 |
| 1880-1889 | 302 | 1,256 | 4.16 |
| 1890-1899 | 203 | 832 | 4.10 |
| 1900-1909 | 169 | 645 | 3.82 |
| 1910-1919 | 89 | 314 | 3.53 |
| 1920-1929 | 27 | 96 | 3.55 |

SOURCE: Probate records of the California Agency, including records from the Carson Agency in Nevada; the females are listed according to the decade in which they were born.

A brief summary of several types of data is now possible. These are the birth-death ratio, the fertility ratio, the number of children produced by white and Indian women in two sample years, and the average number of children ever had by Indian women whose estates were probated during the past eighty years. The rise in birth-death ratio and that of the fertility ratio, together with the increase in family size as shown by the mean number of children, all indicate not only a profound fall in death rate among the Indians but also a sharp improvement in reproductivity. In the latter characteristic the California Indian has come clearly to excel the white man, although he may have reached his maximum potential in the period from 1920 to 1950. If so, he is still maintaining a high level of performance. In any event the conjunction of a much reduced mortality and a greatly improved natality has operated to facilitate the rapid and conspicuous increase in living population which has been noted previously.

## The Mortality Pattern

In the absence of censuses, the vitality status of any population can be approximated by means of a study based upon the age at which its members have died, a very different study from that which is concerned with the age distribution of a living population. Additionally, a great deal can be learned about its demographic character beyond simple rise and fall of numbers or the interplay of crude birth and death rates. Wide application has been made of this principle to ancient populations, knowledge of which consists only of skeletal or burial remains. It may also be used with modern groups for which the death record is known, although we may still be in ignorance of the living age distribution at the time of any actual or potential census. A simple example of this avenue of approach is provided by the California missions.

The death records in the burial books of seven missions were transcribed for me by Mr. Thomas W. Temple, and include San Gabriel, San Luis Obispo, San Miguel, San Carlos, San Juan Bautista, Santa Cruz, and Santa Clara. Some others are in existence but it was not possible to work on them. Those which have been secured, however, probably constitute a fair representation of the whole mission chain. In any event the individual missions among the seven which have been tabulated show no significant variation, and as a group may be considered adequate, although not as large a sample as might be desired.

The record for each of the seven missions is chronologically complete from foundation to extinction with the exception of San Carlos. Here, unfortunately, the Fathers did not include all necessary data during several periods of years. Hence, for this mission there are the records for only the intervals 1771-1792, 1799-1804, and 1819-1829, but since these are quite well spaced and extensive, the deaths which occurred during them may be incorporated in the mission total.

The mission burial books customarily give the serial death number, the year of death, the sex, the age at death (sometimes expressed merely as child or adult), and the baptism number. This last item is especially important because it enables one to check in the corresponding baptism book and thus secure the date of birth and hence age of the individual. Some of the books are internally incomplete. The most serious omissions occur when the baptism number is not given, and the age at death is noted only as child (*parvulo*) and adult (*adulto*). In order to utilize these deaths an indirect calculation is necessary.

For each mission of the seven there is tabulated the age in years at death of all persons for whom this information is given. The age groups are in five-year periods up to the interval 20-24. The older groups are in ten-year periods, 25-34 and so on, due to inaccuracy of the record, heaping at the even decades, and the ignorance on the part of the missionaries of the exact age of the gentile converts. In addition there are recorded the total number of those whose age is indicated only by the terms child and adult. Then, since the word *parvulo* was applied only to children under 10 years of age, the number of children was prorated according to the relative number of persons who fell exactly in the age groups 0-4 and 5-9. The prorated values were then added to those directly known and an adjusted total secured for each age group. The total number of adults was prorated in the same manner for age group 10-14, and so on to 85 plus. The adjusted values for each age group were then added and thus the aggregate secured for the seven missions collectively. This is a rather ad hoc procedure, but its use appears justified by the consistency and reasonableness of the results.

The critical value is the total number of deaths which occurred in the seven missions between their establishment at various dates from 1771 to 1798 and their final dissolution in 1833. Unlike similar formulations pertaining to ancient, medieval, or aboriginal cultures, it is very well known that the population at hand varied greatly with respect to its age composition, its replacement, and its mortality rates. Hence the hypothesis cannot be invoked that the mission population was stationary, or even stable, but the average state throughout seventy years must be taken as the standard of reference. Since the pressure of disease and economic stringency was not significantly relieved prior to the end of the mission period, the burial-book data may be regarded as representing the mission environment as a whole, and as such capable of comparison with other states of the Indian population, at other epochs of its history.

Table 20 is an abridged life table for those who died as baptized gentiles in the seven missions between 1772 and 1832. The absolute number of deaths for each age group is given in the column of the table headed $D_x$. These figures may also be expressed as percentage of the total decedents. Thus close to 35 percent of the deaths fell in the category 0-4 years. About 6 percent survived after 64 years, and nearly 16 percent lived after 50 years. This is a much better record than is made by McCown's aboriginal skeleton series.

*Table 20.* ABRIDGED LIFE TABLE OF THOSE WHO DIED AS BAPTIZED GENTILES IN SEVEN CALIFORNIA MISSIONS FROM 1772-1832

| $x$ | $D_x$ | $d_x$ | $l_x$ | $q_x$ | $L_x$ | $T_x$ | $e_x$ |
|-----|-------|-------|-------|-------|-------|-------|-------|
| 0-4 | 7,402 | 35,238 | 100,000 | 0.3524 | 411,905 | 2,371,620 | 23.71 |
| 5-9 | 1,330 | 6,332 | 64,762 | 0.0979 | 307,980 | 1,959,715 | 30.26 |
| 10-14 | 1,181 | 5,622 | 58,430 | 0.0962 | 278,095 | 1,651,735 | 28.27 |
| 15-19 | 1,241 | 5,908 | 52,808 | 0.1119 | 249,270 | 1,373,640 | 26.01 |
| 20-24 | 1,391 | 6,622 | 46,900 | 0.1412 | 217,945 | 1,124,370 | 23.97 |
| 25-34 | 2,307 | 10,982 | 40,278 | 0.2727 | 347,870 | 906,425 | 22.50 |
| 35-44 | 1,916 | 9,121 | 29,296 | 0.3116 | 247,350 | 558,555 | 19.08 |
| 45-54 | 1,698 | 8,084 | 20,175 | 0.4007 | 161,330 | 311,205 | 15.43 |
| 55-64 | 1,287 | 6,127 | 12,091 | 0.5067 | 90,270 | 149,875 | 12.40 |
| 65-74 | 769 | 3,660 | 5,964 | 0.6137 | 41,340 | 59,605 | 9.99 |
| 75-84 | 342 | 1,629 | 2,304 | 0.7070 | 14,890 | 18,265 | 7.92 |
| 85+ | 142 | 675 | 675 | 1.0000 | 3,375 | 3,375 | 5.00 |

Distribution by percentage    0-4 years: 35.24    50+ years: 16.13 app.

5-14 years: 11.95    65+ years:   5.96

75+ years:   2.30

Other indices may be utilized which are found in the life table (Table 20). Thus the values of $q_x$, the age-specific death rates, or the probability of death in certain age groups, are all high by modern standards and the expectation of life at birth (23.7 years) as well as at subsequent ages, is very low. Nevertheless, the results obtained here are not discrepant with many others found with primitive populations throughout space and time. On the whole, these tabulations indicate that the native Californians were demographically as well off under the mission administration as populations of other races in Europe and America.

It is necessary at this point to digress in order to discuss briefly the use of life tables in the examination of mortality records. When the life table form is used in this manner, ordinarily the operative assumption is that the population concerned is in a demographically stable condition, that is, that the rates of addition and removal do not change during a period of several generations. Hence the birth and death rates are constant, and there is no significant in-migration and out-migration. Such a state can not be claimed for either the Indian or the white population of California at any time in its history. Nevertheless, it is possible to make use of the data for comparative purposes and for the establishment of strictly empirical indices. One device is simply to determine the relative number of individuals who are dying at certain ages, such as zero years, zero to four years, or over sixty-four years. The base may be the entire population who die, or it may be any fraction of those dying, for instance adults and children, males and females. A second device consists of the construction of a life table which shows the age-specific death rates ($q_x$) and the expectation of life of those who die within a given time period. In the *absence of stability* this cannot be a complete life table of the living, or census population, but it can provide much information concerning the mortality which occurred within the population. It is in this sense that the life table technique is used here.

It must be recognized that these indices, the distribution of age at death, the age-specific death rate, the expectation of life at x years, are by no means precise. They are influenced by random fluctuations in the sample, which itself is frequently small. They also depend upon local and sporadic changes in health conditions which unpredictably alter the number of births and deaths. It follows, therefore, that not too much reliance can be placed upon a single index, such as the proportion of all deaths which occurred within a certain age group. On the other hand, the composite force of several indices, all pointing in the same direction, may be considerable, and if an aggregate is used, the result may be accorded confidence.

If the missions be now reconsidered it is found that the situation in these establishments may be compared with more modern conditions in California. For example, Table 21 shows the mortality in the state at 1870. The data are from the United States Census of that date and produce a pattern which, when expressed in life table form, is very similar to that found with the mission death records. Indeed the survivorship among the neophytes appears to have been as high as in the white population of the state forty years after the missions had disappeared.

*Table 21.* ABRIDGED LIFE TABLE FOR THOSE IN THE TOTAL
POPULATION OF CALIFORNIA WHO DIED DURING THE YEAR 1870

| $x$ | $D_x$ | $d_x$ | $l_x$ | $q_x$ | $L_x$ | $T_x$ | $e_x$ |
|------|--------|---------|---------|--------|---------|-----------|-------|
| 0-4 | 3,450 | 38,970 | 100,000 | 0.3897 | 402,575 | 2,289,070 | 22.89 |
| 5-9 | 568 | 6,416 | 61,030 | 0.1051 | 289,105 | 1,886,495 | 30.89 |
| 10-14 | 233 | 2,632 | 54,614 | 0.0482 | 266,490 | 1,597,390 | 29.25 |
| 15-19 | 253 | 2,858 | 51,982 | 0.0550 | 252,765 | 1,330,900 | 25.60 |
| 20-24 | 403 | 4,552 | 49,124 | 0.0927 | 234,240 | 1,078,135 | 21.95 |
| 25-34 | 1,102 | 12,448 | 44,572 | 0.2793 | 383,480 | 843,895 | 18.93 |
| 35-44 | 1,311 | 14,808 | 32,124 | 0.4610 | 247,200 | 460,415 | 14.33 |
| 45-54 | 862 | 9,737 | 17,316 | 0.5623 | 124,475 | 213,214 | 12.31 |
| 55-64 | 381 | 4,304 | 7,579 | 0.5679 | 54,275 | 88,740 | 11.71 |
| 65-74 | 199 | 2,248 | 3,275 | 0.6864 | 26,510 | 34,465 | 10.52 |
| 75-84 | 66 | 745 | 1,027 | 0.7254 | 6,545 | 7,955 | 7.75 |
| 85+ | 25 | 282 | 282 | 1.0000 | 1,410 | 1,410 | 5.00 |

| Distribution by percentage | 0-4 years: 38.97 | 50+ years: 12.45 app. |
|---|---|---|
| | 5-14 years: 9.05 | 65+ years: 3.28 |
| | | 75+ years: 1.03 |

NOTE: Column heads used in Tables 20-23 are explained in the text discussion Chapter Four, under the head "The Mortality Pattern."

SOURCE: United States Census of 1870, Vol. II, pp. 6-7.

There are also shown the life tables in the same form which are derived for the total population of California at two other dates, 1900 and 1967 (see Tables 22 and 23). The distribution of deaths according to age group, in terms of the percentage of total deaths, is also given with each life table. It is evident from these figures, as also from the values of $q_x$ and $e_x$, that although the proportion of young persons who died in the missions and in the total population of California in 1870 is approximately equal, by way of contrast the total population in 1900 shows a profound change. There is a sharp reduction in the proportion of those dying in youth, a corresponding rise in the number of those who lived to become old, and a significant increase in the expectation of life at birth. These trends are even more pronounced in the abridged life table for 1967. This movement since 1870 is of course a well-recognized demographic phenomenon.

*Table 22*. ABRIDGED LIFE TABLE OF THOSE WHO DIED IN THE TOTAL
POPULATION OF CALIFORNIA DURING THE YEAR 1900

| $x$ | $D_x$ | $d_x$ | $l_x$ | $q_x$ | $L_x$ | $T_x$ | $e_x$ |
|---|---|---|---|---|---|---|---|
| 0-4 | 3,788 | 17,009 | 100,000 | 0.1701 | 457,475 | 4,162,560 | 41.63 |
| 5-9 | 628 | 2,820 | 82,991 | 0.0340 | 407,905 | 3,705,085 | 44.65 |
| 10-14 | 402 | 1,835 | 80,171 | 0.0229 | 396,340 | 3,297,180 | 41.13 |
| 15-19 | 655 | 2,941 | 78,366 | 0.0375 | 384,475 | 2,900,840 | 37.02 |
| 20-24 | 1,118 | 5,020 | 75,425 | 0.0666 | 364,575 | 2,516,365 | 33.36 |
| 25-34 | 2,502 | 11,234 | 70,405 | 0.1596 | 647,880 | 2,151,790 | 30.56 |
| 35-44 | 2,589 | 11,625 | 59,171 | 0.1965 | 533,580 | 1,503,910 | 25.42 |
| 45-54 | 2,526 | 11,342 | 47,546 | 0.2385 | 418,750 | 970,330 | 20.41 |
| 55-64 | 2,764 | 12,411 | 36,204 | 0.3428 | 299,985 | 551,580 | 15.24 |
| 65-74 | 3,050 | 13,695 | 23,793 | 0.5756 | 169,455 | 251,555 | 10.57 |
| 75-84 | 1,779 | 7,988 | 10,098 | 0.7910 | 61,040 | 82,140 | 8.13 |
| 85+ | 470 | 2,110 | 2,110 | 1.0000 | 21,100 | 21,100 | 5.00 |

Distribution by percentage    0-4 years: 17.01    50+ years: 41.88 app.
                                    5-14 years:   4.66    65+ years: 23.79
                                                                  75+ years: 10.10

SOURCE: United States Census of 1900, Vol. IV, Part II, P. 66.

*Table 23.* ABRIDGED LIFE TABLE FOR THOSE IN THE TOTAL
POPULATION OF CALIFORNIA WHO DIED
DURING THE YEAR 1967

| $x$ | $D_x$ | $d_x$ | $l_x$ | $q_x$ | $L_x$ | $T_x$ | $e_x$ |
|------|--------|--------|---------|--------|---------|-----------|--------|
| 0-4 | 7,752 | 4,994 | 100,000 | 0.0499 | 487,515 | 6,419,965 | 64.20 |
| 5-14 | 1,497 | 904 | 95,006 | 0.0095 | 945,540 | 5,932,450 | 62.44 |
| 15-24 | 3,620 | 2,308 | 94,102 | 0.0245 | 929,480 | 4,986,910 | 52.99 |
| 25-34 | 3,407 | 2,172 | 91,794 | 0.0237 | 907,280 | 4,057,430 | 44.20 |
| 35-44 | 6,923 | 4,414 | 89,622 | 0.0493 | 874,150 | 3,150,150 | 35.15 |
| 45-54 | 15,049 | 9,595 | 85,208 | 0.1126 | 804,105 | 2,276,000 | 26.71 |
| 55-64 | 24,831 | 15,832 | 75,613 | 0.2094 | 676,970 | 1,471,895 | 19.47 |
| 65-74 | 35,406 | 22,575 | 59,781 | 0.3776 | 484,930 | 794,925 | 13.30 |
| 75-84 | 38,910 | 24,809 | 37,206 | 0.6668 | 248,010 | 309,995 | 8.33 |
| 85+ | 19,445 | 12,397 | 12,397 | 1.0000 | 61,985 | 61,985 | 5.00 |

| Distribution by percentage | 0-4 years: 4.99 | 50+ years: 80.41 app. |
|---|---|---|
| | 5-14 years: 0.90 | 65+ years: 59.78 |
| | | 75+ years: 37.21 |

SOURCE: *Vital Statistics of the United States, Vol. II, Mortality,* Part B, Table 7-3.

With respect to the Indian population, the fact has been emphasized repeatedly that subsequent to the destruction of the missions in 1833 no birth or death records of any kind were kept until the end of the century. From the period beginning near 1880 data may be found which become more and more copious up to the present day. The successive volumes of the United States Census constitute one of the earlier sources.

The censuses of 1870, 1880, 1890, and 1900 contained mortality tables for the Indians of the United States. The material contained in the 1870 census is wholly inadequate and must be disregarded. In 1880 there were 892 Indian deaths reported for the entire country, 150 of which were from California. The sample is very small but the record for the United States is usable. In 1890 and 1900 there were respectively 3,013 and 4,717 deaths in the nation. California was not segregated as a separate entity.

*Table 24.* AGING AND SURVIVORSHIP INDICES FOR
THE INDIAN POPULATION OF THE UNITED STATES IN
1880, 1890, AND 1900

| Percentage of deaths in age groups | 1880 | 1890 | 1900 |
|---|---|---|---|
| 0-4 | 28.21 | 33.52 | 35.11 |
| 5-14 | 10.54 | 27.69 | 15.05 |
| 50 and over | 16.25 | 15.60 | 18.74 |
| 65 and over | 8.52 | 8.27 | 10.50 |
| 75 and over | 5.38 | 4.35 | 5.51 |
| | | | |
| Age-specific death rate | | | |
| $q_0$ (at birth) | 0.1278 | 0.1122 | 0.1522 |
| $q_{25}$ (at 25 years) | 0.1622 | 0.1355 | 0.1144 |
| | | | |
| Expectation of life at birth ($e^0$) in years | 25.67 | 22.50 | 24.20 |

SOURCES: United States Censuses: 1880, Vol. II, Table IV, pp. 16-17; 1890, Vol. IV, Part III, Table 13, pp. 636-637; 1900, Vol. IV, Part 2, Table 9, pp. 686-687.

The indices calculated from the corresponding data, in part from abridged life tables, are given in Table 24. It is clear that the results are erratic and that no refined conclusions can be drawn from them. At the same time two features emerge which carry reasonable assurance. First, the range of the indices falls most closely with those found for the mission Indians and the California total population in 1870. From this fact may be deduced the corollary that the Indian population of the United States was aging and dying in conformity with a pattern which was commonly found among primitive populations in the middle of the nineteenth century. Unfortunately we cannot specify the behavior of the native Californians as compared with the native national population, but there is no reason to expect a serious deviation from the latter. Second, there is little or no evidence in the indices shown in Table 24 that there was any significant change during the two decades 1880-1900. However, if there was no clear improvement, there was likewise no deterioration. This condition of stability is to be expected if the Indian population was at or near the low point of its decline due to warfare and disease, and had not yet undergone the transition toward a better demographic status.

The next step was to examine the file of microfilm at the Bureau of Vital Statistics, which displays the death certificates of all those who have died in California since registration was initiated. Attention was focused on the Indians who had died in 20 selected counties. (These counties were as follows: in the north and center, Butte, Del Norte, Fresno, Humboldt, Inyo, Kern, Lake, Lassen, Madera, Mendocino, Modoc, Mono, Plumas, Shasta, Siskiyou, Trinity, Tulare; in the south, Riverside, San Bernardino, San Diego). At the outset the year 1910 was chosen because this year was as early as could be expected to furnish a fully representative file of Indian deaths. In the 20 counties examined there were only 85 deaths which were attributed to Indians. Clearly the registration at that time was inadequate. Next the year 1920 was inspected. During these twelve months only 206 Indian deaths were on file. Consequently the examination was extended so as to include the years 1921, 1922, and 1923. In this four-year period there were 593 deaths registered in the 20 counties. This number is barely adequate for the purpose of establishing indices, but to enlarge it significantly would have involved an inordinate amount of time and effort.

There are two sources of error which could affect adversely the completeness of these reports. In the first place, registration was a new and unwelcome procedure, even to the white population, and it is highly probable that many Indians ignored the requirement. Particularly in the more remote areas, the natives may well have failed to comply with the regulations, especially if no medical or police authority was present who could act as a coercive agent. In the second place, the designation of "Indian" was applied as the result of the personal judgment of doctor or clerk who made the entry on the certificate. Although the designation was usually correct, if the decedent were only part Indian, or if the relatives for any reason wished to conceal his ethnic origin, the word "white" might be used, and thereby the Indian association would be forever deleted from the record.

How serious were these omissions and falsifications cannot now be estimated quantitatively. However, an approximate analysis of the record for the year 1920 can be made. If we know the total recorded deaths for the year in the 20 counties and also their probable Indian population, we can get an estimate of the crude death rate and compare

*Table 25.* INDIAN DEATHS IN CALIFORNIA BY COUNTY IN 1920, AND
INDIAN POPULATION IN 1910, 1920, AND 1930

| County | Deaths, 1920 | Population, 1910 census | Population, 1920 census | Population 1930 census | Mean of 3 Censuses Number | Rate per 1,000 |
|---|---|---|---|---|---|---|
| Butte | 7 | 298 | 225 | 377 | 300 | 23 |
| Del Norte | 1 | 337 | 524 | 499 | 453 | 2 |
| Fresno | 8 | 313 | 380 | 652 | 448 | 18 |
| Humboldt | 35 | 1,652 | 1,829 | 2,174 | 1,885 | 19 |
| Inyo | 12 | 792 | 632 | 736 | 720 | 17 |
| Kern | 8 | 252 | 271 | 531 | 351 | 24 |
| Lake | 18 | 433 | 294 | 377 | 368 | 49 |
| Lassen | 3 | 410 | 331 | 308 | 350 | 9 |
| Madera | 8 | 419 | 392 | 520 | 444 | 18 |
| Mendocino | 29 | 1,170 | 1,056 | 1,154 | 1,127 | 26 |
| Modoc | 3 | 546 | 475 | 561 | 527 | 6 |
| Mono | 0 | 386 | 252 | 293 | 310 | 0 |
| Plumas | 7 | 380 | 332 | 251 | 321 | 22 |
| Riverside | 5 | 1,590 | 1,958 | 1,327 | 1,625 | 3 |
| San Bernardino | 5 | 573 | 1,029 | 468 | 690 | 7 |
| San Diego | 14 | 1,516 | 1,352 | 1,722 | 1,530 | 9 |
| Shasta | 20 | 756 | 610 | 687 | 684 | 29 |
| Siskiyou | 10 | 1,109 | 624 | 964 | 899 | 11 |
| Trinity | 2 | 227 | 99 | 280 | 202 | 10 |
| Tulare | 11 | 204 | 216 | 351 | 257 | 43 |
| Total | 206 | 13,363 | 12,881 | 14,232 | 13,491 | |

Mean death rate per 1,000
   3 southern counties   6.2
   17 northern counties 18.9
   Total, 20 counties    15.3

this with what might be expected at the stated place and time. In Table
25 are shown the number of certificates filed for Indians in each county
in the year 1920. The total population is taken from the Federal Censuses of 1910, 1920, and 1930. From each census is obtained a figure
which purports to show the Indians in each county. As was mentioned
in another place, these values are highly erratic and probably widely in

error. In order to equalize the deviations to some extent, the figures in the three censuses are averaged for each county (shown in Table 25). Then the death rate is expressed as the ratio of deaths to population times 1,000.

The three-census average for the 20 counties is 13,491 Indians. There are 206 death certificates dated 1920. Thus the death rate was 15.3 per thousand. Now, in 1920 the death rate for the non-white fraction of the entire national population was close to 20 per thousand. The Indians of California may be regarded as being fairly typical non-whites. Certainly their health status was on a par with Negroes and Orientals. Hence their death rate in the restricted sample obtained here is too low.

Further light is shed by splitting the sample geographically. The three southern counties, Riverside, San Bernardino, and San Diego, with 3,845 persons, show only 24 deaths, or 6.2 per thousand, whereas the corresponding figures for the 17 northern counties are 9,646 persons and 182 deaths, or 18.9 per thousand. Clearly the north and center of the state yield a value not far removed from the national average, but for the southern area the death rate is badly defective. If the northern portion is examined in detail it will be noted that the north-eastern area, embracing Siskiyou, Lassen, and Modoc Counties, the home of the Pit River and Modoc tribes, had 16 deaths in a population of 1,776 persons, or a death rate of 9.0 per thousand. On the other hand the western group, Humboldt, Mendocino, and Lake Counties had 82 deaths and 3,380 people, a rate of 24.3 per thousand, while Butte and Plumas Counties, close to the first three mentioned, showed a death rate of 22.6 per thousand. There is no alternative but to conclude that, whatever the reasons may have been, some regions in 1920 were failing to register properly the deaths among the Indian population. It follows, therefore, that the true number of deaths was greater than the file indicates, and may have reached close to 25 per thousand.

In addition to the deaths which were registered during the years 1920 to 1923, another group was studied—the deaths which were recorded during 1965 and 1966, the latest for which microfilm of the certificates is available. The treatment was the same, except that the counties were somewhat different. Owing to the paucity of deaths the three southern counties were omitted, but the county of Sonoma was added. There were thus 18 counties with a total for the two years of

350 deaths. The key indices for both groups of deaths are found in Table 26. The primary features of Indian mortality are quite apparent.

There was a slight improvement between 1900 and 1920 if it may be assumed that the national data for 1880, 1890, and 1900 simulate the corresponding data for Californa alone. Child and infant deaths were fewer and deaths among the aged relatively greater. Consequently a reduction in infant mortality and an aging of the population must be postulated. Although the age-specific death rates are exceptional in showing a reversal, the expectation of life at birth ($e_0$) is distinctly greater in 1920 than in 1880-1900. The trends toward aging and toward reduction in mortality are accentuated in the period 1920 to 1965. With respect to distribution, the preponderance of deaths is moved strongly to the later age groups, while the age-specific death rates at birth and at 25 years of age both fell sharply and the expectation of life at birth rose from 39 to 53 years.

Although the mortality status of the Indians had improved greatly by 1965, it still lagged behind that of other races. This fact may be appreciated by making a rough comparison between the Indian indices in 1965 and those of the total population of the state in 1900 and 1967 (Tables 22 and 23). In general the Indian population seems to have reached in 1965 approximately the level of the total population in 1920 or a little later, say 1930. Further analysis of this condition is necessary.

In order to pursue this objective I have assembled the data for age at death of the total population of the state as they are found in the successive reports of the Bureau of Vital Statistics since the year 1880. In order to present these figures in condensed form, three indices have been selected: the proportion of persons dying in age groups 0-4 years and 65 years and over, together with the expectation of life at birth ($e_0$ in the corresponding life table). For the purpose of putting the trends and differences in a form which is more easily visualized than are tables, the values are represented graphically in Figures 1 and 2. All the calendar years are here except those from 1897 to 1904, during which time the reports omitted the age distribution of mortality.

The changes in the three indices are very clear, despite numerous minor fluctuations from year to year. The relative number of persons dying in infancy and early childhood (age group 0-4 years) has steadily fallen, whereas the relative number of persons who died in old age has increased. Likewise, the expectation of life among those who died has constantly risen. These phenomena are well recognized, of course, as depicting processes which have been in operation for a century throughout the Western World. Their presentation here is merely for the purpose of providing a background against which to place the behavior of the Indian population.

The indices calculated for the Indians of the United States from the censuses of 1890 and 1900 and given in Table 24 have been added to figures 1 and 2 in a large circle for age group 0-4 years and a large, solid dot for the age group 65 years and over. Similarly $e_0$ for these dates is shown as a large, solid dot. The same indices are drawn in the figures in the same way for 1921 and 1965, as calculated from the death certificates of selected counties of California, as previously described (see Table 26).

*Table 26.* AGING AND SURVIVORSHIP INDICES FOR
THE INDIAN POPULATION OF CERTAIN COUNTIES
IN CALIFORNIA, 1920-1923 AND 1965-1966

| | Percentage of deaths | |
| --- | --- | --- |
| Age groups | 1920-1923 | 1965-1966 |
| 0-4 | 23.10 | 9.43 |
| 5-14 | 10.46 | 1.43 |
| 50 and over | 38.11 app. | 60.57 app. |
| 65 and over | 28.67 | 34.86 |
| 75 and over | 22.09 | 21.43 |
| | | |
| Age-specific death rate | | |
| $q_0$ (at birth) | 0.2310 | 0.0943 |
| $q_{25}$ (at 25 years) | 0.1524 | 0.0686 |
| | | |
| Expectation of life at birth ($e_0$) in years | 38.97 | 53.12 |

NOTE: The indices for 1920-1923 are based upon the counties shown in Table 25. Those for 1965-1966 are based upon the same counties with the addition of Sonoma and the deletion of Riverside, San Bernardino, and San Diego. The 1920 list contains 593 deaths; that for 1965 contains 350 deaths.

SOURCE: Death certificates on file at the Bureau of Vital Statistics, Sacramento.

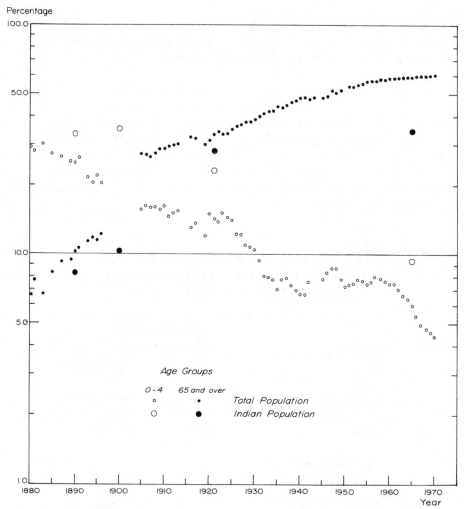

**Figure 1.** Mortality indices for the total population of California and for its Indian population. Circles represent the proportion of deaths occurring to the age group 0-4 years, dots the age 65 years and over. Small symbols represent total population, large symbols Indian population. Ordinate is values of indices in percent of all deaths. Abscissa is calendar year of occurence. For detail, see text.

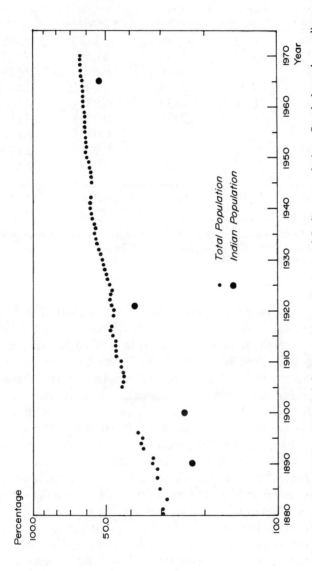

**Figure 2.** Expectation of life at birth ($e_o$) for total population and Indian population. Symbols and coordinates are as in Figure 1.

*Table 27.* AGING AND SURVIVORSHIP INDICES FOR THE INDIAN
POPULATION OF CALIFORNIA, 1961-1970

| Date | Percent of deaths 0-4 years | Percent of deaths 65 and over | Life expectation at birth $(e_o)$ | Age- specific death rate at birth $(q_o)$ | death rate at 25 yrs. $(q_{25})$ |
|------|------|------|------|------|------|
| 1961 | 15.41 | 34.93 | 49.66 | 0.1130 | 0.0991 |
| 1963 | 10.35 | 41.72 | 53.95 | 0.0759 | 0.1205 |
| 1964 | 13.46 | 32.38 | 48.69 | 0.0996 | 0.1161 |
| 1965 | 12.17 | 32.90 | 50.50 | 0.0987 | 0.1028 |
| 1966 | 9.45 | 28.01 | 49.37 | 0.0814 | 0.1000 |
| 1967 | 8.33 | 34.33 | 50.22 | 0.0633 | 0.1120 |
| 1968 | 8.79 | 30.77 | 49.44 | 0.0843 | 0.1295 |
| 1969 | 7.09 | 30.74 | 50.71 | 0.0338 | 0.1260 |
| 1970 | 6.23 | 34.27 | 52.06 | 0.0592 | 0.1164 |
| 1961-1970 | 9.91 | 33.85 | 50.83 | 0.0778 | 0.1124 |

SOURCE: Derived from data contained in the file of reports of the Bureau of Vital
Statistics, Department of Public Health, Sacramento. The distributions of age at death
are not given in the report for 1962.

The crosses placed at the year 1966-1967 are derived from the
distributions of age at death for all Indians of the State of California
which are given in the Reports of the Bureau of Vital Statistics in the
years 1961 to 1970 inclusive (except 1962). With the exception of the
odd years 1950 and 1951, the Reports of the Bureau of Vital Statistics
do not contain age distributions for Indians as a separate race prior to
1961. The life tables and corresponding indices for the ensuing decade
give little evidence of anything but random variation. The sole exception is the sharply decreasing proportion of infant deaths which is
manifested in the behavior of age group 0-4 and the expectation of life
at birth (see Table 27). Consequently the deaths during the nine years
may be consolidated and the indices determined for the decade as a
whole. They are indicated by crosses in the figures in order to dif-
ferentiate this source from those utilized for dots and circles. It will be
noted that these indices are very close to the ones calculated from the
actual death certificates of the years 1965-1966. This correspondence
is evidence for the essential correctness of both methods, for the
ultimate origin of the data is the same.

Figures 1 and 2 depict graphically the conclusion previously drawn. The Indian population has in its mortality behavior followed consistently that of the general population, who are mostly of the white race. Even before 1900 it had begun to do so. At the same time the rate of change has remained at about the level of the whole, such that in absolute terms the Indian component has never caught up with the main stream of the population, but still lags three or four decades behind it. This condition is in strong contrast to the relationship which exists with respect to birth and reproduction.

These conclusions are based upon consideration of mortality as it is recorded for an entire population, whether the total for the state or the total for the Indian component. There is no segregation according to any characteristic. An instructive procedure, however, is to make a distinction with respect to age and to follow separately the changes which have occurred in the adult and in the infant fraction of the whole California population and of the Indian sub-population. This task may be accomplished first by constructing the abridged life tables for both groups using only those who died at the age of 25 years or older, and second, by tabulating or plotting the infant death rates in those years for which both the infant deaths and total births have been published.

What we know about the adult population is condensed in Table 28, where the customary indices are employed. If the condensation were not drastic a vast and confusing set of life tables and other figures would have to be presented. The table is divided into three parts. The first gives the data for the total population of California which died at an age of 25 or older. The indices are the proportion of deaths which have occurred respectively in the age groups 50, 65, and 75 years and over, the age-specific death rate at 25 years ($q_{25}$), and the expectation of life at age 25 ($e_{25}$). The annual figures published in the Reports of the Bureau of Vital Statistics are abbreviated so as to show seven groups of three years each. Thus the first group consolidates the deaths in 1911, 1912, and 1913, the second those in 1919, 1920, and 1921, and so on as indicated in the table.

The second part of Table 28 embraces the deaths reported in the records filed in the Office of the Indian Probate Hearings Branch, Sacramento, California. These figures are restricted to persons who died at ages of 25 years or older and have been divided into four groups according to the pair of decades in which each individual died: 1890-1909, 1910-1929, 1930-1949, 1950-1969. The third part contains

*Table 28.* AGING AND SURVIVORSHIP INDICES FOR THREE TYPES
OF ADULT POPULATION

| Date | Number of deaths[a] | Percent died 75 plus | Percent died 65 plus | Percent died 50 plus | Age— specific death rate $q_{25}$ | Expectation of life $(e_{25})$ |
|---|---|---|---|---|---|---|
| I. TOTAL POPULATION OF CALIFORNIA[b] | | | | | | |
| 1911-1913 | 83,116 | — | 39.33 | 64.35 | 0.1303 | 32.46 |
| 1919-1921 | 108,218 | — | 40.87 | 66.62 | 0.1189 | 33.27 |
| 1929-1931 | 164,881 | — | 46.68 | 73.87 | 0.0767 | 36.21 |
| 1939-1941 | 213,358 | — | 53.23 | 80.55 | 0.0472 | 38.62 |
| 1949-1951 | 271,903 | 31.98 | 58.63 | 84.39 | 0.0329 | 41.42 |
| 1959-1961 | 357,478 | 38.44 | 64.19 | 86.97 | 0.0240 | 43.63 |
| 1968-1970 | 451,724 | 41.66 | 65.61 | 87.97 | 0.0257 | 44.51 |
| II. INDIAN ADULT POPULATION[c] | | | | | | |
| 1890-1909 | 804 | 16.79 | 37.95 | 64.69 | 0.0746 | 32.38 |
| 1910-1929 | 1,312 | 29.19 | 50.99 | 72.41 | 0.0579 | 37.16 |
| 1930-1949 | 1,884 | 31.58 | 52.04 | 75.07 | 0.0441 | 38.28 |
| 1950-1969 | 1,527 | 28.49 | 48.13 | 75.70 | 0.0268 | 37.87 |
| III. INDIAN ADULT POPULATION[d] | | | | | | |
| 1920-1923 | 328 | 39.94 | 51.83 | 68.90 | 0.1524 | 38.54 |
| 1965-1966 | 293 | 25.60 | 41.64 | 72.35 | 0.0614 | 36.71 |
| 1961-1970 | 2,215 | 24.33 | 41.04 | 66.37 | 0.1124 | 34.79 |

[a] All populations include persons who died at the age of 25 years or older.
[b] Consolidated by three-year periods, from the reports of the Bureau of Vital Statistics.
[c] According to date of death in twenty-year periods, from the files of the Office of Indian Probate Hearings Branch.
[d] The first two items are from microfilm of death certificates; the third is from reports of the Bureau of Vital Statistics.

the figures obtained from the death registration of the Indians, either directly from the certificates, (in 1920-1923 and 1965-1966), or from the annual reports of the Bureau of Vital Statistics. Obviously the third part, which is drawn from the entire Indian population of the state, is more comprehensive that the second part, which depicts only a selected portion of that population.

The first part of Table 28 shows trends in the indices for the total population of California which might be expected from consideration of previous discussion and of Tables 21, 22, and 23, as well as of Figures 1 and 2. The proportion of deaths in the older age groups increased steadily, the age-specific death rate at 25 years ($q_{25}$) diminished consistently, and the expectation of life ($e_{25}$) rose from 32 to 44 years. According to Table 28 the Indian population reacted differently, although the figures are somewhat equivocal in certain respects.

The probate series shows a severe dislocation at the first interval: between those who died in the years 1890-1909 and those who died in 1910-1929. In this context the fact should be repeated that those persons over forty years in 1900 were born in 1850 or before, and therefore would be survivors of the devastation of Indian life which occurred during the mining-settlement era. It is likely, therefore, that their youthful experience is reflected in the mortality behavior of those who were relatively old in the period 1890-1909. If so, this group of decedents must be considered abnormal from the standpoint of the modern population.

If attention is restricted to those in the probate records who died in 1910 or thereafter, it is evident that very little movement is suggested by the indices. There may have been a slight rise, followed by a slight fall, but on the whole very little change is indicated, certainly nothing which resembles the trends which characterize the total population.

The data from the death certificates resemble what is found with the probate series, both in absolute values and in trends. The figures for 1965-1966, taken from the certificates filed in twenty counties, in some instances demonstrate a smaller proportion of elderly decedents than the same area in 1920-1923. The expectation of life at age 25 years is less, although the age-specific death rate appears also to be reduced. The values for the consolidated deaths in 1961-1970, from the Reports of the Bureau of Vital Statistics, are even smaller. Nevertheless, the numerical differences in the indices utilized among the groups of Indians are all relatively minor. The important point is that the Indian adults have not displayed the marked progress toward a longer life and preponderance of the aged component that has been displayed by the total population during the past sixty years.

Infant mortality presents a very different picture. It will be remembered that the pattern of death for all ages showed the Indian component undergoing improvement throughout the past seventy or eighty years, but at the same time always remaining behind the bulk of the population. This condition is manifested particularly by the adult segment of the age scale. What has happened with regard to infants can be observed in Table 29. Here the infant deaths for the few years which have been reported in publication are given, together with the births of Indians and the consequent mortality rates. For the purpose of comparison the mortality values of the total population for the same years are also given. The trend is clear, but, in order to exploit the situation fully, the same data are presented graphically in Figure 3. In this figure the known points for the Indian fraction are indicated by circles, those for the total population by dots. Moreover all the points for the total

*Table 29.* INFANT MORTALITY AMONG THE
INDIAN POPULATION

| | Indian population | | | State total |
|---|---|---|---|---|
| Date[a] | Births | Infant deaths | Deaths per 1,000 births | Deaths per 1,000 births |
| 1926 | 221 | 39 | 176.5 | 62.9 |
| 1927 | 236 | 47 | 199.2 | 62.5 |
| 1928 | 315 | 41 | 130.2 | 62.4 |
| 1929 | 314 | 44 | 140.1 | 63.1 |
| 1930 | 329 | 56 | 170.2 | 58.6 |
| 1931 | 329 | 48 | 145.9 | 56.6 |
| 1932 | 336 | 51 | 151.8 | 52.8 |
| 1933 | 376 | 46 | 122.2 | 53.4 |
| 1934 | 362 | 60 | 165.7 | 51.6 |
| 1935 | 401 | 44 | 109.7 | 49.5 |
| 1950 | 848 | 42 | 49.6 | 24.9 |
| 1953 | 889 | 37 | 41.7 | 24.5 |
| 1956 | 1,282 | 31 | 24.2 | 24.0 |
| 1961 | 1,756 | 33 | 18.8 | 23.3 |
| 1963 | 1,841 | 22 | 11.9 | 22.3 |
| 1964 | 1,826 | 28 | 15.3 | 21.8 |
| 1968 | 1,687 | 23 | 13.6 | 19.0 |
| 1969 | 1,799 | 10 | 5.6 | 18.3 |
| 1970 | 1,868 | 19 | 10.2 | 17.2 |

[a] Years for which figures are published in the reports of the Bureau of Vital Statistics. In these years the corresponding rates are given for the total population of the state. Other rates are omitted here but are shown in Figure 3.

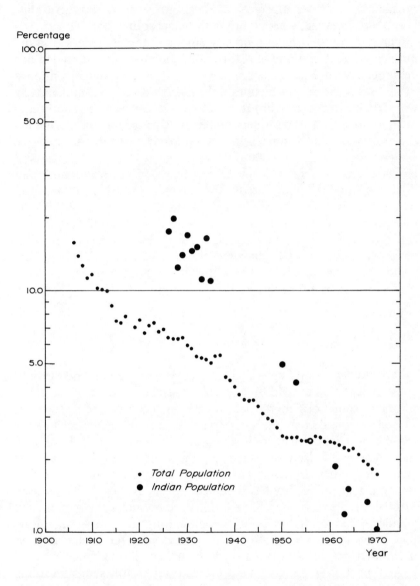

**Figure 3.** Infant mortality. Dots represent total population, circles Indian population. Ordinate is percent of infant deaths in total number of births for each year shown. Abscissa is calendar year of occurrence. For details, *see text.*

population, representing most of the years since death registration began, are included, whether or not they appear in Table 29.

The reduction in infant mortality among the white race was in full progress at the beginning of registration, and must have started from a very high level at least half a century previously. The fall has continued in almost logarithmic fashion until the present decade but undoubtedly will stabilize in the near future at somewhere between ten and twenty infant deaths per year per thousand births. Meanwhile our information concerning the Indians extends backward only to 1926. At this time the rate was clearly in a state of sharp decline. However it was still higher than the general level. Owing to the very small number of deaths reported the points are badly scattered. Nevertheless the reduction is clear as is also the distance above the non-Indian level. The further progress of the Indians is remarkable. Even from the few points between 1950 and 1970 it is evident that the rate of decline in infant mortality is little short of phenomenal and has far exceeded that of the white race. It has now fallen below the level of the total population and may remain there in the future.

## Summary

At this juncture it will be desirable to recapitulate certain findings. The Indian population of California, since the establishment of more or less favorable conditions in the late nineteenth century, has undergone several profound changes. These may be summarized as including a significant increase in reproductivity and an equally great decrease in mortality, particularly of infants. At the same time the aging in the adult fraction has not kept pace with that found in the white race. This improvement in viability has been demonstrated by explosive increase in birth-death ratio, by rising fertility ratio, and by larger natural families. The result has been an accelerating increase in aggregate population and a marked rejuvenation referable to the greater number of children and the fact that vastly fewer of them die in infancy.

A suggestion was made in a previous essay in this series regarding the age distribution of the living Indian population. It was concluded that the demographic transition of this people had taken the form of a reversion to an early phase wherein there was a high and stable birth rate coupled with a falling death rate. We are now able to confirm this suggestion and to add two further comments. The first is that the rate of reproduction or replacement has not merely remained stable but has sharply increased. The second is that the reduction in death rate not only has affected the population at large but has been concentrated in the first year of life, such that the number of living souls has been further augmented.

# V. DEGREES OF BLOOD

The expression "degree of blood" is a barbarism in the view of the geneticist and the demographic purist. Nevertheless, it is universally employed by those who deal with the Indian on the day-to-day, practical level and by the Indians themselves. Because of its wide popular acceptance it is retained here. To be sure, the words denote in fact the relative inheritance possessed by a person which is derived from the Indian stock, or the proportion of Indian characters to be found in the genetic constitution of the individual. Thus the expression "full-blooded" connotes a condition of racial purity and may be used to describe any species or other hereditary unit. "Half-blooded" or any other fractional term states the proportion of his whole genetic complement which has been inherited by the individual from the race under examination. With the basic meaning understood, we can proceed to discuss the degree of blood found in the California Indian at present and in the past.

In California racial mixing began early and in some instances has proceeded very far. A question therefore arises concerning the point to which we should carry the dilution of the original Indian genetic strain. The Bureau of Indian Affairs has been obliged to contend with this problem at various times and has sought various solutions, none of which has been completely satisfactory to all parties. Clearly the first generation off-spring of a union between Indian and non-Indian is a half-blood who retains many obvious Indian traits. Similarly a quarter-blood displays unmistakable Indian characteristics. However, when we reach an eighth or a sixteenth, the Indian traits tend to be submerged, and the person involved exists in a twilight zone where he can certainly regard himself as part Indian, but where he may also pass as a member of another race. This point is attained by common consent at the level of one-sixteenth Indian inheritance. We therefore, in this study, consider this the critical degree of blood and accept as appropriate for this type of analysis any person possessing at least one-sixteenth Indian in his genetic constitution.

When we make this decision we are forced to discard from the 1928 Roll several score persons whose degree of blood is given as one thirty-second, one sixty-fourth, and one-one hundred twenty-eighth Indian. There are 168 of these, about 0.8 percent of the total number of enrollees. It is a curious finding that almost all of them announced their tribal affiliation as Mission Carmel. We know from historical records that at least one Spanish soldier in the garrison at Monterey married an Indian neophyte in the first days of the mission. The fruit of this union was numerous offspring and the number of descendants who appear on the 1928 Roll is not surprising. On the other hand, the possibility is opened that there may be many hundred persons living in California today who could, if they wished, claim similar descent from other missions. The fact that they have not done so renders suspect any of our data which involves persons of less than one-sixteenth Indian blood.

Another phenomenon which has appeared conspicuously in the evolution of the Indian population is back-crossing. It is quite to be anticipated that a half-blood who has been brought up to maturity in an Indian community will marry an Indian rather than a member of another race. This union will produce a three-quarter blood. If the latter, in turn, marries a pure Indian the result is a seven-eighths blood, or if the marriage is with a half-blood the result is a person of five-eighths Indian descent. In this manner all gradations may be produced within a very few generations, indeed in four generations from the original Indian and non-Indian couple. The California natives have now reached the point at which there occur widely all possible combinations from 1 to 16 if the process is carried only to fractions expressed as sixteenths. There are many more if we go to thirty-seconds and sixty-fourths. As mentioned above, however, the 1928 Roll and other available documents require only that the limit be set at sixteenths.

The documentary sources for study of degree of blood are severely limited. The mission books are of no help for two reasons. First, the marriage records have not been available, nor have the baptismal records of those who were of mixed descent. Second, there were very few marriages between Spaniards or Mexicans and native women. Although illicit unions occurred, their number was of little significance prior to 1845. Subsequent to that date the Americans recorded no data concerning racial origin until the agency censuses of the early twentieth century. Then we have a few, such as that from Hupa Reservation in 1910. Not until 1940 was there adequate coverage by most of the agencies. In the meantime the necessity of proving California descent forced the determination of exact degree of Indian blood for inclusion in the Roll of 1928. This Roll therefore constitutes the foundation for most of our knowledge of Indian racial composition. Its importance in this respect is magnified by the unfortunate fact that neither the Roll of 1950 nor that of 1970 includes information concerning this matter, and even the contemporary Indian Service is obliged to consult the 1928 Roll for evidence bearing upon personal ancestry.

In a paper written over thirty years ago (Cook 1943e), I examined the racial composition of the California Indians according to certain areas, or regions within the state, for considerable differences appeared to exist according to locality. The present reexamination of the data confirms the general validity of these differences, but suggests a somewhat altered alignment of territory.

With respect to genetic history, the California natives may be allocated to three primary groups. The first is an eastern division on the far side of the Sierra Nevada, extending north and south in a narrow band from Modoc County to and including Inyo County. The second is a north central division which embraces the entire state from the Oregon line to the Tehachapi Mountains, with the exception of the mission strip along the coast from San Francisco to Santa Barbara. The third division includes the coastal mission area plus the entire southern portion of the state.

The first division is designated Group 1. The second is separated roughly into a northern portion, Group 2; and a southern portion, Group 3. The third is further divided into three parts, Group 4, the northern mission area; Group 5, the southern mission area; and Group 6, the interior desert. Further detail may be given.

*Group 1.* Transmontane California. Here are the Paiute, Washo, and Shoshone.

*Groups 2 and 3.* North central California, including many linguistic stocks and tribelets. From this aggregate we have selected the following specific components.

    *Group 2A.* The northwest coast and the Klamath-Trinity basin. The principal tribes are the Yurok, Hupa, Wiyot, and Karok.

    *Group 2B.* The northeastern interior, principally the watershed of the Pit River. The Indians are almost exclusively the Pit Rivers (Achomawi and Atsugewi), with a few Yana and Maidu.

    *Group 3A.* Here are the Pomo and neighboring peoples

(the Yuki and Wylackie). They lived primarily in Mendocino and Sonoma Counties.

*Group 3B.* The southern San Joaquin Valley and adjacent foothills. The tribes are the remnants of the Yokuts and the Western Mono.

These four groups, 2A, 2B, 3A, and 3B have been selected from the north-central region in order to obtain a more precise comparison among areas of different history and characteristics.

*Group 4.* The northern missions from San Francisco to San Luis Obispo. There were several hundred persons in 1928 who claimed descent from neophytes at these missions.

*Group 5.* The southern missions from the Santa Barbara Channel to San Diego. We include only those persons who gave their tribal affiliation as pertaining to a mission. The same is true with respect to Group 4. It is evident that Groups 4 and 5 are segregated on a cultural as well as a geographical basis. There is only a vague territorial line between Group 3 and Group 4, as well as between Group 5 and Group 6. The cultural distinction, however, between mission and non-mission influence is very clear.

*Group 6.* Here are the non-mission, unconverted, desert tribes of southern California, principally the Cahuilla. The Yuma are not included.

From the study made several years ago (Cook, 1943e) two conclusions could be drawn. The California Indians have been steadily losing the native genetic character since their first encounter with European civilization, and this change has been determined and modified by conditions operating within the boundaries of restricted geographic and political areas. Specifically, the rapidity of reduction in degree of blood has been dependent upon the intensity, duration, and nature of contact with the Caucasian race. In order to refute or confirm these conclusions, the 1928 Roll has been subjected to a new and detailed analysis, certain other data have been added, and different methods have been applied.

The first and perhaps the most important method has been to examine the relationship between the degree of blood and the age of those Indians who appear in the 1928 Roll. This relationship is then placed in the context of the region which was the ancestral home. Hence, for each region or group listed above, the degree of blood was tabulated and plotted against the age of the persons concerned.

The age was organized by decades, but those who were born between January 1 and May 30 in the year 1928 were omitted. This procedure was adopted, as in the previous study of age distribution, in order to avoid the necessity for splitting years, an undesirable complication. Thus we work with ten decades, beginning with the cohort 1-10 years old in 1928, or those persons born from 1918 to 1927 inclusive. The last cohort begins with 91 years and extends to an indefinite upper limit.

The degree of blood is based upon the assumption that the smallest value would be that of one-sixteenth Indian inheritance. Therefore, as was previously suggested, those persons with a smaller fraction of Indian blood had to be excluded. For those of one-sixteenth or greater only the numerator of the fraction is employed. Thus to a full blood is assigned the rating of 16 (or 16/16), to a half-blood one of 8 (or 8/16), and so forth. In this way the use of fractions is obviated.

Within each regional group and within each age group, we wish to determine the average degree of blood. To do this we might sum the number of cases, also the degrees of blood (expressed as whole numbers on the scale of 16), and find the quotient. However, the degree of blood follows, from one generation to another, a geometric, not an arithmetic progression: 16, 8, 4, 2, 1. In order to compensate for the distortion we derive the geometric mean, which is the antilogarithm of the mean of the logarithms of the individual cases. Having thus calculated the mean degree of blood on the scale of 16, we convert to percent of comparisons. The same procedure may be used to find the mean degree of blood for persons of all ages in any area or region. As an example we may use Region 1. There are 502 persons on the 1928 Roll from this region, in the age group 1-10 years. The average logarithm of the degree of blood pertaining to these individuals is 1.07730. The mean degree of blood indicated is 11.97. This is 74.68 percent of 16, or of the full-blooded condition. Likewise the mean degree of blood for the entire 1,884 persons in Region 1 is 13.12, or 82.00 percent. These data are taken from the detailed presentation in Table 30.

Even a cursory examination of this table demonstrates that whereas the mean degree of blood existing in 1928 varied widely among the regions studied, the direction of change with age, in all these regions,

*Table 30.* DEGREE OF BLOOD OF THE CALIFORNIA
INDIANS AS SHOWN BY THE ROLL OF 1928
(The mean degree of blood is on the scale of 16; the percent
of full blood is on the scale of 100.)

| Age group | Number of cases | Mean degree of blood | Percent of full blood |
|---|---|---|---|
| | | Region 1 | |
| 1-10 | 502 | 11.950 | 74.68 |
| 11-20 | 386 | 12.120 | 75.75 |
| 21-30 | 281 | 13.180 | 82.37 |
| 31-40 | 193 | 13.210 | 82.56 |
| 41-50 | 179 | 14.580 | 91.12 |
| 51-60 | 144 | 14.810 | 92.56 |
| 61-70 | 106 | 15.890 | 99.31 |
| 71-80 | 68 | 16.000 | 100.00 |
| 81-90 | 17 | 16.000 | 100.00 |
| 91 and over | 8 | 16.000 | 100.00 |
| All ages | 1,884 | 13.120 | 82.00 |
| | | Region 2A | |
| 1-10 | 1,000 | 6.606 | 41.28 |
| 11-20 | 780 | 7.831 | 48.94 |
| 21-30 | 543 | 8.371 | 52.31 |
| 31-40 | 411 | 8.504 | 53.15 |
| 41-50 | 300 | 10.100 | 63.12 |
| 51-60 | 280 | 10.395 | 64.97 |
| 61-70 | 196 | 11.763 | 73.51 |
| 71-80 | 70 | 14.034 | 91.46 |
| 81-90 | 26 | 16.000 | 100.00 |
| 91 and over | 6 | 14.255 | 89.09 |
| All ages | 3,612 | 8.279 | 51.75 |

*Table 30 (continued)*

| Age group | Number of cases | Mean degree of blood | Percent of full blood |
|---|---|---|---|
| Region 2B | | | |
| 1-10 | 182 | 11.365 | 71.03 |
| 11-20 | 148 | 13.213 | 82.58 |
| 21-30 | 128 | 14.775 | 92.34 |
| 31-40 | 107 | 13.855 | 86.59 |
| 41-50 | 79 | 14.421 | 90.13 |
| 51-60 | 80 | 14.958 | 93.49 |
| 61-70 | 61 | 15.257 | 95.36 |
| 71-80 | 43 | 15.482 | 96.76 |
| 81-90 | 9 | 15.765 | 98.53 |
| 91 and over | 9 | 16.000 | 100.00 |
| All ages | 846 | 13.650 | 85.31 |
| Region 3A | | | |
| 1-10 | 786 | 6.807 | 42.54 |
| 11-20 | 589 | 7.855 | 49.09 |
| 21-30 | 464 | 8.557 | 53.48 |
| 31-40 | 317 | 8.968 | 56.05 |
| 41-50 | 228 | 10.047 | 62.79 |
| 51-60 | 196 | 10.908 | 68.18 |
| 61-70 | 156 | 11.021 | 68.88 |
| 71-80 | 89 | 14.125 | 88.28 |
| 81-90 | 36 | 15.692 | 98.08 |
| 91 and over | 4 | 16.000 | 100.00 |
| All ages | 2,865 | 8.489 | 53.06 |
| Region 3B | | | |
| 1-10 | 438 | 8.064 | 50.40 |
| 10-20 | 368 | 9.534 | 59.89 |
| 21-30 | 251 | 9.227 | 57.67 |
| 31-40 | 183 | 9.628 | 60.18 |
| 41-50 | 157 | 11.536 | 72.10 |
| 51-60 | 88 | 11.955 | 74.72 |
| 61-70 | 82 | 12.951 | 80.94 |
| 71-80 | 41 | 15.730 | 98.31 |

*Table 30 (continued)*

| Age group | Number of cases | Mean degree of blood | Percent of full blood |
|---|---|---|---|
| 81-90 | 23 | 16.000 | 100.00 |
| 91 and over | 6 | 16.000 | 100.00 |
| All ages | 1,637 | 9.715 | 60.72 |

### Region 4

| Age group | Number of cases | Mean degree of blood | Percent of full blood |
|---|---|---|---|
| 1-10 | 95 | 4.871 | 30.44 |
| 11-20 | 85 | 6.796 | 42.48 |
| 21-30 | 57 | 6.267 | 39.17 |
| 31-40 | 41 | 7.888 | 49.30 |
| 41-50 | 30 | 7.565 | 47.28 |
| 51-60 | 30 | 7.817 | 48.86 |
| 61-70 | 27 | 7.519 | 46.99 |
| 71-80 | 11 | 6.870 | 42.94 |
| 81-90 | 4 | 6.727 | 42.04 |
| 91 and over | 0 | — | — |
| All ages | 380 | 6.323 | 39.52 |

### Region 5

| Age group | Number of cases | Mean degree of blood | Percent of full blood |
|---|---|---|---|
| 1-10 | 305 | 3.727 | 23.29 |
| 11-20 | 306 | 4.617 | 28.86 |
| 21-30 | 182 | 6.251 | 39.07 |
| 31-40 | 156 | 7.371 | 46.07 |
| 41-50 | 112 | 8.272 | 51.70 |
| 51-60 | 86 | 9.191 | 57.44 |
| 61-70 | 49 | 10.667 | 66.67 |
| 71-80 | 27 | 10.387 | 64.92 |
| 81-90 | 5 | 12.126 | 75.79 |
| 91 and over | 4 | 11.314 | 70.71 |
| All ages | 1,232 | 5.696 | 35.60 |

### Region 6

| Age group | Number of cases | Mean degree of blood | Percent of full blood |
|---|---|---|---|
| 1-10 | 711 | 7.354 | 45.96 |
| 11-20 | 593 | 9.059 | 56.62 |
| 21-30 | 510 | 10.194 | 63.71 |
| 31-40 | 424 | 11.523 | 72.02 |
| 41-50 | 301 | 12.167 | 76.04 |

*Table 30 (continued)*

| Age group | Number of cases | Mean degree of blood | Percent of full blood |
|---|---|---|---|
| 51-60 | 233 | 13.057 | 81.61 |
| 61-70 | 168 | 13.754 | 85.96 |
| 71-80 | 80 | 14.621 | 92.63 |
| 81-90 | 34 | 16.000 | 100.00 |
| 91 and over | 19 | 15.426 | 96.41 |
| All ages | 3,073 | 10.072 | 62.93 |

Regions 2 and 3, entire

| Age group | Number of cases | Mean degree of blood | Percent of full blood |
|---|---|---|---|
| 1-10 | 3,613 | 6.448 | 40.30 |
| 11-20 | 2,889 | 7.633 | 47.71 |
| 21-30 | 2,108 | 8.282 | 51.76 |
| 31-40 | 1,578 | 8.859 | 55.37 |
| 41-50 | 1,193 | 9.949 | 62.18 |
| 51-60 | 960 | 10.714 | 66.96 |
| 61-70 | 745 | 11.467 | 71.67 |
| 71-80 | 362 | 14.290 | 89.31 |
| 81-90 | 141 | 15.906 | 99.41 |
| 91 and over | 39 | 15.717 | 98.23 |
| All ages | 13,628 | 8.275 | 51.61 |

Regions 4, 5, and 6, entire

| Age group | Number of cases | Mean degree of blood | Percent of full blood |
|---|---|---|---|
| 1-10 | 1,111 | 5,891 | 36.82 |
| 10-20 | 984 | 7.165 | 44.78 |
| 21-30 | 749 | 8,722 | 54.51 |
| 31-40 | 621 | 10.045 | 62.78 |
| 41-50 | 443 | 10.665 | 66.66 |
| 51-60 | 349 | 11.458 | 71.61 |
| 61-70 | 244 | 12.224 | 76.40 |
| 71-80 | 118 | 12.718 | 79.49 |
| 81-90 | 43 | 14.293 | 89.33 |
| 91 and over | 23 | 14.616 | 91.35 |
| All ages | 4,685 | 8.362 | 52.26 |

California, entire

| Age group | Number of cases | Mean degree of blood | Percent of full blood |
|---|---|---|---|
| 1-10 | 5,226 | 6.712 | 41.95 |
| 11-20 | 4,259 | 7.844 | 49.03 |
| 21-30 | 3,138 | 8.741 | 54.63 |

*Table 30 (Continued)*

| Age group | Number of cases | Mean degree of blood | Percent of full blood |
|---|---|---|---|
| 31-40 | 2,392 | 9.453 | 59.08 |
| 41-50 | 1,815 | 10.507 | 65.67 |
| 51-60 | 1,453 | 11.243 | 70.27 |
| 61-70 | 1,095 | 12.016 | 75.10 |
| 71-80 | 548 | 14.134 | 88.34 |
| 81-90 | 201 | 15.553 | 97.21 |
| 91 and over | 70 | 15.379 | 96.12 |
| All ages | 20,197 | 8.660 | 54.13 |

has been toward a reduction of the Indian component. At the same time, the rate of this reduction appears to have been a function of the environment surrounding the natives within each region. Consequently it is desirable to discover some device for expressing the value of this rate. To this end the mean degree of blood has been plotted for each region, or group, in the form displayed by Figures 4 to 15, inclusive.

In each of these figures the mean degree of blood is shown on the ordinate, with age at the time of the 1928 Roll on the abscissa. Although the degree of blood is readily stated as the mean for each ten-year cohort, the parameter of age has, for greater clarity, been altered. Instead of age in years we have employed the calendar year of birth. The transformation is simple. The group 1-10 years old in 1928 was born in the years from 1918 to 1927. Thus we place the point showing the mean degree of blood for this group at the year 1923, which is approximately the midpoint of the decade. The preceding cohort, 11-20 years old, was born in the decade 1908-1917, with the midpoint at 1913. The progression continues as far as the earliest decade, which is taken for convenience as 1818-1827, with the midpoint at 1823.

The average degree of blood found in the California Indians throughout the century which terminated in 1928 can be read from the data in Table 30. However, the course of change, particularly in restricted areas, is difficult to ascertain, not to mention interpret, from the table alone. For this purpose it is more satisfactory to use the graphs in Figures 4 to 15. Here we encounter the fact that it is necessary to represent in numerical terms the trend or movement of the points through the decades during which the 1928 enrollees lived.

To do this we employ the conventional regression coefficient, *b*. By this means a number is obtained which at least will serve as an index for the purpose of making comparisons among regions and among different time intervals within a region. In the figures are shown several trend lines which have thus been determined. The corresponding values of *b* are summarized in Table 31.

Without exception the trend lines were descending in the decade 1918-1927, a feature which indicates a progressive dilution of the Indian blood up to and including that period. In view of the total absence of concrete information since 1928, it is very tempting to extrapolate these lines. Thus we might predict that throughout California the average degree of Indian blood would sink below the one-sixteenth level not long after the year 2000 A.D. But such extrapolation is extremely dangerous. The change, which had been almost linear for nearly a century prior to 1928, may have become curvilinear in the past fifty years and may still be altering its character in response to new social and economic conditions. Therefore, we can say little concerning degree of blood in the future. On the other hand, what happened during the nineteenth and early twentieth centuries may be deduced from the age series provided by the 1928 Roll.

From the numerical values in Table 30, and from Figure 4, it may be concluded that at the end of the mission period, about 1830, the native population of California outside the sphere of mission influence was pure-blooded Indian. Nevertheless, within that sphere, a few percent of the genetic constitution had been derived from other races, almost exclusively Ibero-American, and interracial mixing had already begun. The amalgamation spread to the entire state and there continued at a consistent rate until 1928. The value of *b* for the century 1828-1928 is -0.646 (see Table 31), a number which may be taken as a standard of comparison. In 1928 the level of Indian blood in the population of more than 21,000 who reported for the Roll of that year reached only approximately 40 percent. No doubt it has further declined in recent decades.

Of the primary divisions of the state we first encounter Region 1, the arid strip beyond the mountains and the home of the Paiute and Washo. This area remained relatively undisturbed for it functioned only as an expanse of desert to be traversed by immigrants as rapidly as they could manage. It was not until the Nevada silver and gold rush of the early 1860s that there occurred extensive, permanent settlement

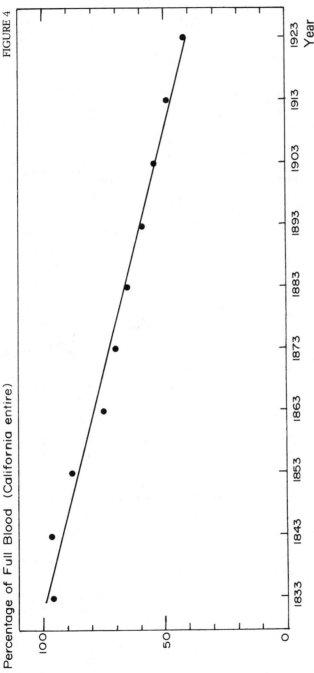

FIGURE 4

Percentage of Full Blood (California entire)

Year

**Figures 4 to 15.** These figures show, for several regions in California, the mean degree of blood, according to decade of birth. In all cases the ordinate is the mean degree of blood, expressed as a percentage of full blood. The abscissa shows calendar year of birth of the successive cohorts by decade. Each decade is indicated by the approximate single central year, e.g., 1833 designates the decade of birth 1928-1837 inclusive. The trend lines are placed according to the value of $b$, or slop of the points as calculated and shown in table 31. They extend between the dates given in Table 31. The regions correspond to the figures as follows:

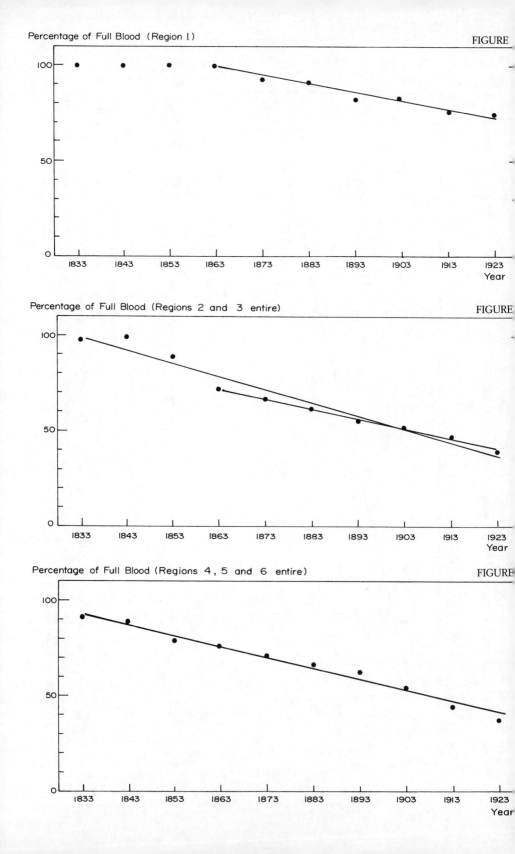

Percentage of Full Blood (Region 1)

FIGURE

Percentage of Full Blood (Regions 2 and 3 entire)

FIGURE

Percentage of Full Blood (Regions 4, 5 and 6 entire)

FIGURE

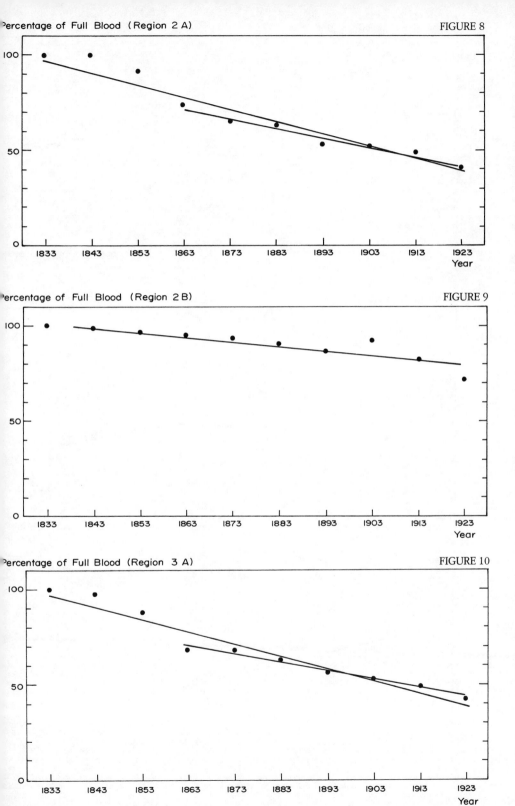

Percentage of Full Blood (Region 2 A)

FIGURE 8

Percentage of Full Blood (Region 2 B)

FIGURE 9

Percentage of Full Blood (Region 3 A)

FIGURE 10

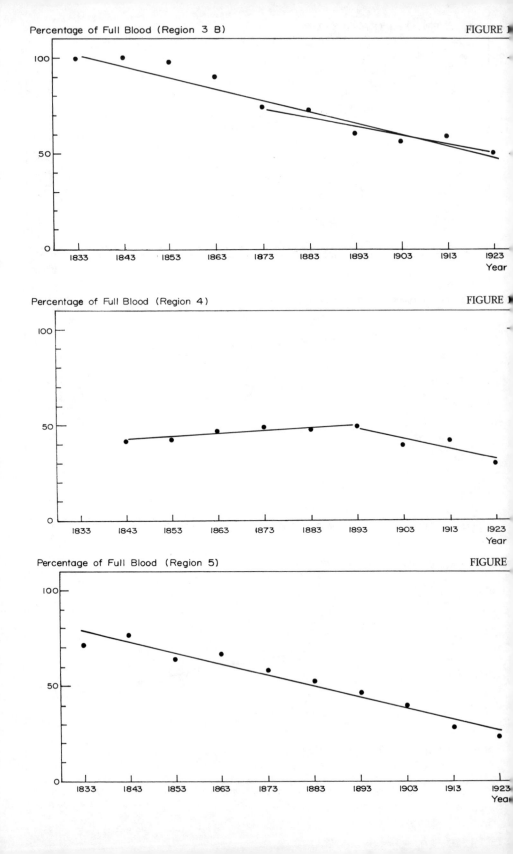

Percentage of Full Blood (Region 3 B)    FIGURE

Percentage of Full Blood (Region 4)    FIGURE

Percentage of Full Blood (Region 5)    FIGURE

FIGURE 14

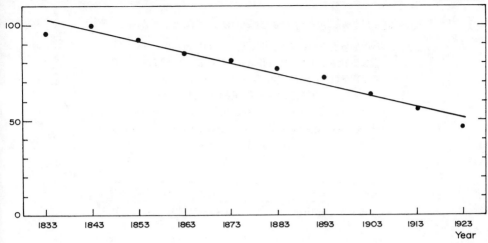

Percentage of Full Blood (Region 6)

FIGURE 15

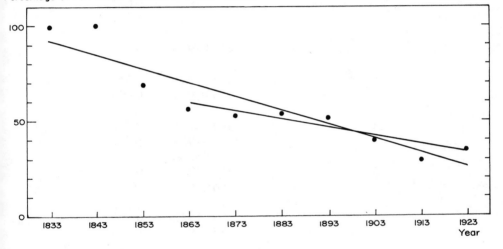

Percentage of Full Blood (Kroeber's "extinct" tribes)

*Table 31.* THE VALUE OF *b*, WHICH IS AN INDEX
TO THE SLOPE OF THE TREND LINE FOR DEGREE
OF BLOOD SHOWN WITH EACH REGION IN
FIGURES 4 THROUGH 15.
(All values are negative unless otherwise indicated. The
inclusive decades of birth are indicated by the single central
year of the decade.)

| Region | Decades of birth | *b* |
|---|---|---|
| California, entire | 1833-1923 | 0.646 |
| 1 | 1863-1923 | 0.415 |
| 2 and 3 entire | 1833-1923 | 0.682 |
| | 1863-1923 | 0.511 |
| 4, 5, and 6, entire | 1833-1923 | 0.590 |
| 2A | 1833-1923 | 0.634 |
| | 1863-1923 | 0.498 |
| 2B | 1833-1923 | 0.249 |
| | 1863-1923 | 0.331 |
| 3A | 1833-1923 | 0.653 |
| | 1863-1923 | 0.451 |
| 3B | 1833-1923 | 0.604 |
| | 1873-1923 | 0.462 |
| 4 | 1843-1923 | 0.011 |
| | 1843-1893 | + 0.146 |
| | 1893-1923 | 0.533 |
| 5 | 1833-1923 | 0.577 |
| 6 | 1833-1923 | 0.576 |
| Kroeber's extinct tribes | 1833-1923 | 0.739 |
| | 1863-1923 | 0.442 |

by the Americans. Probably for this reason all the Indians over 70 years old who are reported in the 1928 Roll from this territory were full-blooded, and those in the cohort 61-70 (106 of them) were at the level of 99 percent Indian. Subsequently the Indian genetic fraction suffered attrition (the value of $b$ is -0.415) at a rate which was moderate to slow, but linear, as seen in Figure 5.

Here is a clear instance of a relatively large Indian population living under rural conditions alongside a white population which remained very sparse after the immediate rush of miners had been dissipated. The rate of interbreeding was reduced to a minimum through lack of contact between the two races, and the relative separation of the mining communities and the Indian villages. This situation undoubtedly obtained throughout Nevada, although we have no information concerning dilution of Indian blood in the interior of that state.

The second primary division consists of all cis-montane California north of the Tehachapi Mountains and the Santa Barbara Channel, but excludes all Indians who were descendants of former mission neophytes. From it were reported approximately 13,600 Indians on the 1928 Roll, the data for whom are shown in Tables 30 and 31, as well as in Figure 6. If we examine the graph in Figure 6 we note that the cohorts born in the decades 1828-1837 and 1838-1847 possessed close to 100 percent Indian blood. At this time, therefore, apart from the missionized natives, there had been very little marital contact between the Hispano-Mexican population and the aboriginal inhabitants of the northern coast and the central interior. Among those born in the next two decades (1847-1868) there was a sudden fall in the percentage value to the level of roughly 70 percent Indian blood. After 1868 the rate of decline stabilized and remained at a value for $b$ of -0.511 (see Figure 6). If $b$ is calculated for the entire century its value is greater, 0.682. The course of the change is readily explained. After the invasion by the Americans the rate of interbreeding, mainly illicit, increased explosively, thus producing many mixed bloods in the 1850s and 1860s. When the social atmosphere had cleared somewhat, and the most undesirable element had been liquidated, the white agricultural population established a rather steady level of racial intercourse which was contingent upon the relative number and propinquity of the two races.

Within the limits of this primary division there have been segregated four minor regions, numbered Region 2A, 2B, 3A, and 3B, the tribal composition of which has been set forth previously. Those designated 2A and 3A produce a quite similar pattern when the relationship between date of birth and degree of blood is plotted (see Figures 8 and 10), and this behavior in many respects is reflected in the composite graph for Northern California as a whole. Both Region 2A and Region 3A are characterized by nearly pure (100 percent) Indian blood in the 1840s, a sharp decline between 1843 and 1863, and finally a steady reduction in degree of Indian blood lasting to the end of the record in 1928. The values for $b$, in the two periods 1833-1923 and 1863-1923, conform closely to each other and to those found in Figure 6 for the entire territory.

The sequence of events in Regions 2A and 3A can be read from the graphs. In these areas were concentrated some of the worst manifestations of the behavior which is visibly reflected in the graph of even the state as a whole and which has been mentioned in the preceeding paragraphs. The debauchery of Indian women not only on the coast but throughout northern California was carried to an extreme which has often been described and which has merited much derogatory comment. What is not so well appreciated is the demographic impact. The offspring of these white-Indian unions, all of them half-bloods, together with their immediate progeny, were sufficiently numerous to bring the mean degree of Indian blood in all the northern and central tribes from close to 100 percent to 70 percent in the short space of one generation. This means that in the most heavily affected areas, such as those of the Yurok, Hupa, and Pomo, nearly one-half of the Indian women of reproductive age must have been impregnated by white men. Such a wholesale prostitution of a race has seldom been observed on this continent.

The inhabitants of the Pit River basin, in Region 2B, displayed a breeding pattern which differed markedly from that which characterized the tribes further west. It resembled much more closely that of the Paiute and Washo. Beginning with a condition of genetic purity, the Achomawi and Atsugewi either strongly resisted the influence of the settlers or were not so violently confronted by them. For, if not by miners *en masse*, their home was invaded by white farmers and ranchers in a steady, if rather slow stream. In any event the result was only a gradual decline in mean degree of Indian blood, which is expressed by a falling trend line of gentle slope, and a value for $b$ of only

-0.249 between 1833 and 1923 (see Figure 9). Indeed the mean degree of blood in 1928 was as high as 70 or 80 percent.

Region 3B, which embraced the remains of the valley Yokuts and the foothill Mono, falls into a position intermediate between 2A and 3A on the west and 3B to the north. From Figure 11 it is evident that from a starting point of near 100 percent Indian blood in the 1840s, the value of this percentage fell sharply but less rapidly than in Regions 2A and 3A, until the 1870s, when it, like the others, stabilized at a lower rate ($b$ equals -0.604 for 1833-1923, and -0.462 for 1873-1923).

This trend of the mean degree of blood follows the historical experience of the southern valley tribes. This portion of the state was blessed with a lack of gold and hence attracted few miners. In the 1850s it began to fill up with settlers who pursued farming and stock raising. The Indians were badly treated, nevertheless, and interbreeding was relatively common during the later phases of settlement. The stabilization at a lower, but constant rate did not occur until the 1870s. Hence Region 3B followed in its genetic course that which characterized Regions 2A and 3A, but the changes occurred one or two decades later, and perhaps the strain was less severe because the density of the white population was lower.

The consolidated data for the third primary division of the state, the mission area and the south, are illustrated in Figure 7. The mean degree of blood in the 1840s rises scarcely above 90 percent, unlike the 98-100 percent found in the north and center. However, the trend 1843-1923 is nearly linear until the mean degree of blood reaches approximately 40 percent in the 1920s. There is no trace of the precipitous decline during the period of intensive occupation between 1845 and 1865. This treatment of the entire region as a single area, however, completely masks certain interesting differences which are manifested by the component parts of the aggregate.

Restricted Region 4 embraces the survivors of the mission neophytes who were drawn from the Costanoan and Salinan strip of coast between San Francisco Bay and San Luis Obispo. In this sample their former mission was principally San Carlos, with a few from San Jose. Unfortunately, there are only 380 individuals whose names appear on the 1928 Roll and who claimed at least one-sixteenth Indian blood. Nevertheless their genetic history is reasonably well depicted in the tables and in Figure 12. Of those born prior to 1838 there are no survivors who were included in the Roll. There are four who were born in the decade 1838-1847; one full blood, two who were one-half Indian, and one who was one-eighth Indian. The mean degree of blood is 42 percent. Subsequent to this decade the mean degree of blood increased until for the cohort born 1888-1897 it reached 49 percent. Thereafter this value fell to 30 percent in the decade 1918-1927. The coefficient $b$ for the time segment 1843-1893 equals +0.146 and for the segment 1893-1923 equals -0.533. The overall change from 1843 to 1923 is almost zero.

Here we see the behavior of a group to which interracial, legal marriage had long been familiar. From 1770 to 1840 there had been a steady amalgamation of the Indian and non-Indian (that is, Hispano-Mexican) which was socially sanctioned. The result was a set of people who were derived almost equally from the two ethnic stocks. This condition persisted, with perhaps a slight reverse trend toward the Indian, until the end of the nineteenth century. Then new influences began to be felt and the mean degree of Indian blood diminished. These people lived in the relatively friendly, more or less congenial environment provided by the central coast counties. There was little invasion of their rights or disturbance of their strictly rural existence. On a very small scale there was a repetition of what has happened in Mexico and other Latin-American countries where racial fusion has proceeded steadily for centuries. Had not an overwhelming flood of Anglo-Americans invaded the area, the ultimate outcome would probably have been the complete mestization of the local native element.

In Region 5 are the survivors of the southern missions, almost exclusively San Fernando, San Gabriel, San Juan Capistrano, San Luis Rey, and San Diego. They have contributed a large fraction to the inhabitants of the reservations under the Mission Agency and designate their tribal affiliation in the 1928 Roll as Mission San Gabriel, Mission San Diego, and so on. Their history is one of struggle on the lowest social level, but without the physical destruction which was visited upon their northern brethren. In Figure 13 the course of their change in degree of blood may be observed (see also Tables 30 and 31). Despite some irregularity in the points, it is clear that in the decades 1828-1847 their degree of Indian blood had already decreased to a mean of 70 or 80 percent. In this feature they resemble the group from the northern missions, although the dilution of the Indian component was not as great. It is therefore also evident that a great deal of intermarriage with non-Indians (almost entirely Mexicans) had taken place between the foundation of the missions and the entrance of the Americans in the 1840s.

From the 1840s onward the mean degree of blood continued to decline, but at a consistent rate (*b* equals -0.577) as late as the Roll of 1928, at which time the mean degree of blood had fallen below 30 percent. Here, as in the northern mission area, interracial fusion has gone ahead rapidly. In the majority of cases the non-Indian element is Mexican, but since 1928 there has been an increase in crossings with other ethnic components, such as Puerto Rican, Filipino, and Negro.

Region 6 covers much the same area as Region 5, but the sample is restricted to those who inscribed their tribal affiliation as non-mission, mostly Cahuilla. Here are the more remote desert communities which stretch eastward from the San Bernardino and the San Jacinto Mountains. The graph of their mean degree of blood follows a trend which is almost identical in form with that seen in Region 5 (see Figure 14). However, there is one important difference. The mean degree of Indian blood in the decades 1828-1847 is close to 100 percent in Region 6, whereas it is 70 to 80 percent in Region 5. This difference is clear evidence that prior to the American occupation there had been very little racial mixing which involved the Cahuilla and allied tribes. In other words, the intermarriage which was promoted by the missions did not extend to the east of the mountains. The reason was probably simply geographical separation, and the failure of the Spanish-Mexican civilization to penetrate far into the arid interior. Not until the expanding agriculture based upon irrigation and the advancing cattle industry entered the desert were these tribes subjected to the domestic pressure of the white man.

This comparison between north and south in California shows how the Anglo-American and the Hispano-American cultures brought about much the same results insofar as dilution of the Indian genetic stock is concerned, but by very different methods. The Anglo-American population attacked the Indians physically and used their women for casual and common law purposes. This activity has always been most intense when (1) the American component was at its roughest and most brutal, as in the gold rush, and (2) when the density of the white population in the Indian areas was greatest. At any event, the interracial intercourse was one-sided and compulsive, at least until recent decades. On the other hand, the Hispano-American population entered into legal and socially acceptable contact with the native. The contract of union was sanctified by the Church, and as a rule involved the mutual consent of both parties. Therefore the density factor alone was operative in determining the rapidity with which interracial fusion occurred. These two factors, compulsion and density, are reflected in the tabulations and graphs of the relation between age and mean degree of Indian blood.

This discussion may be terminated by a reference to a small group of Indians who, in spite of their inadequate numbers, are of great ethnographic interest. In preparing his testimony for the Indian Claims Cases, the late Prof. Alfred L. Kroeber went to Sacramento and inspected the 1928 Roll. Among other groups of significance, Kroeber found the names of 285 persons who claimed affiliation with several tribes in northern California which had been considered totally extinct by anthropologists. Kroeber noted the ages of these people and their degree of Indian blood, with other information, on cards which are now preserved by the Department of Anthropology in Berkeley. Through the kindness of Prof. Robert F. Heizer, I was permitted to examine these.

A tabulation and graphing of data pertaining to these members of ''extinct'' tribes yields the results seen in Table 31 and Figure 15. The points for mean degree of blood in the decade cohorts are rather erratic, as would be expected in such a small sample, but the trend is evident. Here is an extreme case of the dilution of Indian blood during the mining era, followed by a rapid decline to approximately 30 percent. No wonder that these little tribes and tribelets were considered extinct. Any of their culture which survived would be obliterated by the overwhelming infusion of non-Indians who made up their families and occupied their homes.

Two other indices to the degree of racial mixing which has occurred among the California Indians are the extent of back-crossing and the proportion of full-bloodedness retained by the population. Both of these may be evaluated from the data contained in the 1928 Roll.

By back-crossing we mean the union of the person whose genetic constitution is only part Indian, for example a half-blood, with another who is either a full blood, or whose descent is heavily weighted toward the Indian component. If the dividing line be taken as eight-sixteenths Indian, then we may compare the number of progeny who are eight-sixteenths full-blooded Indian with those who are eight-sixteenths to zero Indian. In the aggregate after several generations of experience, if the number of those in the former group exceeds those in the latter group, it may be concluded that the pressure on the reproductive behavior of the population was in the direction of a return to the original condition of a purely Indian community. Conversely, if the number of the latter exceeds that of the former, the pressure is seen to be driving the surviving Indians toward amalgamation with other races.

A simple numerical expression for the group tendency is the ratio of the high Indian to the low Indian component as found in a census, or a count such as the 1928 Roll. Since eight-sixteenths is the dividing line, and since it is inadvisable to introduce either pure Indians or pure whites, the number of persons who are fifteen-, fourteen-, thirteen-, and twelve-sixteenths Indian may be used as the numerator of a fraction, or ratio, the denominator of which is the number of those four-, three-, two-, and one-sixteenth Indian. If the ratio exceeds unity then the tendency toward back-crossing to the Indian is held to predominate over the tendency toward forward crossing to the white, or other non-Indian race. The converse is true if the ratio is less than unity.

The direction of the trend may change at any time, by virtue of the operation of many factors—density of either race, compulsion, personal preference, economic advantage, social pressures. What we see in the Roll or census is the cumulative effect of past influences. If the detailed history of backward and forward crossing were to be elucidated it would be necessary to have samples of much greater size than those at our actual disposal.

The other index depicts the extreme state of resistance on the part of the Indians to fusion with other races, for it shows the relative number of persons none of whose ancestors have married outside their own ethnic group. If the proportion of pure bloods is high, one may deduce that there never has been a serious assault upon the racial integrity of the people. If it is low then for one reason or another, and at one time or continuously, there has been strong pressure toward interracial union. The simple percentage of surviving persons who are sixteen-sixteenth Indian is adequate to express this factor. Both back-crossing ratio and percent of full-blooded Indians are given for the previously indicated regions in Table 32.

*Table 32.* BACK-CROSSING AND RETENTION OF
FULL-BLOODEDNESS IN CALIFORNIA AND ITS
CONSTITUENT REGIONS

| Region | Backcrossing[a] degree of blood ratio 15-12/4-1 | Retention[b] Percent of persons 16/16 Indian descent |
|---|---|---|
| California, entire | 0.566 | 36.2 |
| 1. | 1.988 | 71.0 |
| 2 and 3 entire | 0.607 | 29.9 |
| 4, 5 and 6, entire | 0.353 | 40.5 |
| 2A. | 0.667 | 25.7 |
| 2B. | 2.300 | 77.5 |
| 3A. | 0.854 | 28.1 |
| 3B. | 0.656 | 45.6 |
| 4. | 0.136 | 26.6 |
| 5. | 0.181 | 16.9 |
| 6. | 0.595 | 51.7 |
| Kroeber's extinct tribes | 0.262 | 23.9 |

[a] Extent of backcrossing is shown by the ratio of persons appearing in the 1928 Roll as 15, 14, 13, and 12 sixteenths Indian to persons who were 4, 3, 2, and 1 sixteenths Indian.

[b] Retention of full-bloodedness is expressed as the percent of full bloods in the 1928 Roll.

The data in this table present a clear picture of conditions within the state of California. Regions 1 and 2B, the home of the Paiute and Pit Rivers, are set widely apart from the other areas. Both have very high ratios in favor of back-crossing. Both still (in 1928) have over 70 percent pure-blooded members. In both regions there has been some but relatively little mixture with other races, and the pressure to marry back into the Indian stock has been strong.

In the north, Regions 2A and 3A lie at the opposite extreme, as do the mission descendants in both north and south. In all of these the percent of surviving pure bloods is below 30, and the tendency to marry non-Indians is accentuated. However, the ratios of degree of blood diverge, although all are less than 1.0. In Regions 2A and 3A they are respectively 0.667 and 0.854; in Regions 4 and 5 they are 0.136 and 0.181. The difference is probably referable to time and to the type of contact with the various branches of the Caucasian race. In the north there was no contact prior to 1845, after which date the mixing process went on rapidly for two or three decades. Compulsion was present. Dilution of the Indian blood occurred to a significant extent, but the preference for Indian consorts over the white males brought into being numerous back-crosses as soon as the white invasion mitigated its intensity. Hence the ratios shown in Table 32 did not fall far below unity. In the south the entire process was gradual but consistent. Racial mixture began with the missions and continued at least up to 1928. There was little compulsion and much less animosity toward non-Indians. Forward crossing with whites, particularly of Iberian origin, was facilitated in many ways, and in nearly two centuries the ratios of degree of blood have sunk very low indeed.

The members of the tribes which have disappeared ethnographically (Kroeber's "extinct" tribes) represent the interracial fusion in the north carried almost to its limit. Persons of pure Indian descent are very few, and crossing with the whites has gone much further than would be implied by the values of the ratios in Regions 2A and 3A. Perhaps there is a reciprocal cause and effect. Perhaps the attenuation of Indian blood shown by a ratio of 0.262 facilitated the loss of the aboriginal culture while the loss of the culture promoted closer relations with the Anglo-Americans. Much the same considerations apply elsewhere in Regions 2 and 3.

In the south there is a clear distinction between the mission descendants in Region 5 and the unconverted people to the east, in Region 6.

The former, with Region 4, show very low ratios and small survival of full bloods. The latter has a much higher, although still quite small ratio, and contained in 1928 at least one half full-blooded Indians. The causes of the difference lie in the greater exposure time afforded the mission descendants and their closer contact with a relatively sympathetic branch of the white race.

Apart from the 1928 Roll, which was a very broad sampling of the entire population of California Indians, there are a few censuses of a more local nature. They were taken by the several agencies of the Bureau of Indian Affairs. Three of them, all from the year 1940, are of particular interest, for they may be used as a check on the data secured from the Roll of 1928. I was permitted to examine them at the headquarters of the three agencies in 1940, where I excerpted the pertinent information in numerical form. In Table 33 the principal direct indices are summarized ($b$ is omitted). Those from Hupa, Mission, and Carson agencies may be compared respectively with the indices obtained from Region 2A, Regions 5 and 6, and Region 1. They vary to some extent from the values which would be predicted on the basis of the 1928 Roll as shown in Tables 30, 31, and 32, as well as in Figures 4 to 15.

Two consistent features of the comparison will be observed. The geographical areas involved bear the same relation to each other in both sets of data, with the exception of the figure for the back-crossing ratio in the southern district. Here the value is very low in the 1928 Roll, but intermediate between the other two districts in the agency censuses. At the same time all nine pairs of values in Table 33 agree in that the index for the agency census is numerically greater than the corresponding index for the 1928 Roll. Since a larger index of any kind always implies a higher level of Indian blood than a smaller one, it may be stated first that both sources of data show the greatest degree of Indian blood in the transmontane region, with the least in the northwest, and, second, that the agency censuses show a higher level of Indian blood than does the 1928 Roll.

The reason underlying all these divergencies is simply that different groups of people are being sampled. In the eastern area the 1928 Roll admitted only strictly Californian Paiute and Washo. The Carson Agency census of 1940 included also the Nevada Indians who lived at Fallon, Schurtz, Pyramid Lake, and Walker River. The latter communities are probably more isolated and their inhabitants more con-

*Table 33.* COMPARISON OF CERTAIN INDICES FOR DEGREE OF BLOOD
BETWEEN THREE AGENCY CENSUSES OF 1940 AND THE
CORRESPONDING REGIONS ESTABLISHED WITH THE 1928 ROLL

| Agency or region | Number of persons | Mean degree of blood, all ages | Back crossing ratio[a] | Percent of persons of full Indian blood |
|---|---|---|---|---|
| Hupa Agency | 1,927 | 59.75 | 1.241 | 29.4 |
| Region 2A | 3,612 | 51.75 | 0.667 | 25.7 |
| | | | | |
| Mission Agency | 3,059 | 66.45 | 1.430 | 63.2 |
| Regions 5 and 6 | 4,305 | 53.48 | 0.385 | 41.7 |
| | | | | |
| Carson Agency | 5,230 | 84.45 | 3.845 | 71.4 |
| Region 1 | 1,884 | 82.00 | 1.988 | 71.0 |

[a] Explained in Table 32, note a.

servative in their social attitude than would be found across the boundary of California.

In the northwest is demonstrated the contrast between the Indians who lived on reservations or otherwise under the direct control of the Bureau of Indian Affairs and those who were partially or completely independent. The portion on reservations contained more older people and in general represented those who had least contact with the white society of Humboldt and Trinity Counties. They were the ones who were counted in the Hupa Agency census. The others were not included, but on the other hand they knew about and applied for the financial assistance promised by Congress in the late 1920s.

The situation in the south was more complex. If Region 4, the northern missions, is left out of consideration, the Indians below Santa Barbara fell into two categories during the period 1928-1940. One consisted of the offspring of the former mission neophytes which have been segregated in Group 5, and the non-mission natives who were placed in Group 6. The two groups differ sharply in their degree of Indian blood, the mission component showing relatively little, the desert people having retained a substantial percentage. These two groups have to be combined in order to get indices for comparison with the Mission Agency census, for the latter contains reservation Indians from both sources in considerable number. In order to duplicate the 1928 Roll there must be added also the hundreds of southern Indians who were not attached to the Mission Agency at all, but who lived at large in the city of Los Angeles and scattered through the southern counties. These persons possessed a low average level of Indian blood. The final result is that the indices for the Mission Agency census represent a selected population which is characterized by an abnormally high level of Indian blood. On the whole, therefore, it may be concluded that the Agency censuses of 1940 confirm the distribution of residual Indian blood among the survivors of that race in the period 1920 to 1940.

There is still another type of information contained in the 1928 Roll which tends to support the data hitherto discussed concerning attenuation of the Indian genetic strain in modern times. In the Roll the arrangement on the page is such that, although the names run in alphabetical order throughout the Roll, the family organization is preserved. The head, the spouse if any, and the children, are listed together, with subordinate order according to age. On the contrary the 1950 and 1970 Rolls are set in strictly alphabetical order by individuals. Families are broken up, and, indeed, family relationship is not mentioned.

Because of this organization of the 1928 Roll it is easy to distinguish the head of the family and the spouse. In the majority of cases both these are of Indian descent, with the degree of blood also stated. However, frequently the spouse, male or female, is non-Indian in origin. Such a person did not qualify for a federal subvention and consequently his or her name and all other personal data are omitted. At the same time the fact of existence is noted by the phrase "married to a non-Indian" or words to that effect. From these statements it becomes possible to determine how many heads of families were living in union with a member of another race. Past experience is of course ignored, and the Roll describes only the marital situation as it existed in 1928. The head of a family was considered to be the husband regardless of the origin of the wife; the wife was taken as the head when the husband was a non-Indian or when there had been a separation.

A direct count showed that there were 5,076 persons listed as the head of a family, male or female. Of their spouses 3,139 were Indian and 1,937 were stated explicitly to be non-Indians. In other words, 38.15 or let us say 38 percent of the heads of families were married, legally or in common-law to non-Indians. This figure cannot account for casual, illegitimate unions. However, the latter would probably not change the percentage value by a very significant factor for most of the contacts not sanctioned by either white or Indian law would already have been included, and the consort would have been dignified by the designation of husband or wife. In any event 38 percent must be regarded as minimal, admitted estimate of interracial mixing. It means that in 1928 two out of every five family heads of California Indian descent had produced children by persons of other ethnic origin.

It is of interest to test whether the statement of interracial marriage derived from the 1928 Roll is capable of reconciliation with the figures already presented for degree of blood. In order to carry out this test it is necessary to make the assumption that the average generation among the California Indians was of twenty years' duration. This period may be too short, but is needed in order to avoid making the calculation too intricate. Let us consider the data for California as a whole and focus attention upon the two cohorts who were 21 to 40 years of age in 1928. These were the survivors of those born in the twenty years between 1888 and 1907. There were 5,330 persons of this age whose names are on the 1928 Roll. During the period 1908-1927 they produced 9,485 children who had survived to that date. The 1888-1907 group had a mean degree of blood which was 56.50 percent of pure Indian. Now, if 38 percent of the married couples included a non-Indian, the mean degree of blood of their progeny would have been one half of 56.50 percent, or approximately 28.25 percent Indian. In the meanwhile the remaining 62 percent of the heads of families in the 1888-1907 cohorts would have mated with California Indians whose mean degree of blood was the same as their own, 56.50 percent. Their progeny also would have averaged 56.50 Indian blood. Of the 9,485 children in the group born 1908-1927, 3,604 would have been derived from the first fraction, and 5,881 from the second component. The two components may be combined according to the expression:

$$\frac{3,604 \times 28.25\% + 5,881 \times 56.50\%}{9,485} = 45.77 \text{ percent}$$

The mean degree of blood of the younger generation therefore should be 45.77 percent.

If alternatively we calculate the mean degree of blood from the data used for California entire in Table 30, it is 44.99 percent. The closeness of the correspondence may be accidental but it creates the probability that both sets of data are substantially veracious. It also means that during the first half of the twentieth century nearly two-fifths of the reproductively active California Indians were crossing with non-Indian races, and that the mean degree of Indian blood was diminished at the rate of over 10 percent per generation.

Certain data which support the findings drawn from the 1928 Roll may be derived from the Statistical Reports of the California Department of Public Health. In the published reports of the Bureau of Vital Statistics for the years 1955, 1957, 1958, and 1959 are to be found tabulations by race of all marriages in California. For Indians, in each year are given the numbers of brides and grooms who married other Indians and who married members of other races. It thus becomes possible to get the total number of marriages in which Indians participated during the four years, together with the number in which both parties were Indian and the number in which only one party was Indian. The detailed figures are in Table 34.

*Table 34.* MARRIAGES OF CALIFORNIA INDIANS WITH OTHER
INDIANS OR WITH NON-INDIANS

| Year | Marriages between two Indians | Marriages between an Indian and a non-Indian | Total marriages |
|------|------|------|------|
| 1955 | 49 | 104 | 153 |
| 1957 | 78 | 115 | 193 |
| 1958 | 68 | 145 | 213 |
| 1959 | 74 | 149 | 223 |
| Total | 269 | 513 | 782 |
| Percent | 34.40 | 65.60 | 100.00 |

SOURCE: Statistical Reports of the California Department of Public Health. The data are found for the years mentioned in the corresponding reports: 1955, p. 12, Table 2; 1957, p. 22, Table 6; 1958, p. 26, Table 6; 1959, p. 26, Table 6.

From the table it will be observed that out of 782 marriages, 513 or 65.60 percent involved an Indian and a non-Indian. The proportion of mixed unions is thus very much greater than was indicated by the 1928 Roll (38.15 percent), and the figures for racial dilution which were based upon the 1928 Roll would have to be extended correspondingly. There are several reasons for this difference, any or all of which may be operative.

1. These are unquestionably legal marriages, since the information is ultimately derived from the central file of marriage certificates. No Indian Custom, or common-law matrimony can be included. On the other hand, as has been intimated, many of the husbands and wives recorded in the Roll of 1928 were such by virtue of the latter type of ceremony. In general, one would expect a non-Indian to insist upon the legal rather than the common-law procedure. As a result it would be anticipated that a series of legal marriages would show a relatively high proportion of non-Indians to be concerned.

2. The reports of the Bureau of Vital Statistics refer, obviously, to the persons who designated themselves Indians, without reference to their geographical or tribal origin. The total therefore must include many who were born outside the state, and who, consequently would not have been eligible for enrollment in 1928 or at any other time. This component of the Indian population would consist of persons who had no local ties, who indeed would probably be living in an urban environment, and who would select a mate from the predominantly non-Indian community. The number of these immigrants, many of them young adults, who entered California after the Second World War, was very considerable.

3. There was a time lapse of more than twenty-five years between the 1928 Roll and the data obtained from the Public Health Reports. During this interval the pressure toward racial fusion certainly did not diminish and the atmosphere was conducive to interracial marriage. We can not document this effect because there are no matrimonial data available in published form which apply to a homogeneous group over a sufficient length of time. But we know that it existed and we know that the result must have been favorable to an increase in the relative number of marriages which involved the union of Indian with non-Indian.

Extension of these results to the period prior to 1928 is of questionable validity. We see from Table 30 and Figure 4 that the fall in degree of Indian blood throughout the state was close to linear from the 1860s to 1928. On the other hand, we have no direct information pertaining to the proportion of interracial crosses similar to the figures on the 1928 Roll. We know also that the numerical value for the proportion of interracial marriages in the entire state is a composite in which different areas with different historical experiences are represented. On the whole it is better not to attempt any reconstruction of the past in the absence of concrete information.

Concerning what has occurred since 1928 we have only the Public Health marriage data which have been shown in Table 34. Whether or not these figures can be reconciled with those seen in the 1928 Roll, it is highly unlikely that events in the second half of this century will cause a reversal and will induce Indians to marry only other Indians. With all society moving toward closer contact with advancing technology, and with continually increasing urbanization, it is probable that the rate of racial fusion will increase. In the end the Indian race in its California aspect will almost have vanished as an independent genetic entity.

# VI. DISTRIBUTION OF THE
# INDIAN POPULATION

For many years it has been a well-recognized fact that the Indians of California were joining other races in a broad movement towards a metropolitan environment. To the extent permitted by their numbers they have contributed to the urbanization which becomes more acute with each passing year. Thirty years ago (Cook 1943d) I published a brief article in which I pointed out that much progress had been demonstrated by the Indians up to that time, and correlated the movement to the cities with the age, tribal affiliation and other characteristics of the participants. It would be fruitless to repeat the conclusions formulated at that time, for they are still valid. It is, however, worthwhile to bring the story up to date, and examine in detail the pattern of migration which has been unfolding during the past century. This pattern is peculiar to the Indian, if only because the Indian is the single minority race which has been in full occupation of the terriroty known as California from time immemorial and had fully adapted to its exigencies long before there was disturbance through the intrusion of other peoples.

In the aboriginal condition the Indian population of California had penetrated every corner of the state in its pursuit of an adequate food supply. As with all hunter-gatherer cultures, the density was a direct function of the volume of readily obtainable food. Thus there was a heavy settlement along the course of the fish-bearing streams, near the estuarine and marsh lands on the seacoast, and in the oak forests of the lower hills and valleys. The intricate relations between the population and the subsistence level of the countryside have been analyzed by numerous ethnographers, such as Kroeber (1925) and Baumhoff (1963).

With the coming of the whites, the equilibrium was deeply disturbed. The Spanish-Mexican incursion moved the tribes of the central and southern coast to the mission establishments. For those people the distance of transfer was not great, although the change in the mode of life was profound. Moreover, upon secularization of the missions, many of the former neophytes reverted to their ancient habitat.

The American invasion produced a much greater effect. In almost every instance the places occupied by the natives became the most valuable and the most preferred by the whites. As a result the former inhabitants were driven out. They found refuge in two types of locality. One was the reservation where they were aggregated in a manner wholly foreign to their cultural background, and where they lived in a state of complete dependence upon the federal government. The other type of refuge was sought by the majority, and consisted of enclaves in the more remote regions where disturbance by the Americans was at a minimum. Therefore, aside from the reservations, the surviving Indians adhered to their ancestral style of living.

By the period between 1880 and 1910 the population was fairly well established under the new conditions. The people lived in small rancherias or as separate families in the oak belt or in desert oases, much as did their ancestors. Some remained near white settlements and worked as casual farm labor. To these may be added the residents of the reservations, Hupa, Round Valley, Tule River, and the many colonies of Mission Indians in the south. All of them derived their subsistence from the land, not so much by hunting and gathering as from the agriculture taught them by the whites.

Regardless of economic and social status, however, the characteristic common to all the Indian population was that it was completely rural. Few, if any, of the native race lived in a town or city. A simple method for evaluating the shift toward urbanization and at the same time for comparing the Indian with the total population in this respect, is to examine the number of urban and rural inhabitants of the state who were reported in the successive censuses. These values appear in Table 35 and have been expressed graphically in Figure 16. Since the relative number of Indians has been very small, the two populations have been placed upon a common basis by taking for each the ratio of urban to rural numbers.

In 1890 and 1900 there were only 200-300 Indians who were described as living in an urban community. This number constituted only one or two percent of all the Indians reported in the census, whereas the total population was more or less evenly divided between the two types of habitat. After 1900 the Indians began to simulate the behavior of other races. In 1910 there were 831 living in towns, in both absolute and relative terms close to three times as many as in 1890-1900. The table and graph demonstrate that the increase has continued with astonishing rapidity and has not ceased in 1970. Meanwhile the urbanization of the total population has been proceeding, although not with the speed displayed by the Indian. Figure 16 shows very clearly two facts: first, that the Indian has urbanized much faster

Ratio, Urban to Rural Inhabitants

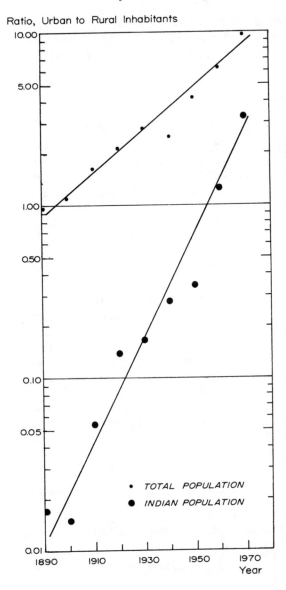

**Figure 16.** The ratio of urban to rural inhabitants of California, shown on the ordinate as the logarithm of the ratio, at the dates given on the abscissa. The dots represent the total population, circles the Indian population.

*Table 35.* SEPARATION OF CALIFORNIA'S TOTAL
POPULATION AND INDIAN POPULATION INTO
THEIR URBAN AND RURAL COMPONENTS

| Census date | Urban population | Rural population | Ratio urban/rural |
|---|---|---|---|
| | I. Total Population of the State | | |
| 1890 | 589,464 | 623,934 | 0.945 |
| 1900 | 777,699 | 707,354 | 1.099 |
| 1910 | 1,469,739 | 907,810 | 1.619 |
| 1920 | 2,331,729 | 1,095,132 | 2.129 |
| 1930 | 4,160,596 | 1,516,655 | 2.743 |
| 1940 | 4,902,265 | 2,005,122 | 2.445 |
| 1950 | 8,539,420 | 2,046,803 | 4.172 |
| 1960 | 13,576,812 | 2,144,048 | 6.332 |
| 1970 | 18,136,045 | 1,817,089 | 9.981 |
| | II. Indian Population of the State | | |
| 1890 | 281 | 16,343 | 0.017 |
| 1900 | 221 | 15,156 | 0.015 |
| 1910 | 831 | 15,540 | 0.054 |
| 1920 | 2,118 | 15,242 | 0.139 |
| 1930 | 2,736 | 16,476 | 0.166 |
| 1940 | 4,078 | 14,597 | 0.279 |
| 1950 | 5,094 | 14,853 | 0.343 |
| 1960 | 22,874 | 18,279 | 1.252 |
| 1970 | 69,802 | 16,476 | 3.288 |

SOURCES: The decennial United States Censuses, as follows:

1890, 1900, 1910, *Total population and Indian population:*
    13th Census, 1910, Population, Vol. II, California, Table
1, p. 157.
1920, *Total population:*
    14th Census, 1920, Population, Vol. III, California, Table
1, p. 106.
1930, *Total population:*
    15th Census, 1930, Population, Vol. III, Table 1, p. 233.
1940, *Total population:*
    16th Census, 1940, Population, Vol. IV, California, Table
1, p. 171.

SOURCES *(continued)*

1920, 1930, 1940, *Indian population:*
  16th Census, 1940, Population, Vol. IV, California, Table 6, p. 518.
1950, *Total population and Indian population:*
  17th Census, 1950, Population, Vol. II, Part 5, California, Table 14, p. 5-57.
1960, *Total population:*
  18th Census, 1960, Vol. I, Characteristics of the Population, Part 6, California, Table 38, p. 6-231.
1960, *Indian population:*
  18th Census, 1960, Non-white Population by Race, Report PC (2)-1C, Table 51, p. 202.
1970, *Total population:*
  19th Census, 1970, General Population Characteristics, California, Report PC1-B6, Table 20, p. 6-89.
1970, *Indian population:*
  The same, Table 17, p. 6-86.

than the non-Indian; and second, that he has nevertheless, not yet reached the high level of his competitors.

A glance at Figure 16 demonstrates a further interesting fact. Since the points for both Indians and total population appear to run in an approximately linear fashion, when plotted on semi-log paper, it follows that the urbanization process between 1890 and 1970 has pursued an exponential course. Furthermore, the constant which would describe the trend of the process for the Indians is greater than that characteristic of the total population. If extrapolation were permissible, one might predict that in a few decades the entire population would be living in urban areas, and that the Indian would be among the first to arrive at this happy condition.

Even though the general direction of flow is fully recognized, it is still desirable to analyze in greater detail the geographical movement of the Indian population within the state, and to explore the mechanics of the process. A convenient territorial unit by which to achieve this purpose is the county.

Prior to 1900 there was very little long-range displacement of the natives. The journey in search of a refuge was likely to be short. Moreover, the attempt to relocate whole tribelets and settle them on reservations met with substantial failure, and the distances traversed by those who remained on the reservations seldom involved more than two or three counties. Hence in the great majority of cases the Indians in 1880 or 1900 lived in close propinquity to the local residence of their ancestors. It is fortunate that our best source of county statistics, the United States decennial censuses, reach back with adequacy, if not with complete accuracy, to 1880.

From 1880 we may skip the very bad census of 1890 and go to 1900. Thereafter, all the censuses may be utilized to and including that of 1970. It is a relatively simple clerical task to tabulate the reported number of Indians living in each of the present 58 counties as published in the nine censuses concerned. Very few entries are lacking, seven in 1880, two in 1900, two in 1910, and one in 1920. From this tabulation the changes in the absolute and relative numbers of Indians may be traced for each county. However, the very large number of entities leads to confusion. Consolidation is essential.

The first level of aggregation rests upon some degree of homogeneity among groups of counties. It has been possible to distinguish nine of these. They resemble to a considerable extent the groups employed in the discussion of degree of blood but differ very much in detail.

*County group I.* The transmontane and Great Basin area of the Paiute, Washo, and part of the Achomawi includes Modoc, Lassen, Mono, Inyo, and Alpine counties.

*County group II.* The coastal northwestern and interior northern hill region embraces, perhaps somewhat arbitrarily, Del Norte, Humboldt, Mendocino, Sonoma, Lake, Napa, Trinity, Shasta, Siskiyou, and Tehama. Numerous tribes are involved, most prominent of which are the Shasta, the Karok, the Hupa, the Yurok, the Wiyot, the Athabascans, the Yuki, the Pomo, and the Wappo.

*County group III.* The Sierra Nevada foothill strip in the good mining country, together with an extension to the northeast, was occupied by part of the Achomawi, the Yana, the Maidu, and the Miwok. The counties are Plumas, Sierra, Placer, Nevada, El Dorado, Amador, Calaveras, Tuolumne, and Mariposa.

*County group IV.* Here the objective is to set apart the flat land of the Sacramento and lower San Joaquin Valleys, although it is difficult to exclude some of the foothills bordering on both east and west. Here are ten counties, Glenn, Colusa, Butte, Sutter, Yuba, Yolo, Sacramento, San Joaquin, Stanislaus, and Merced.

*County group V.* Here is the upper, or southern San Joaquin Valley, together with the southern Sierra foothills, the Tehachapi Mountains, and an expanse of desert in Kern County. The entire region is relatively arid but covers both hills and valley floor. There is relatively little reason for segregating it except that the county boundaries so dictate, and that this region was only to a small degree molested by the gold miners. The native tribes include the Western Mono, the Yokuts not found in group IV, the Tubatulabal, and a few desert Paiute. The counties are Madera, Tulare, Fresno, Kern, and Kings.

*County group VI.* These seven counties surround San Francisco Bay and have always constituted a demographic as well as a geographic unit. The native tribes, almost extinguished in Hispano-Mexican times, were the Coast Miwok, some Patwin, and a large fraction of the Costanoans. The counties are Marin, Solano, Contra Costa, Alameda, Santa Clara, San Mateo, and San Francisco.

*County group VII.* Here have been placed the south central counties of the coast, Santa Cruz, Monterey, San Benito, San Luis Obispo, Santa Barbara, and Ventura. Their indigenous population—Costanoan, Salinan, and Chumash—was completely missionized and nearly extirpated before the American occupation.

*County group VIII.* Los Angeles County, alone, constitutes this group. To set it apart as an independent entity is necessary because of the presence and growth of the City, and the great number of Indians who now live there.

*County group IX.* This is southern California excepting Los Angeles County. The present five counties, San Bernardino, Orange, Riverside, San Diego, and Imperial include the state from the coast to the Colorado River, a very diverse habitat. It is, however, an area which has been subject to the same political and social influences since the white man first appeared, and which may be most profitably compared with group V, the southern San Joaquin Valley and its adjacent highlands.

By the use of these groups the behavior of the Indian population of the individual counties may be reduced to a reasonably simplified form. Nevertheless the data, for which reference may be made to Table 36, are still too extensive for easy comprehension, and further consolidation is advisable. For this purpose there may be established three extended or comprehensive county groups at a second level of aggregation.

The first combines county groups I, II, and III. Thus is put together most of the hill and mountain region of Northern California, which was not entered by the Spaniards, which was badly oppressed by the gold miners, and which even yet is essentially rural in character. The thin white population has engaged in farming and in timber cutting. No large and few small cities have been established. In many senses this is the most conservative portion of the state.

*Table 36.* INDIAN POPULATION OF
CALIFORNIA ACCORDING TO CENSUSES
FROM 1880 TO 1970

| County Group[a] | Indian population | Relative number[b] | Percent of all Indians[c] |
|---|---|---|---|
| | | 1880 CENSUS | |
| I | 1,406 | 0.598 | 8.64 |
| II | 6,746 | 1.165 | 41.45 |
| III | 1,907 | 1.489 | 11.72 |
| IV | 1,081 | 2.290 | 6.64 |
| V | 1,244 | 0.834 | 7.64 |
| VI | 459 | 3.502 | 2.82 |
| VII | 755 | 3.645 | 4.64 |
| VIII | 316 | 4.580 | 1.94 |
| IX | 2,360 | 0.660 | 14.50 |
| | | 1900 CENSUS | |
| I | 2,355 | 1.000 | 15.32 |
| II | 5.787 | 1.000 | 37.63 |
| III | 1,287 | 1.000 | 8.37 |
| IV | 472 | 1.000 | 3.07 |
| V | 1,491 | 1.000 | 9.70 |
| VI | 131 | 1.000 | 0.85 |
| VII | 207 | 1.000 | 1.35 |
| VIII | 69 | 1.000 | 0.45 |
| IX | 3,578 | 1.000 | 23.27 |
| | | 1910 CENSUS | |
| I | 2,228 | 0.945 | 13.59 |
| II | 6,124 | 1.058 | 37.36 |
| III | 1,447 | 1.124 | 8.83 |
| IV | 685 | 1.451 | 4.18 |
| V | 1,188 | 0.796 | 7.25 |
| VI | 134 | 1.024 | 0.82 |
| VII | 106 | 0.512 | 0.65 |
| VIII | 97 | 1.405 | 0.59 |
| IX | 4,382 | 1.225 | 26.73 |

*Table 36 (continued)*

| County Group[a] | Indian population | Relative number[b] | Percent of all Indians[c] |
|---|---|---|---|
| | 1920 CENSUS | | |
| I | 1,792 | 0.761 | 10.32 |
| II | 5,520 | 0.953 | 31.80 |
| III | 982 | 0.763 | 5.66 |
| IV | 571 | 1.210 | 3.29 |
| V | 1,289 | 0.864 | 7.43 |
| VI | 286 | 2.183 | 1.65 |
| VII | 125 | 0.604 | 0.72 |
| VIII | 281 | 4.075 | 1.62 |
| IX | 6,514 | 1.820 | 37.52 |
| | 1930 CENSUS | | |
| I | 2,002 | 0.850 | 10.42 |
| II | 6,821 | 1.179 | 35.50 |
| III | 1,196 | 0.929 | 6.22 |
| IV | 992 | 2.102 | 5.16 |
| V | 2,054 | 1.380 | 10.69 |
| VI | 587 | 4.480 | 3.05 |
| VII | 128 | 0.619 | 0.67 |
| VIII | 997 | 14,449 | 5.19 |
| IX | 4,438 | 1,240 | 23.10 |
| | 1940 CENSUS | | |
| I | 1,867 | 0.782 | 10.01 |
| II | 5,751 | 0.994 | 30.83 |
| III | 1,140 | 0.886 | 6.11 |
| IV | 1,401 | 2.968 | 7.51 |
| V | 1,571 | 1.056 | 8.42 |
| VI | 646 | 4.933 | 3.46 |
| VII | 270 | 1.314 | 1.45 |
| VIII | 1,378 | 19.971 | 7.39 |
| IX | 4,631 | 1.295 | 24.82 |
| | 1950 CENSUS | | |
| I | 1,665 | 0.707 | 8.35 |
| II | 5,870 | 1.104 | 29.43 |
| III | 1,153 | 0.896 | 5.78 |

*Table 36 (continued)*

| County Group[a] | Indian population | Relative number[b] | Percent of all Indian[c] |
|---|---|---|---|
| IV | 1,235 | 2.617 | 6.19 |
| V | 1,984 | 1.333 | 9.95 |
| VI | 1,452 | 11.080 | 7.28 |
| VII | 281 | 1.357 | 1.41 |
| VIII | 1,671 | 24.217 | 8.38 |
| IX | 4,636 | 1.296 | 23.24 |
| 1960 CENSUS | | | |
| I | 1,840 | 0.782 | 4.72 |
| II | 7,754 | 1.303 | 19.87 |
| III | 1,165 | 0.906 | 2.99 |
| IV | 2,638 | 5.589 | 6.76 |
| V | 3,060 | 2.057 | 7.84 |
| VI | 4,588 | 35.023 | 11.76 |
| VII | 1,441 | 6.960 | 3.89 |
| VIII | 8,109 | 117.500 | 20.98 |
| IX | 8,419 | 2.353 | 21.58 |
| 1970 CENSUS | | | |
| I | 1,979 | 0.839 | 2.17 |
| II | 10,258 | 1.774 | 11.27 |
| III | 2,179 | 1.693 | 2.39 |
| IV | 7,035 | 14.905 | 7.73 |
| V | 6,656 | 4.470 | 7.31 |
| VI | 17,107 | 130.600 | 18.80 |
| VII | 4,228 | 20.420 | 4.65 |
| VIII | 24,509 | 355.800 | 23.93 |
| IX | 17,067 | 4.720 | 18.75 |

SOURCES: Same as listed for Table 37.

[a] Roman numerals refer to the nine areas, or groups, of counties described in the text.

[b] The relative number is the ratio of Indian population in the census year to Indian population in 1900.

[c] Total Indian population in the census year specified.

The second extended group includes county groups V and IX. This area was occupied by the Ibero-Americans, either lightly or intensively. Much of it, particularly in the south, was missionized. Since 1849 the open plains and arid hills have been utilized primarily for agriculture and stock raising. The native inhabitants have been moderately exposed to the influences of American culture. A few cities were developed early, such as Fresno, San Bernardino, and San Diego, but in recent decades their growth has been significant.

The third group is urban par excellence and has been supported by industry and intensive agriculture. It includes the metropolitan areas of Los Angeles and San Francisco, together with numerous smaller towns and cities in county groups IV, VI, VII, and VIII. Any movement of the Indian population toward the large centers should be expressed by an increase in the number of Indians in this aggregate.

The data for the three extended groups will be found in Table 37. The rise in Indian population during the present century is obvious. Furthermore, the fact that this increase has been of greatest magnitude in the third extended group and least in the first extended group is equally evident. It is desirable, however, to express these differences more precisely. This may be done by two methods. One shows on a relative scale the changes which occurred within each of the three primary areas. The other compares the three areas from point to point in time since 1880.

In order to calculate the relative change in the population of any group, simple or extended, we must have a common basis for estimate. The most satisfactory such basis is the minimum value of the population within recent times, a value which for most territorial units was that found in or near the year 1900. If this value is taken as unity for each group then the relative difference at any other census date may be expressed as the ratio of the population at this date to that found in the year 1900. Hence a ratio of 2.0 for group X in 1920 means that the Indian population doubled between the two dates. These indices of relative change are given in Tables 36 and 37 under the heading "relative number."

The comparison of areas may be based upon the total Indian population shown by a census of the state. Since the nine groups together or the three extended groups together comprise the entire population, it is simple to determine what percentage of the total is contributed by each unit. These figures are given under the heading "percent of all Indians."

*Table 37.* INDIAN POPULATION OF
CALIFORNIA ACCORDING TO EXTENDED
COUNTY GROUPS FOR THE CENSUS YEARS
1880 TO 1970
(County groups and other magnitudes as in Table 36)

| Census year | Indian population | Relative number | Percent of all Indians |
|---|---|---|---|
| First Extended Group: I, II, III | | | |
| 1880 | 10,059 | 1.067 | 61.81 |
| 1900 | 9,429 | 1.000 | 61.32 |
| 1910 | 9,799 | 1.038 | 59.78 |
| 1920 | 8,294 | 0.880 | 47.78 |
| 1930 | 10,019 | 1.062 | 52.14 |
| 1940 | 8,758 | 0.929 | 46.95 |
| 1950 | 8,688 | 0.822 | 43.56 |
| 1960 | 10,759 | 1.141 | 27.58 |
| 1970 | 14,416 | 1.529 | 15.84 |
| Second Extended Group: V, IX | | | |
| 1880 | 3,604 | 0.712 | 22.15 |
| 1900 | 5,069 | 1.000 | 32.96 |
| 1910 | 5,570 | 1.100 | 33.98 |
| 1920 | 7,803 | 1.540 | 44.95 |
| 1930 | 6,492 | 1.281 | 33.79 |
| 1940 | 6,202 | 1.224 | 33.25 |
| 1950 | 6,620 | 1.315 | 33.19 |
| 1960 | 11,479 | 2.265 | 29.42 |
| 1970 | 23,723 | 4.680 | 26.06 |
| Third Extended Group: IV, VI, VII, VIII | | | |
| 1880 | 2,611 | 2.970 | 16.04 |
| 1900 | 879 | 1.000 | 5.72 |
| 1910 | 1,022 | 1.163 | 6.24 |
| 1920 | 1,263 | 1.437 | 7.28 |
| 1930 | 2,704 | 3.076 | 14.07 |
| 1940 | 3,695 | 4.204 | 19.81 |
| 1950 | 4,639 | 5.278 | 23.26 |
| 1960 | 16,776 | 19.085 | 43.00 |
| 1970 | 52,879 | 60.158 | 58.10 |

SOURCES: The decennial United States censuses, as follows:

1880: 10th Census, 1880. Table V. Population, by Race and by Counties, California, Vol. I, p. 382.
1900: 12th Census, 1900. Census Reports, Vol. I., Table 19, p. 531.
1910: 13th Census, 1910. Abstract of the Census with Supplement for California. Table 17, p. 596.
1920: 14th Census, 1920. Vol. III, Population, Table 7, p. 109.
1930, 1940: 16th Census, 1940. Population, Vol. II, Part I, Table 25, p. 567-568.
1950: 17th Census, 1950. Characteristics of the Population, Vol. II, Part 5, Table 47, p. 5-179.
1960: 18th Census, 1960. Characteristics of the Population, Vol. I, part A, California, Table 28, p. 6-195 to 6-199.
1970: 19th Census, 1970. General Population Characteristics, Vol. 6, Table 34, pp. 6-310 to 6-311.

From the tabulations it is clear that, with respect to the population in the year 1900, there was little relative change to be seen in the first extended group; in the second there was a moderate increase which accelerated slightly after 1950; in the third there was a steady increase which became very significant in 1960 and 1970. At the same time the proportion of the total Indian population of the state declined consistently in the first extended group, remained more or less constant in the second, and increased remarkably in the third. These relationships are depicted visually in Figures 17 to 22, where the differences among the various geographical entities are strikingly demonstrated.

What this all signifies in terms of differential Indian population growth is that the counties of the hill, coast, and mountain area in northern and central California have remained essentially static with respect to the number of Indians they contain since the low point was reached at or near 1900. The Indian stock has been multiplying, with a high birth rate and a declining death rate, but the excess human production has been draining off into other areas. Meanwhile there has been little if any immigration by Indians into this region. This has meant that, whereas in 1900 the first extended county group (with 24 northern counties) contained approximately 61 percent of the California Indians, in 1970 it contributed scarcely 16 percent of the total number.

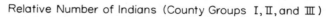

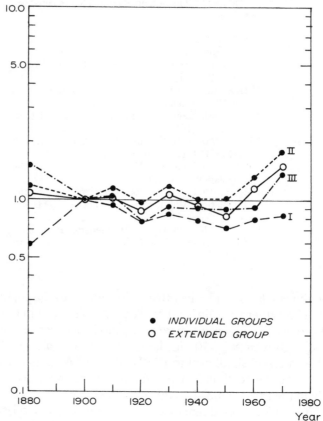

**Figure 17.** The relative number of Indians in county groups I, II, and III. The ordinate is the percent of the absolute number existing in 1900 (when it was zero percent), expressed as the logarithm of the number, at the date shown on the abscissa. Dots represent the individual groups, circles the values for the extended group, which is the total of the simple groups.

Relative Number of Indians (County Groups Ⅴ and Ⅸ)

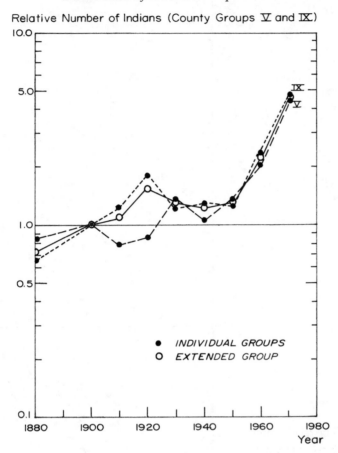

**Figure 18.** The relative number of Indians in county groups V and IX. Ordinate, abscissa, and symbols as in Figure 17.

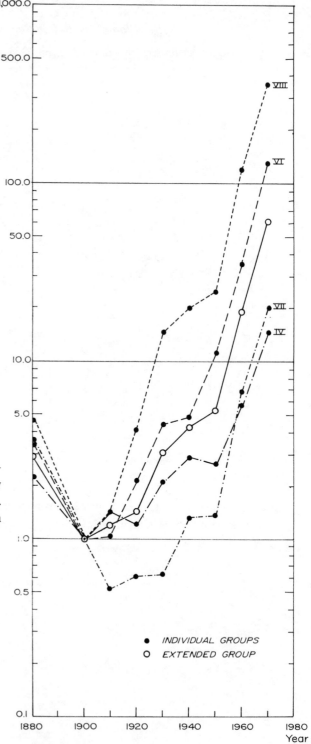

**Figure 19.** The relative number of Indians in county groups IV, VI, VII, and VIII. Coordinates and symbols as in Figure 17.

Percentage of Total (County Groups I, II, and III)

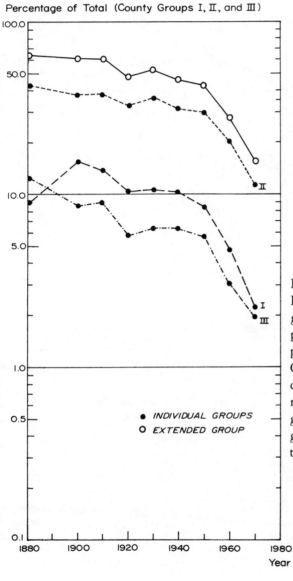

Figure 20. The number of Indians in each of county groups I, II, and III, expressed in logarithmic form as percent of all Indians in California at the dates indicated on the abscissa. Dots represent the individual groups, circles the extended group, which is the total of the single groups.

Percentage of Total   (County Groups Ⅴ and Ⅸ)

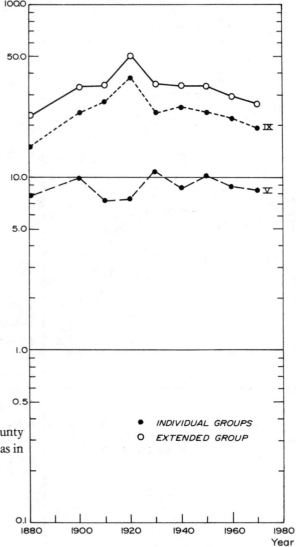

**Figure 21.** Data for county groups V and IX, plotted as in Figure 20.

Percentage of Total  (County Groups Ⅳ,Ⅵ,Ⅶ, and Ⅷ)

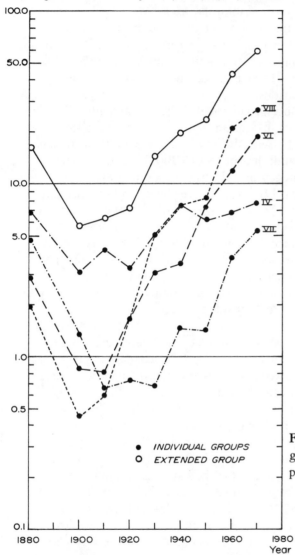

**Figure 22.** Data for county groups IV, VI, VII, and VIII plotted as in Figure 20.

The second extended county group, the southern San Joaquin Valley and the southern part of California, exclusive of Los Angeles, has made a steady growth throughout the twentieth century, with the rate accelerating during the past twenty years. In addition to the natural increase, which appears to have been consistently retained in the area, there must have been a moderate immigration, perhaps mostly to the urbanized portions.

The third extended county group covers both the agricultural and the metropolitan regions of the central valley and the south central coast. Groups IV and VII, after having lost most of their Indian inhabitants during the great decline of 1845-1900, have made a strong recovery during the present century. But the most sensational increase has come in the two major urban areas, the regon of San Francisco Bay and the City and County of Los Angeles. Here both the tables and the graphs depict a rise in Indian population from nearly zero in 1900 to almost 40,000 in 1970. Since there was no appreciable reservoir of Indians at the beginning, the increase must be due to immigration. The movement has been of a dual character, a migration of Californians from the interior, rural counties (as in the first extended county group), and an immigration from outside the state.

Although it is at present impossible to make an accurate numerical distinction between these two sources of people, the internal and external, considerable light can be shed upon the course of events by means of a comparison between the national censuses and the three Rolls compiled by the Bureau of Indian Affairs. The Rolls were inscribed with cut-off dates not far removed from the three census years 1930, 1950, and 1970. Consequently the censuses taken at these dates may be set off directly against the corresponding Rolls. When this is done certain discrepancies appear between the two types of enumeration which are confusing but at the same time illuminating.

It is also possible with the Rolls alone to trace the movement of the strictly California Indians, those who were descendants of Indians living in the state in 1849. In order to examine this sub-population, it will be necessary to digress from consideration of the censuses and discuss some of the features of the Rolls.

The three Rolls differ considerably in their style, with certain information available in one but not in the others, and with some types of treatment practicable for less than the full number. As a result a consistent tabulation of population categories is not feasible and the essential data must be presented in a semi-cursive form, as in Table 38. Some of the controversial points which are pertinent here may be mentioned as follows.

*Table 38.* RESIDENCE OF CALIFORNIA INDIAN DESCENDANTS,
ACCORDING TO THE ROLLS OF 1928, 1950, AND 1970

| Roll and residence | Number | | Percent |
|---|---|---|---|
| ROLL OF 1928 | | | |
| Total enrolled | 21,977 | | |
| Yuma excluded | 777 | | |
| *Total counted* | 21,200 | | 100.00 |
| Living outside the state | 69 | | 0.32 |
| | | | |
| Bay area . . . . . . . . . . . . . . . . 599 | | 2.82 | |
| Los Angeles County . . . . . . . . 388 | | 1.83 | |
| Street address elsewhere . . . . 1,201 | | 5.66 | |
| Total urban | 2,188 | | 10.31 |
| Rural (non-urban) | 18,943 | | 89.37 |
| | | | |
| ROLL OF 1950 | | | |
| Total enrolled | 33,200 | | |
| Yuma excluded | 579 | | |
| *Total counted* | 32,681 | | 100.00 |
| Living outside the state | 2,912 | | 8.91 |
| | | | |
| Bay area . . . . . . . . . . . . . . . 1,982 | | 6.06 | |
| Los Angeles County . . . . . . . 1,913 | | 5.85 | |
| Street address elsewhere . . . . 5,950 | | 18.20 | |
| Total urban | 9,845 | | 30.11 |
| Rural (non-urban) | 19,924 | | 60.98 |
| | | | |
| ROLL OF 1970 | | | |
| *Total enrolled* (Yuma included) | 69,911 | | 100.00 |
| Living outside the state, remote | 4,367 | | 6.25 |
| Living outside the state, adjacent | | | |
| Oregon . . . . . . . . . . . . . . . . 3,214 | | | |
| Nevada . . . . . . . . . . . . . . . 1,327 | | | |
| Arizona . . . . . . . . . . . . . . . . 861 | | | |
| Total adjacent . . . . . . . . . . . 5,402 | | | 7.73 |
| Total outside the state | 9,769 | | 13.98 |
| | | | |
| Bay area . . . . . . . . . . . . . . . 5,989 | | 8.57 | |
| Los Angeles County . . . . . . . 5,389 | | 7.71 | |
| Total living in California | 60,142 | | 86.02 |

1. In the 1928 and 1950 Rolls it has been possible to exclude the Yuma because this tribe is indicated as such. In the 1970 Roll, however, the spaces for tribal affiliation of those persons who were Yuma, and who also were Paiute and Washo, were simply left blank. Therefore the Yuma cannot be distinguished from the others, and they all have to be counted.

2. The persons with a street address can be segregated in the 1928 and the 1950 Rolls because for others merely a town or a post office is named. In the 1970 Roll nearly everyone gave a street address, many of which were obviously far from a center of population. This criterion of location consequently could not be used with this Roll.

3. The individuals who were living outside the state when they signed for the 1970 Roll could be separated meaningfully into two groups: (1) those living in adjacent states, Oregon, Nevada, Arizona, some of them very close to the California border, and (2) those living in more remote states, many of them in the Middle West and the East. This division would be possible with the two earlier Rolls but would involve too few people to be of real significance. The majority of the big jumps have occurred within the past twenty years.

With respect to the distance and direction of migration from the rural areas of the state during the past forty years Table 38 shows clearly that the California Indian descendants have moved in two main streams. One is toward the principal metropolitan districts of the state, San Francisco and Los Angeles. This component amounted to at least 16 percent of the total number of persons whose names are on the 1970 Roll. The other is a peripheral stream, going out of the state to not only the nearby territory but also to the much more remote parts of the nation. This portion reaches fourteen percent of the enrollees. Together the two movements have involved close to one third of the native California Indian population.

With the knowledge of how the native Indians have reacted to modern civilization, we can now consider the total Indian population and return to the discrepancy between the figures contained in the Rolls and those given by the censuses. It was pointed out in a previous portion of this essay that the census of 1970 showed approximately 90,000 Indians in California whereas the Roll of 1970 has only 70,000 names listed. Certain possible reasons for the 20,000 excess claimed by the census were adduced, principally the immigration of outside Indians to California. This difference as it appears at the three dates 1930, 1950, and 1970, and as it may be separated into its component parts is shown in Table 39.

*Table 39.* COMPARISON OF POPULATIONS
ACCORDING TO CENSUSES AND ROLLS

| Population | Census | Roll |
|---|---|---|
| | 1930 Census | 1928 Roll |
| Total population | 19,212 | 21,977 |
| Seven Bay Counties | 587 | 599 |
| Los Angeles County | 997 | 388 |
| Living out of state | | 69 |
| | 1950 Census | 1950 Roll |
| Total population | 19,947 | 33,200 |
| Seven Bay Counties | 1,452 | 1,982 |
| Los Angeles County | 1,671 | 1.913 |
| Living out of state | | 2,912 |
| | 1970 Census | 1970 Roll |
| Total population | 91,018 | 69,911 |
| Seven Bay Counties | 17,107 | 5,989 |
| Los Angeles County | 24,509 | 5,389 |
| Living out of state | | 9,769 |

From this table it will be observed that the number of California descendants who were living outside the state in 1970 reached nearly to 10,000. This means that, if a strict comparison is to be made between the Roll and the census of that date, these persons must be deducted from the total of the Roll because they could not under any circumstances be included in the census count. The already wide discrepancy between Roll and census is therefore increased from 20,000 to 30,000 and the problem is to that degree magnified.

The resolution is effected by the metropolitan areas. In 1928-1930, and even in 1950, the disparity between the Roll and the census figures for the Bay Area and for Los Angeles County is not serious, for the failure to coincide may be ascribed to inaccuracy of enumeration and random movement of a few people. But with thousands reported in 1970 the census shows from three to four and one-half times as many Indians in these regions as does the 1970 Roll. The difference can be due only to the multitude of non-California Indians who swarmed in between 1950 and 1970.

In these two areas the total excess by census with respect to the Roll is 41,616 minus 11,378, or 30,238 souls. This is almost the precise difference between census Indians on the one hand and California descendants living in the state on the other. It thus appears that most if not all of the discrepancy between the census and the 1970 Roll can be accounted for by immigration of non-California Indians to the local metropolitan areas.

# SUMMARY AND CONCLUSIONS

Whether or not one subscribes to the figure presented here, 310,000, for the aboriginal population of California, there can be no doubt that it was very large. Our value lies between those of Merriam and Baumhoff, 260,000 and 350,000 respectively. In fact it may be regarded as something of a compromise, although it probably comes near the truth. The area is close to 156,000 square miles and the density would be 2 persons per square mile. If, however, one deletes the uninhabitable desert and mountains, which have an area of approximately 50,000 square miles, the density becomes about 3 persons per square mile. This is a high value for such a great area, but the work of Baumhoff has demonstrated much higher levels for favored areas such as the great river valleys. Indeed, Baumhoff has shown quantitatively the active response of the natives to the enormous food resources of fish, game, and acorns provided in the coastal ranges and central valleys of the state. It is this factor of copious and readily available food supply which raised the carrying capacity of California to such high levels.

The retreat from the initial number began with the entrance of the white man in 1769. The decline may have been in progress even earlier, but certain it is that with the establishment of the coastal missions the native population began to undergo rapid reduction. At first only the local tribes were affected, those subject to immediate conversion. Soon, however, the penetration of the Spanish-Mexican civilization into the interior brought calamity to all the inhabitants of the state except those who lived in the really remote mountains and hills of the north and east. Deterioration was vastly intensified by the invasion of the Americans, whose desire for farms, timber, and gold took them into those precise localities which hitherto had formed a more or less secure refuge. Thus the population decline became catastrophic between 1848 and 1860. The number of Indians fell from the order of 200,000 or 250,000 in twenty years to merely 25,000 or 30,000. The low point was reached between 1880 and 1900 with a recorded number of no more than 20,000 or perhaps 25,000 souls.

During this period three adverse factors controlled the lives of the Indians. The first was the food supply. It has been pointed out that the very great proliferation of numbers aboriginally was a function of the unusually copious reserves of food, in particular the acorn and small game on land and the fish in the many rivers and along the seacoast.

These supplies were cut off by the white man and the Indian was left with no alternative but to pursue a European agriculture which he did not understand.

The second factor was disease. In addition to chronic, endemic ailments of a respiratory or gastrointestinal nature, there were widespread epidemics. It is now known that epidemics cut the indigenous population of the continent in half. California was no exception, a fact attested by the experience of the missions as well as by the appearance of lethal plagues, especially of smallpox and malaria.

A third factor, which strongly intensified the effect of the other two, was the social and physical disruption visited upon the Indian. He was driven from his home by the thousands, starved, beaten, raped, and murdered with impunity. He was not only given no assistance in the struggle against foreign diseases, but was prevented from adopting even the most elementary measures to secure his food, clothing, and shelter. The utter devastation caused by the white man was literally incredible, and not until the population figures are examined does the extent of the havoc become evident.

As seen above in Chapter Two, since 1900 there has been a sensational reversal in the numerical trend of the Indian population. From that date to 1970 the rise in numbers has been approximately fourfold, from 20,000 to 90,000 according to the United States census. The natural increase of the native Californians will account for nearly 60,000. The remainder comes from immigration. Altogether the total has moved from about 6 or 7 percent of the aboriginal value to nearly 30 percent. However, with the increase in numbers has gone a parallel change in the character of the economy and the environment.

In nutrition and food preparation there has been a complete shift to modern methods and requirements. Resistance to the European diseases has risen and is on a par with that demonstrated by other racial groups. In the area of physical and social oppression by non-Indian elements there has been great alleviation, although many Indians feel that there is still much room for improvement. By comparison with aboriginal conditions, and certainly with those obtaining in the nineteenth century, the California Indian is in a decidedly healthy state. At the same time he has not yet reached a position which is in all respects as satisfactory as that enjoyed by other races. The demographic characteristics which determine and express the existing status are analyzed in Chapters Three and Four of this volume.

A study of the age distribution of the Indian population since 1910 shows a consistent increase in the proportion of the young children and infants with reduction of the relative number of old people. At the same time the natality, or replacement rate has risen faster than even that of the white race, although Indian mortality has not improved with great rapidity. These facts may be considered with reference to the status of the Indian population in the demographic revolution which is now in progress throughout the world.

It is generally recognized that in the pre-industrial or relatively primitive condition, any group of people has tended and does tend to show a high birth rate coupled with a high death rate. Under these circumstances a stable or even stationary population may be achieved. It has been the experience of many peoples that an advance in economic condition and in technology is accompanied first by a fall in death rate. As a result the gross number increases, until at the end the birth rate also falls and equilibrium is again secured. After the process has run to completion the total number of persons will be much greater than it was initially.

The North American and specifically the Californian Indian, however, has been subjected to a rather unique course of events. He began, in 1770, at the end of a long period of demographically primitive conditions: high birth rate, high mortality especially among infants, and a relatively stable population. But instead of first showing a diminishing mortality in response to betterment in health conditions as did many European and Asiatic groups, the Indian community exhibited a tremendously increased mortality, probably together with a reduction in birth rate. This reversal of the usual state of affairs continued until the end of the nineteenth century and was accompanied not by an increase but by a severe diminution in numbers, the theoretical termination of which was complete extinction.

Nevertheless the Indian did not become extinct. Ultimately the forces which ran counter to the normal trend abated and the Indian population was left badly depleted in the mass, but thoroughly capable of recovery. At this point the replacement rate began to rise and the mortality began to fall, although in only a moderate fashion. A rising birth rate with an unchanging mortality would have returned the Indian population to its original state: high birth rate, high death rate. However, the actually falling death rate, with a constant or even rising natality simulates the course of the demographic revolution in its earliest stages, as it has been observed with various races during the past two centuries. In other words, the California Indian has been in the process of restoring his original viability while at the same time initiating the changes which will eventually bring him into line with other ethnic components of the total population. These two trends will undoubtedly be reconciled within the next generations when the death rate declines still further and natality reaches a maximum and begins to decline. Thus the demographic revolution in the long run completes itself. Meanwhile the obvious result will be a very sensational increase in numbers.

The degree of blood characteristic of the Indian race in California has been diminishing for decades, a fact which is evident from the many types of information set forth in Chapters Five and Six of this series. With a severely declining population, the gene pool of pure Indian stock contracted in proportion to the decline. At the same time several pressures favored miscegenation. In modern times the process has been accentuated by the spatial attenuation of the Indian people through mass movement to an urban environment. The recent population explosion has been at the expense of the Indian's genetic integrity. Under existing conditions it is difficult to see how this integrity can be indefinitely maintained.

# REFERENCES

Note: The publication *Contributions of the University of California Archaeological Research Facility* is abbreviated U.C.A.R.F.

Acsadi, Gy., and J. Nemeskeri
  1970      History of Human Life Span and Mortality. Akademiai Kiado, Budapest.
Baumhoff, Martin A.
  1963      Ecological Determinants of Aboriginal California Populations. University of California Publications in American Archaeology and Ethnology, Vol. 49: 155-236.
Brown, Alan K.
  1967      The Aboriginal Population of the Santa Barbara Channel. Reports of the University of California Archaeological Survey, No. 69: 1-99.
Bureau of the Census
  1960      Statistical Abstract of the United States, 1960. 81st Edition. Department of Commerce, Washington, D.C.
  1960      Historical Statistics of the United States, Colonial Times to 1957. A Statistical Abstract Supplement. Department of Commerce, Washington, D.C.
  1968      Statistical Abstract of the United States, 1968. 89th Edition. Department of Commerce, Washington, D.C.
Cook, Sherburne F.
  1940      Population Trends among the California Mission Indians. University of California Publications: Ibero-Americana, No. 17: 1-48.
  1943a     The Conflict between the California Indian and White Civilization. I. University of California Publications: Ibero-Americana, No. 21: 1-194.
  1943b     The Conflict between the California Indian and White Civilization. II. University of California Publications: Ibero-Americana, No. 22: 1-55.
  1943c     The Conflict between the California Indian and White Civilization. III. University of California Publications: Ibero-Americana, No. 23: 1-115.
  1943d     Migration and Urbanization of the Indians in California. Human Biology, Vol. 15: 33-45.
  1943e     Racial Fusion among the California and Nevada Indians. Human Biology, Vol. 15: 153-165.
  1955a     The Aboriginal Population of the San Joaquin Valley, California. University of California Publications: Anthropological Records, Vol. 16: 31-80.
  1955b     The Epidemic of 1830-1833 in California and Oregon. University of California Publications in American Archaeology and Ethnology, Vol. 43: 303-326.
  1956      The Aboriginal Population of Alameda and Contra Costa Counties, California. University of California Publications: Anthropological Records, Vol. 16: 81-130.
  1957      The Aboriginal Population of Alameda and Contra Costa Counties, California. University of California Publications: Anthropological Records, Vol. 16: 131-156.
  1964      The Aboriginal Population of Upper California. Actas y Memorias, XXXV International Congress of Americanists, Mexico, 1962. Vol. 3: 397-403.
Cook, Sherburne F., and Robert F. Heizer.
  1965      The Quantative Approach to the Relation between Population and Settlement Size. Reports of the University of California Archaeological Survey, No. 64, Chap. IV: 17-21.
Dixon, Ronald B.
  1907      The Shasta. Bulletin of the American Museum of Natural History, Vol. 17: 381-498.
Engelhardt, Charles Anthony (Zephyrin)
  1913      The Missions and Missionaries of California. 4 volumes. James H. Barry Co. San Francisco.

Heizer, Robert F., and Thomas R. Hester
    1970a     Names and Locations of some Ethnographic Patwin and Maidu Villages.
             U.C.A.R.F., No. 9. Chap. V: 79-93.
    1970b     Spanish Exploring Expeditions to Sacramento Valley, 1821. U.C.A.R.F., No. 9,
             Chap. V: 97-106.
    1970c     Shasta Villages and Territory. U.C.A.R.F:, No. 9, Chap. VI: 119-147.

Kelsey, C. E.
    1971      Census of Non-Reservation California Indians, 1905-1906. Edited with intro-
             duction by Robert F. Heizer. U.C.A.R.F., No number, v plus 118 pages.

Kniffen, Fred B.
    1928      Achomawi Geography. University of California Publications in American
             Archaeology and Ethnology, Vol. 23: 297-332.

Kroeber, Alfred L.
    1925      Handbook of the Indians of California. Bureau of American Ethnology, Bulletin
             No. 78.
    1929      The Valley Nisenan. University of California Publications in American Arch-
             aeology and Ethnology. Vol. 24: 253-290.
    1932      The Patwin and their Neighbors. University of California Publications in
             American Archaeology and Ethnology, Vol. 29: 253-423.

Maloney, Alice B., editor
    1945      Fur Brigade to the Bonaventura. John Work's California Expedition, 1832-1833.
             California Historical Society, San Francisco.

Merriam, C. Hart
    1905      The Indian Population of California. American Anthropologist (n.s.) Vol. 7:
             594-606.
    1968      Village Names in Twelve California Mission Records. University of California
             Archaeological Survey, Reports, No. 74: 1-175.
    1970      Indian Rancheria Names in Four Mission Records. U.C.A.R.F., No. 9, Chap. III:
             29-58.

Rogers, David B.
    1929      Prehistoric Man of the Santa Barbara Coast. Santa Barbara Museum of Natural
             History.

Rosset, Edward
    1964      The Aging Process of Population. 478 pages. Translated from the Polish. The
             MacMillan Company, New York.

In addition, the decennial censuses of the United States, 1860 to 1970, and the
three Great Rolls of California Indians (1928, 1950, and 1970), prepared by the
Bureau of Indian Affairs, have been used. The later were consulted in copies at
the California Indian Agency in Sacramento.

# INDEX

Achomawi: location, 2, 4, 45-46, 180; population density, 3, 4, 16; population distribution, 3, 180; aboriginal population counts, 4, 42; number of villages, 5; in county groups I and III, 180. *See also* Pit River Indians

Achomawi, western: related to Yana and Yahi, 16

Adults. *See* Age categories

Age categories, 79, 80, 82

Age distribution: as index to natality and mortality, 78; sources, 78, 82, 85, 87, 94, 95, 96, 100, 101; of aboriginal population, 81, 92; of mission population, 85-92; in 1860, 1870, and 1910 censuses, 85-87, 94-95; and demographic transition, 92-94, 103; in agencies and reservations (1887-1920), 95-101; according to Rolls, 101-103; changes since 1910, 200-201

Agencies: vital statistics recorded by, 95, 96. *See also* Reservations

Aging and survivorship indices, 126, 130, 131, 134, 136

Agriculture: demographic effect, 199-200

Alameda County: earlier studies of, 1, 20, 21; aboriginal population count, 25; baptisms to aboriginal population ratio, 25; total baptisms, 28; population counts, 51, 54, 56; in 1880 census, 64; in county group VI, 181

Alliklik: aboriginal population count, 38

Alpine County: Washo in, 46; population counts, 51, 54, 56, 65; in county group I, 180

Amador County: population counts, 54, 56; in 1880 census, 63; Digger reserve in, 66; in county group III, 180

American River: as Sacramento Valley boundary, 1, 6, 8; number of villages on, 17; persons per river mile, 18

Anza-Font expedition, 25

Archaelogical data: as demographic source, 80-81, 85

Area: of San Joaquin and Sacramento Valleys compared, 19; of northern mission strip, 33; of southern mission strip, 42; of aboriginal population, 199. *See also* Methodology, area-density

Argüello expedition, 7, 8-9

Arizona: border tribes, 46

Athabascans: in county group II, 180

Atsugewi: location, 2; number of villages, 5. *See also* Pit River Indians

Ausai-ma, 34

Back-crossing, 143, 164-168

Baja California: border tribes, 46

Bancroft, H. H.: had mission records transcribed, 6, 21, 22, 82. *See also* Bancroft Transcripts

Bancroft Library: mission records at, 6, 22, 27, 85; Ordaz diary at, 7

Bancroft Transcripts: total baptisms, northern missions, 27-33 *passim;* reliability, 31, 33; total baptisms, southern missions, 39, 40, 41; as source for vital statistics, 82, 83, 104, 107; age composition in, 91-92

Baptism books: as demographic source, 6, 7, 21, 22-24, 27-33, 35, 39-41; 85, 88, 104, 120; missions available for, 6, 88; reliability, 21, 22-24, 120; village names in, 34

Baptisms: in Southern Patwin tribelets, 7; recorded by Engelhardt, 22 in Santa Barbara Channel, 25, 26; to aboriginal population (ratios), 25-27, 33, 36, 37, 41; mission totals, 27-33, 35-36. *See also* Conversions; Neophytes

Barrett, Samuel A.: used informants, 12

Baumhoff, Martin A.: used subsistence data, 1, 18; aboriginal population count by, 1, 43, 199; studied population distribution, 18, 175, 199